To Hank with best wishes

Roger Wilmut

Tony Hancock – 'Artiste'

'His face was indeed largely his fortune—the sagging jowls, the bushy eyebrows, the poached-egg eyes fitted perfectly the sartorial appearance of a seedy Shakespearean actor of the old school, with the Homburg hat, the fur-collared overcoat that needed cleaning, and the general air of failure. And there was the protesting and disgruntled voice to go with this ensemble. How agreeable to learn that on occasion he himself could laugh so violently that he had to sit down on the floor and clutch his sides. . . .

'Roger Wilmut deals tactfully with the less attractive side of this rare comedian, from the first tentative beginnings in radio, when he was suitably housed in a Barons Court bedsitter, to the hugely successful days of a more famous residence, Railway Cuttings, East Cheam.' Arthur Marshall *The Sunday Telegraph*

'. . . scholarly . . . excellent on technicalities.' Michael Billington *The Guardian*

'. . . contains many hilarious extracts from Hancock scripts and many behind-the-scenes details of his relations with other artists which have never been published before . . . eminently worth reading.' *Western Evening Herald*

TONY
HANCOCK

'ARTISTE'

A Tony Hancock Companion

Roger Wilmut

with a preface by Harry Secombe

METHUEN

A Methuen Paperback

TONY HANCOCK—'ARTISTE'
ISBN 0 413 50820 X

First published in 1978
by Eyre Methuen Ltd

© 1978 by Roger Wilmut
Preface © 1978 by Harry Secombe

This paperback edition first published in 1983
by Methuen London Ltd
11 New Fetter Lane
London EC4P 4EE

Cover photograph by Don Smith
(Reproduced by kind permission of *The Radio Times*)

Script extracts by kind permission of:
Tony Hancock Enterprises Ltd. (p. 15); Mrs
Diana Hewitt (for Larry Stephens) (pp. 21,
29–30); Michael Bentine, Frank Muir and
Denis Norden (pp. 23–5); Eric Sykes and
Sid Colin (pp. 33–4); John Muir and Eric
Geen (pp. 152–5, 157, 162–4); Jimmy
Grafton (pp. 158–61); and Ray Galton and
Alan Simpson (all extracts from pp. 37–128).
'Hancock's Half-Hour Theme' (p. 47) by
kind permission of Angela Morely.

Filmset and printed in Great Britain by
BAS Printers Limited, Over Wallop, Hampshire

Contents

Acknowledgements

This book would have been quite impossible to write without the help I received from many people. Firstly, particular thanks are due to Roger Hancock, for constant encouragement and practical help, and for screening the ATV series for me. Thanks are also due to Thomas Porter for allowing me to see the telerecordings held by Jack Hylton Ltd; to Gareth Morris and John Sellers of the BBC Film Library for arranging screenings of their Hancock material; to E. E. Stancliffe of BBC Transcription Services for allowing me access to their recordings; and to D. Jeremy Stevenson for the loan of many rare tapes.

The script extracts in the book are an essential part of the examination of Hancock's career, and I am most grateful to the following for permission to quote from their scripts: Ray Galton and Alan Simpson; Michael Bentine, Frank Muir and Denis Norden; Eric Sykes and Sid Colin; John Muir and Eric Geen; Jimmy Grafton; and to Mrs Diana Hewitt for permission to quote from material written by the late Larry Stephens. I am also grateful to Angela Morley for permission to quote 'The Hancock Theme'.

Those who kindly talked to me or took the trouble to look up details included Alan Simpson and Ray Galton, Dennis Main Wilson, Alan Tarrant, John Muir, Hugh Stuckey, Edward Joffe, Billy Marsh, Glyn Jones, Peter Eton, Johnny Vyvyan, George Fairweather, Peter Brough, W. G. Cleverly and Richard Dingley; and the documentary research was done with the aid of BBC Radio and Television Script Libraries and Registries, Sound Archives, Written Archives Centre at Caversham, and News Information Department; and the British Film Institute.

Finally, special thanks to Graham Woodford for doing the picture research; and to my colleagues Peter Copeland, who gave considerable help with the research and criticized the typescript as it progressed; Deirdre Palmer, who typed my notes; and Tim Smith, who checked through the typescript and compiled the index.

Roger Wilmut
March 1978

vi

Preface

Comedy is the business of a comedian and laughter is the prerogative of his audience. It follows, therefore, that whereas a comedian must deliver his comedy, the audience does not have to give up its laughter. He is then, at the beginning of his act, in a state of conflict with his audience.

To understand a comic one has first of all to analyse the requirements of his job. He must have a certain mental toughness, a quick wit, the ability to shrug off a bad reception, and at the same time possess the sensitivity to be aware immediately of the mood of his audience. Two options are open to him—either he gives them what he wants or he provides them with what they want. If he takes up the former he is liable to finish up returning to the rice pudding factory from which Hughie Green plucked him.

Yet such are the vagaries of the comedy profession that in the days of radio, one catch phrase repeated often enough by an indifferent performer could pervade the national consciousness and make him a star. The duration of his stardom depended upon his capacity to back up his gimmick with solid comic ability so that when the time came to cash in on his radio popularity in the theatre his act had some kind of substance. The shrewd performer crying 'Open Sesame' as he rubs his magic lamp before the Aladdin's cave of show business should be careful to take out an insurance policy in the event of the non-appearance of the Genie. The comic David facing the Goliath audience has to be prepared with a song and dance routine in case his sling shot misses its mark.

Anyone who does a job of work and at the end of the day has nothing tangible to show for it, apart from his salary, has every reason to feel insecure. You can't frame applause, you can't place cheers on your mantelpiece and you can't plant a chuckle in a pot and expect it to raise laughs. All the average comic is left with at the end of his career are some yellowing newspaper cuttings, perhaps an L.P. or two and a couple of lines in *The Stage* obituary column. But, if he is one of the few greats, he leaves behind a legacy of laughter when he has gone, especially—and such is human nature—if there has been an element of tragedy in his life. The public likes to think that there is drama lurking behind the laughter—agony caused, ironically, by the insecurity induced by the creation of that laughter.

Tony Hancock was one of those rare ones who are bedevilled by success. He was never completely happy in the variety theatre; the strain of doing the same performance night after night and trying to invest it with an apparent spontaneity was more than he could bear. His timing and delivery were never better than when he was doing something fresh—creating and not re-creating. That was why he took to television so well; it removed him from the treadmill of the music hall and the twice nightly revue and gave him new situations in which to work his magic.

Of the rampaging, drunken, self-destroying Hancock depicted in so many stories, I knew very little. I have drunk with him and been drunk with him in the days when we were both young and inexperienced comics fresh from the services, but it was all good-natured tippling then. The truth for which we were searching wasn't far away—it was there in the bottom of the glass.

Strangely enough, the time I remember Tony with most affection was when we were playing on the same bill at Feldman's Theatre, Blackpool in April 1949. 'Out of season' isn't the best time to be in a seaside town, and to make matters worse we were received with indifference by those who formed the small audiences. I was then doing my shaving act and Tony was doing his Gaumont British News impressions and some hesitant patter. On the opening night, Monday 11th April, at about ten past eight I was rushed to the manager's office to receive a phone call telling me that my wife had given birth to our first child, a daughter. I waited until Tony came off—he was further up the bill than I was—and told him the news. 'We'll celebrate, lad,' he cried.

We had about twelve shillings between us and although champagne was out of the question, we were determined to wet the baby's head. It was a most frustrating night because by the time we had taken off our make-up the pubs had shut and the only place open was a fish and chip shop near the theatre. We sat together over our plates of frizzled rock salmon and toasted my first born in Tizer—an aggressively non-alcoholic drink with a high gassy content. Later we wandered down to the sea front, drunk with the occasion and each other's company. We shared the same dreams of success and we argued about what we would do with the world now that we had fought to save it, leaning over the iron bars of the promenade, looking into the dark sea and seeing only brightness.

I met him many times later and at one time stood in for him on his radio show. But I will always think of Tony Hancock as he was then, pristine and shining with ambition at the threshold of his career. What happened to him subsequently is for others to chronicle and argue

viii

about. I found him gentle and self-mocking then. The demands of his profession shaped him, destroyed him and eventually killed him, but he served it well. If anyone paid dearly for his laughs it was the lad himself. May he lie sweetly at rest.

Harry Secombe

BBC Publicity
Hancock improves his mind in 'The Bedsitter' (broadcast 26.5.61)

x

Introduction

This book is a study of the professional career of Tony Hancock, who was surely one of the greatest comics of our age. It is by now common knowledge that his private life, particularly in his final years, was often unhappy; and that while he often hurt those around him, he hurt himself far more.

However, it is not the brief of this book to enquire into his personal affairs except in so far as they directly affected his work. Mention has to be made of some of his difficulties, but the details have been aired often enough. What matters is the legacy of his work, much of the best of which still exists. To study these richly comic performances is to gain an insight into the man, and the reasons why a great comic should decline as he did in his last few years.

The first part of the book traces his career, illustrating its development with script extracts and analyses of some of his performances. The behind-the-scenes stories of his successes and failures are detailed, many of them for the first time in print. For clarity, this section is not arranged purely chronologically, but divides his work into stage, radio and television. After an introductory chapter on Hancock himself, his stage career is traced up to 1955, after which his regular television appearances prevented his making many stage appearances. His radio career is then traced until the end of the last radio series of *Hancock's Half-Hour*, after which his radio broadcasts were almost entirely interviews.

After this, the narrative back-tracks to 1948 to follow his television career, continuing with the film appearances and the later stage and television performances in the 1960s up until the last, incomplete, series made in Australia.

Part Two provides the documentary evidence of his active career by listing all his known stage appearances, broadcasts and films in detail.

A word about titles—most editions of *Hancock's Half-Hour* on both radio and television did not originally have titles, so for convenience I have, where necessary, invented them. A number of script extracts are quoted in Part One, with the kind permission of the various authors.

Wherever possible these have been checked against actual recordings so as to reflect any changes made during rehearsal.

PART ONE

1. Tony Hancock—'Artiste'

For ten years, from 1952, Tony Hancock was one of the most popular comedians in Britain. For four of those years he proved himself to be at the very peak of his profession—and he is one of the few performers on television who is still remembered many years after the original transmissions.

Hancock was in many ways a contradiction in terms; a performer who so wanted to go on the stage that he existed for six months in a bedsitter in Barons Court, living for the most part on a particularly revolting (but cheap) type of heavy sausage because it was filling, but who was so nervous that he was frequently physically sick before going on, and occasionally had to be pushed on-stage. He had an instinctive knowledge of how to perform, how to deliver his lines to their best advantage, what would and what would not be funny in a script; he could reduce a West End theatre audience, or the less relaxed audience in a television studio, to helpless laughter by standing still and doing nothing.

His face was his fortune. The particular set of the features—the heavy jowls, the lightly poached eyes, the shaggy eyebrows—enabled him to express extremes of exasperation or boredom with a comic effect out of all proportion to the actual variations of expression. It is no more possible to describe precisely *why* Hancock's mobile face could be so funny with so little apparent effort than to explain how Buster Keaton could express a wide range of emotions without seeming to move a muscle of his 'stone face'.

He also had an instinctive feel for timing. It has been said that all comedy is a matter of timing, and certainly Hancock was a master of it. He could double or treble the potential laugh on a line simply by delaying it for longer than any other comedian would dare to—or by knowing when to bring his line in immediately, with no pause at all.

Hancock's particular comic techniques—the timing, the set of the face—are not capable of exact analysis. The timing is correct because it is correct—it is funny because it is funny. This was a basic fact that Hancock himself was never able to accept, and his ill-advised search for

13

the secret of his success was one of the contributory factors in his tragic decline into alcoholism in the 1960s, and his eventual suicide. But even when things were at their worst he retained a loyal audience who remembered him at his best and always seemed to be willing him to succeed, and to make them laugh again.

The last three series of *Hancock's Half-Hour* made for BBC Television are legendary, remembered with tremendous affection by those who are old enough to have seen them either in the original transmissions or the mid-1960s repeats; and one of the greatest pleasures of researching the present book was to find that they are still as funny as one remembered them. Time and inferior technical quality have not dimmed these performances, and Hancock's reputation could rest secure on these telerecordings alone. But his radio shows are also landmarks of broadcast comedy; his films, though artistically less successful, have much to commend them; and his stage appearances, though gone for ever, are remembered by those who saw them as magnificently funny—unforgettable use of a medium even more ephemeral than television.

Hancock did not, of course, appear as a fully-fledged comedian overnight. His early work is extremely interesting, if less than perfect— and indeed when he first began as a stand-up comic he was, by all accounts, so bad that no-one could have predicted his eventual brilliance. The story of his rise to success (and his fall)—told from the memories of his friends and colleagues, from recordings, scripts, press cuttings, and the immense collection of paperwork in the BBC's files—is the background against which the famous performances stand out in greater relief—the story of a comedian who could never believe that he really was one of the greatest of his time.

2. Stage, 1941–55

Tony Hancock was born on May 12th 1924, to Jack and Lily Hancock. When he was three, the family left his birthplace, Small Heath, Birmingham, and moved to Bournemouth, where they eventually set up in business running the Railway Hotel. Visiting music-hall artists stayed at the hotel, and this, combined with the fact that his father was a regular entertainer at smoking concerts and masonics, introduced the boy to the atmosphere of Variety.

After leaving school and slipping into—and out of—a few jobs, he began to persuade organisers of smoking concerts to take him on as a 'Confidential Comic' at ten bob a time. His jokes were mostly pinched from Max Miller. Miller's jokes were either very old or very blue—or both—but 'It's the way I tell 'em, lady,' Miller used to say. Miller had the impeccable timing of a born stand-up comic; he could reduce an audience to the point where they would laugh at anything he said, funny or not. The young Hancock had no sense of timing at all.

His mother introduced him to George Fairweather, a professional comic who was a friend of the family. He let Hancock have a small spot in a show he was running for the troops. Fairweather remembers that Hancock was terrible. The boy's mistake at this stage was that he was picking up his jokes in pubs, remembering those which got the biggest (and dirtiest) laughs. At seventeen (and seventeen-year-olds were much more sheltered then) he hardly understood the meaning of any of them.

He got himself an engagement in a show at a Catholic Church Hall. If he did not understand his material, the audience understood it only too well. They walked out. 'Hancock,' said the vicar afterwards, 'I know your parents well, and I'm sure if they had been here they would have been as disgusted as I am.' He never told another dirty joke.

George Fairweather went into the army—though only for a few weeks, due to ill-health—and Hancock took over the running of the Bournemouth War Services Organisation, organising and appearing in shows for the troops. After the experience at the Catholic Church Hall, he wrote his own material, in the form of Billy Bennett-type monologues. Here is part of one of them, *The Sherriff of Toenail City*:

'In the Township of Toenail City
Lived the Sherriff, a man of good class.
But he drank like a fish, did the Sherriff,
'Till his breath burned a hole in the glass.
But the pride of his life was his moustache—
It was famous as Niagara Falls
And his missus when washing on Fridays
Used the moustache to hang out the smalls.
His moustache was so long and whippy
People spoke of it under their breath—
And the old-timers said that the Sherriff once sneezed
And it practically flogged him to death.
But whenever the Sherriff was shaving,
You could see him all covered in gore
His whiskers just blunted the razor,
So he hammered them back in his jaw.'

15

In 1942 Hancock volunteered for the RAF. After some hard service in the concert party at Bournemouth they transferred him to Stranraer, and placed him i/c coal dump. He immediately tried to get into ENSA. Failing this through a fit of nerves, he joined Ralph Reader's Gang Show Number Nine, eventually touring Southern Italy and Greece. At last Hancock was beginning to gain real experience in comedy. Troops are notoriously easy to entertain—and Hancock needed a lot more experience before he would be at all memorable—but in the company of Robert Moreton, Graham Stark, and other aspiring young hopefuls, he was learning his trade. He later paid tribute to the organizer of his show, Fred Stone: 'No matter what he felt personally about anything, it couldn't interfere with a performance. I was only twenty or so at the time, but it was a great example to me.' After the war ended, he awaited demob by assisting a young airman called Peter Sellers with the wardrobe of RAF Light Entertainment.

Hancock was demobilized on November 6th 1946. It was five and a half months before he got a professional engagement—once again with Ralph Reader, who took him on tour with a cast of ex-Forces personnel in a show called *Wings*. As well as comic turns, he sang (straight) a sentimental ballad that went: 'I don't care tuppence 'cos I know darn well/I'm a hero to my mum.' Philip Oakes remembers that 'a production photograph of the act, showing a phenomenally lean Hancock clutching a broom and singing soulfully into the spotlight, was a weapon which could always be used to silence him in arguments about artistic integrity in later years.' Hardly fair. Most performers would prefer to forget some of their early appearances.

Wings toured until September 6th 1947, calling at the New Theatre, Oxford, on the week of August 18th. It was to Oxford that Hancock went that winter for his next engagement—as an Ugly Sister in *Cinderella* at the Playhouse Theatre. 'It was a very intellectual panto,' Hancock recalled later in a series of articles written for *TV Times*. 'Three minutes of Latin in the wood scene—which had to go—and people chatting about Nietzche during the ballroom scene. Lots of philosophical chat. Extremely successful for Oxford.' The run of the panto began on Boxing Day, after a special children's matinée on Christmas Day. The *Oxford Mail* said 'The superb clowning of the Ugly Sisters (John Moffatt and Anthony Hancock) is slapstick of a very high order. They "had a bash" at almost everything and if Cinderella isn't black and blue already it is surprising'. The run ended on January 24th 1948, after which Hancock had another long wait before returning to Oxford on April 26th to play three walk-on parts in the Playhouse Theatre's production of *Peace In Our Time* by Nöel Coward.

In July 1948 he teamed up with pianist Derek Scott and appeared at the Windmill, the famous 'nude show' theatre where the naked girls had

16

to stand stock-still by order of the Lord Chamberlain's Office, and 'artificial aids to vision' were not permitted. As it was a continuous performance, the various comics who worked there over the years found that their turns largely served as an interval from the nudity during which members of the audience in the rear seats could scramble over the rows into any seats vacated in the front.

Hancock and Scott appeared in *Revudeville no 214* from July 12th to August 21st. They did an imitation of a very scruffy end-of-season seaside concert party. The review in *The Stage* commented that they needed to do more work on it; but their performance earned them an audition for BBC Television, which took place on August 14th at Star Sound Studios. They were described in a report on the audition as being not untalented and having verve—and were booked for a TV appearance.

On the same bill with them at the Windmill was a ventriloquist called Harry Worth, and two rather unpolished young Northern comics called Morecambe and Wise.

Hancock and Scott also did their act at the Nuffield Centre, which was a Forces leave centre, where Forces and ex-Forces artists could perform to their mates, who made an appreciative audience. Agents and producers in search of talent sat quietly in the back of the circle and made notes. Among those who saw Hancock and Scott was Dennis Main Wilson, then in charge of auditions for the BBC Variety Department.

In June 1949 Hancock joined *Flotsam's Follies* at the Esplanade Concert Hall, Bognor Regis. The show was run by B. C. Hilliam, for many years 'Flotsam' of 'Flotsam & Jetsam' with Malcolm McEachern. Hilliam asked Hancock to provide five acts. Hancock managed four, replete with props and complications, and Hilliam let him off the fifth. At the end of the run, Hancock picked out the best bits from his material and began to build a regular act from them.

At Christmas 1949 he appeared as Buttons in *Cinderella* at the Royal Artillery Theatre, Woolwich. He had to lead the audience in singing 'Chick, Chick, Chick, Chick, Chicken, Lay a little egg for me'. He hated the pantomime and he hated the song.

On February 23rd 1950 he celebrated election night by appearing at an Election Night Ball at Claridges. The audience studiously ignored him while he gave his all in a corner.

On June 17th he opened in *Ocean Revue* at Clacton, playing against the ear-splitting noises emanating from the nearby scenic railway. While he was working at Clacton he married Cicely Romanis, whom he had met a few months previously.

On December 23rd 1950 he opened at the Theatre Royal, Nottingham, in *Little Red Riding Hood*. He played a character called Jolly Jenkins, whom he hated, and had to lead the audience in singing

'Every Little Piggy has a Curly Tail', which he also hated.

During 1951 the bookings in Variety began to mount up. From May onwards he worked fairly regularly. Not the Big Time yet, but he was slowly working his way up. At the end of 1951 his radio popularity, which had been slow in building, soared as a result of his appearances in the second series of Peter Brough's comedy series *Educating Archie*. From December 21st to January 19th the principals of *Educating Archie* appeared in matinée performances at the Prince of Wales Theatre, London; Hancock also appeared in the revue *Peep Show* at the same theatre in the evenings. At last he had made the West End.

The first three months of 1952 were fully booked with Variety appearances after he finished at the Prince of Wales Theatre. The stage act had now taken the form that it would retain, with a few additions and alterations, for the rest of his life. The concert party was still there from the Windmill days. He would announce the 'Tatty Follies' and sing an 'on with the show' introduction, acting as the entire cast—the comic, the soubrette, the tenor, the impersonator. Then he would imitate each one.

The comic was done in a northern accent: 'I were coming along to the theatre the other day, a fellow come up to me and he says, "Joe", he says, "D'you know why chicken crosses the road?" I says, "Well, I'll tell you, it's for some foul reason" . . . Aye, well, we'll not bother with that one . . .'

It is a dangerous business to get laughs by *not* getting laughs, but Hancock could bring it off.

The final part of the concert party was the impersonator. Eventually Hancock dropped the rest of the concert party routine as he obtained better material, but the impersonations stayed in his act right to the end. The whole point was that they were *intentionally* bad. Hancock had cribbed most of them from George Fairweather, and hammed them up. As time went by they took on a life of their own, until they became clever satirical imitations in their own right.

He would send the whole thing up in his introduction to the first one: 'My first I believe is entirely original, I think I am right in saying that it has never been presented on any stage before, at any time in any country—ladies and gentlemen, I give you Charles Laughton in *Mutiny on the Bounty* . . .'

Everybody did Charles Laughton in *Mutiny on the Bounty*. 'Mis-ter Chris-tian . . . I'll have you *hung* from the *high*-est *yard*-arm in the Navy.'

He always included George Arliss. Arliss was a well-known British actor who appeared in many Hollywood films in the 1930s; he is best remembered for parts such as the title-role in *Disraeli*. He died in 1946. At the time Hancock started impersonating him, most of the audience would at least know who Arliss was, and many would have seen him.

18

Fifteen years later, when Hancock was doing his act at the Talk of the Town, practically no-one in the audience had ever heard of Arliss, and the joke fell flat. Hancock's impression of Arliss lasted five seconds. It consisted of turning his face side on to the audience, raising his eyebrows, looking supercilious around the eyes, and opening his jaw as far as it would go while keeping his lips together, with the result that the tip of his nose turned down. It was a remarkably accurate portrayal of Arliss's long, aristocratic face.

Another impression, which was added to the routine a little later, and stayed to the end, was of Robert Newton in the 1950 Walt Disney (live-action) film of *Treasure Island*. Newton's portrayal of Long John Silver was a masterpiece of shifty piracy, eye-rolling and over-acting. Hancock's eyes would bulge out, so that he took on a definite similarity to Newton, and he would hobble about with his head at a slight angle and on one leg ('How these storks keep this up all day I'll never know'), saying 'Ha-harr, Jim, lad' and getting into arguments with the imaginary parrot on his shoulder. 'Now look here, Jim-lad, I'm goin' ashore . . . get off there, Polly . . . I cannot aboide that bird, most birds I can aboide, but that bird I cannot aboide . . . don't drink all the brandy, and if anyone comes aboard, fire the cannon, ha-harr, arr, ha-harr, oh, ha-ha-harr, arr . . . (*normal voice*) Cor, it doesn't half do your throat in, this one!' This impression carried over into the television *Hancock's Half-Hours* from time to time, and in 'The Knighthood' he demonstrates the fine art of playing excerpts from *Hamlet, Richard III, Julius Caesar* and *Romeo and Juliet* in the style of Long John Silver.

But the high spot of Hancock's act was the Hunchback of Notre Dame. He always claimed to have got the idea from Peter Sellers, whom, during their days in charge of the RAF Light Entertainment Wardrobe, he once found terrifying two WAAFs with a brilliant imitation of the hunchback. Hancock's version was closely based on the Charles Laughton film of 1939. His legs would buckle slightly, a hump would suggest itself on his shoulder, and the left eye would bulge alarmingly and roll about on its own. The voice was a pointed take-off of Laughton's. If you can imagine an upper-class English voice, dropped half an octave in pitch and slowed accordingly, and spoken with one half of the mouth glued together with Sellotape, you will begin to have some idea of Hancock's delivery.

'I'm so ugly,' he would complain. 'I'm so ugly.' The band would agree with him. 'The bells . . . the bells . . . THE BELLS. Nobody loves me . . . sanctuary . . . sanctuary!'

Then he would abruptly straighten up. 'Sanctuary much!'

On Saturday, April 12th 1952 Hancock opened in *London Laughs* at the Adelphi, with Jimmy Edwards and Vera Lynn. Edwards was well-known for his hearty performances in the radio series *Take It From Here*,

19

written by Frank Muir and Denis Norden. Edwards' foil was to have been Dick Bentley, also from *TIFH*, but Bentley stepped out after an argument about the billing.

The show opened with 'Blossom Time in Covent Garden', a musical extravaganza which built up to the first appearance of Edwards and Hancock as 'The Fruity Fruiterers'. After a couple of musical items, Hancock, Edwards and Natalie Raine appeared in a sketch called 'A Seat in the Circle' by Frank Muir and Denis Norden; then, after more music and an 'interruption' by Hancock, the first half finished with 'The Waters of Pamu', a highly spectacular dance number complete with a real waterfall. ('Warriors, Maidens, Gift Bearers perform "The Ritual Dance" to the "Mighty Parana", God of "The Great Cascade", and offer the bride in the "Final Sacrifice".' Intermission.)

In the second half, Hancock, Edwards, Natalie Raine and Pauline Johnson performed 'Polly Does Everything', another sketch by Muir and Norden; Hancock did a solo routine called 'Machine Age', and Edwards donned his mortarboard and gown for his solo spot, 'Wake up at the back, there!' The show finished with a musical tribute to Al Jolson, which included Edwards singing 'About a quarter to nine' and Hancock singing 'Toot, Toot Tootsie'.

During the run of *London Laughs*, Hancock appeared in the Royal Variety Performance, given at the London Palladium on November 3rd

Houston Rogers
Hancock and Jimmy Edwards in London Laughs

Houston Rogers
Hancock and Jimmy Edwards

1952. He imitated a film travelogue of the 'as-the-sun-sinks-slowly-in-the-West' type—on Margate. 'Lovely, lovely Margate, city of love and laughter . . . as far as the eye can see stretches the ay-zure blue of the sky, as the sea slowly laps over the great jagged rocks that form the beach. Sitting on the beach are the natives, wearing the national headgear of a white handkerchief knotted at each corner . . . Let us listen for a moment to the chatter of the natives on the beaches . . . "Edie . . . *Edie!* . . . put that shark down, you don't know where it's been." '

He went on to take a swipe at the Royal Navy. 'Coming to the surface is a British submarine commanded by Lieutenant Commander Pumfret-Pumfret, Royal Navy . . . as he speaks to his men in his rough, sailor-like fashion. (*Upper-class voice*) "Careful there, Johnson, don't bang yourself on that torpedo there . . . Jones, Jones, come away—you'll get your hands covered in grease . . . Up periscope! Put me down, Hathaway . . . no grog for you. Well, it's half-past four, I think we'll pull up for tea. Put the kettle on, Harmsworth . . . what's that? . . . oh, you've *put* the kettle on . . . yes, I see you have . . . yes, I think it suits you, too . . . all right men, prepare to submerge . . . (*imitates warning siren*) . . . Submerge! . . . Well let me get in! . . . Fools!" '

Finally he gave his impression of a curtain speech made by the foreman of a road-mending gang: 'Well, ladies and gentlemen, on be'alf of the entire company I'd like to thank you for the support you've given us this week . . . if you've enjoyed watching us as much as we've enjoyed working for you then it's all been well worth while. Next week we shall be appearing at the corner of Corporation Road and High Street, in a little thing entitled "Getting the Drains Up" . . . and we shall be featuring 'Arry Trubshawe on the steamroller . . . we shall also be featuring a special solo on the pneumatic drill by Charlie Perkins'.

At Christmas 1952, Hancock took part in a special cabaret, arranged

21

by Peter Brough, given at Windsor for the Royal Family and their guests and staff. Years later, in a radio tribute to Hancock, Peter Brough recalled: 'Max Bygraves was also in the show, and Tony had the hard task of following him. He did very well indeed, and towards the end of his act he was getting a lot of laughs; he wanted to back off the stage and take his bow—round the little stage was a great big bank of flowers. In the excitement of the moment, Tony stepped back too far, and stepped right into the middle of all these flowers—pots of geraniums and chrysanthemums—and sent them flying. Quick as a flash he turned round, looked at the Queen, and said "Don't worry, Ma'am—I'll pay for them." Of course the Royal Family dissolved in laughter, and it got him a tremendous finish.'

But meanwhile the strain of appearing twice nightly at the Adelphi was getting too much for Hancock, and eventually he left the show. He could never relax on-stage, and might have done better to have avoided getting caught in the follow-up to *London Laughs*.

But before that, he appeared in his last pantomime—*Cinderella* again, at the Theatre Royal, Nottingham. This time he had to lead the audience in singing 'When Santa Got Stuck Up the Chimney'. Hancock was Buttons. The Dame—in this case 'The Baroness'—was played by George Bolton, a music-hall comic of the old school.

Dennis Main Wilson went to see Hancock at Nottingham. 'Tony didn't know any of the old music-hall routines,' he says. Main Wilson was standing in the wings with Hancock just before the start of the kitchen scene. Bolton went on, saying to Hancock as he went past: 'We'll do the teapots.'

'What?' said Hancock to Main Wilson.

'Something about teapots,' said Main Wilson.

'The teapots' was an old routine, known only to music-hall comics, and not to Hancock. For twelve minutes Bolton performed 'the teapots' as a solo routine, while Hancock just stood there, looking bewildered and resigned, and quite unconsciously getting most of the laughs.

On June 5th 1954 the successor to *London Laughs* opened at Blackpool. Called *The Talk of the Town*, it again starred Jimmy Edwards, with Hancock and Joan Turner.

After three weeks, the strain began to tell on Hancock. He went to a psychiatrist who had an office in Bolton and got a medical certificate to the effect that he should not continue. Jack Hylton, who was running the show in conjunction with George and Alfred Black, was not impressed. 'I was born in bloody Bolton,' he pointed out, and gave a brief sketch of his opinion of any Bolton psychiatrist.

Hancock stayed in the show.

On November 8th they played one week at the New Theatre, Oxford; then opened at the Adelphi on November 17th. One of the comedy highlights of *The Talk of the Town* was the lighthouse-keeper sketch, called 'Send the Relief', adapted by Frank Muir and Denis Norden from the original sketch by Michael Bentine. Edwards is the keeper, and Hancock his assistant, in a lonely storm-beset lighthouse.

EDWARDS: Ninety days—without relief!

HANCOCK: It's no good! I can't stand it any longer! They've forgotten us. They're going to leave us here to die alone!

EDWARDS: Steady, Hancock.

HANCOCK: Why don't they send the relief? Why don't they come and relieve us?

(Hancock panics; Edwards slaps his face to calm him.)

EDWARDS: I'm sorry I had to do that, lad, but we can't have any hysteria 'eria. Remember, all we're here to do is to keep that light burning.

BOTH: The light! (*They salute.*)

ORCHESTRA: FIRST FOUR BARS OF 'RULE BRITANNIA', RAPIDLY.

EDWARDS: That's better, lad. Now come on, help me enter the log. What time is it?

HANCOCK: It's a little after six bells.

EDWARDS (*writing in log*): 'Six bells and a clanger.' Tide—where's the tide? Well, don't just stand there, you lily-livered, chicken-hearted, low-living landlubber. Is it high tide, or is it low tide?

HANCOCK: I'll go and see.

(He opens the window and gets a faceful of water.)

HANCOCK: It's high tide.

EDWARDS: Are you sure?

HANCOCK: Yes.

EDWARDS: High tide. Weather. What's the weather like?

(Hancock looks out of the window again, and gets a faceful of water and several fish.)

HANCOCK: Unsettled.

EDWARDS: Unsettled weather according to Hancock. (*Writes in log*) 'Unsettled *Hancock* according to *me*. The light's still burning brightly, signed, Dan Dan the Lighthouse man.' You know, Hancock, I don't like the look of it at all. It's going to be a dirty night. What does it say on that barometer?

HANCOCK: 'Property of the Strand Palace Hotel'.

Popperfoto

Hancock fights with Jimmy Edwards in the 'Lighthouse Keeper' sketch from The Talk of the Town

The sketch continues, with Hancock getting facefuls of water at every opportunity. He is lowered on a rope to bring in the milk, arriving back with an octopus on his head. He salutes, using one of its tentacles. The light dims, and they put another shilling in the meter. Then an argument develops; Hancock slaps the keeper in the stomach with a flatfish, and gets logged.

EDWARDS: Don't you realize what we're both here for? To keep that light burning!

BOTH: The light! (*They salute.*)

ORCHESTRA: FIRST FOUR BARS OF 'RULE BRITANNIA', RAPIDLY.

EDWARDS: Come over here, and dedicate yourself anew. There she shines. Shine on, me proud beauty! Shine out, across that wind-tossed sea, like a guiding hand, towards haven, safety, and rest. Don't 'ee *ever* go out! Shine on for ever!

(*There is a knock at the door.*)

24

EDWARDS: What the hell was that?
HANCOCK: The relief! It must be the relief!

(He opens the door, and two attractive girls dressed in bikinis and sailor hats enter. They salute.)

HANCOCK: Our relief has arrived—what do we do now?
EDWARDS: Shut that door, and turn that flaming light out!

Hancock used to dread the facefuls of water in the winter, but looked forward to them in the summer as a welcome relief from the stifling temperature on stage.

One thing Hancock was never able to do was ad-lib. Edwards, on the other hand, had a tendency to regard any script as a basis for extemporization. As the run progressed, Edwards got bored with the same lines every night and started throwing in ad-libs. Hancock was lost.

Dennis Main Wilson recalls: 'Jim would throw out some outrageous ad-lib, and get a huge laugh. Tony would just stand there and shut up . . . Tony, shutting up, is the funniest thing you've ever seen—the full "frog face" . . . the more he shut up, the more laughs he got; and the more laughs he got, the more Jim ad-libbed; and the more Jim ad-libbed, the more Tony shut up . . .'

Hancock could never understand why the audience were laughing at *him*. 'Jim's the star, he should be getting the laughs,' he said. This inability to understand how he could be funny by doing nothing was one of the things that began to worry him as time went on.

Something of Hancock's 'frog face' can be seen in the telerecording of *Hancock's Forty-Three Minutes*, televised on December 23rd 1957; Hancock, reacting to an idiot by just standing still and looking at the ceiling, is the funniest thing in the programme.

The strain continued to build up for Hancock. One night in April 1955 he collapsed at the Adelphi with a temperature of 103. He was out of the show for ten weeks, then returned until October 29th.

Despite the behind-the-scenes strain, Hancock's performances in both Adelphi shows were masterpieces of comic stage work, as Main Wilson remembers. Hancock couldn't bear to have friends watching him from the wings. Main Wilson would visit him in his dressing room; Hancock would leave to go on stage, switching off the loudspeaker which relayed the sound from the stage as he went. Main Wilson would immediately turn it on again. 'The laughs,' he recalls, 'never came in the same place twice. He would get huge laughs on lines that were supposed to be straight.' When Hancock came back Main Wilson would try to get out of him just what he had done to get those extra laughs. Hancock could never remember. His performance was always completely intuitive. 'He had tremendous projection,' says Main Wilson. 'In the theatre, he could dominate, and not know that he was dominating.'

Hancock's stage style—and, for that matter, his early radio style— owed a debt to Sid Field. Hancock was a great admirer of Field, a superb comic who, after years in the provinces, had all too brief a career in the West End before his death. Perhaps his most famous act was the golfing sketch, with Jerry Desmonde as the reluctant instructor.

'First you must make the tee,' Desmonde would instruct Field.

'I thought we were going to play golf?'

'No, no—make the tee with sand!'

Field would be outraged. 'Tea with sand? I'm not drinking that stuff! More like co-coa!'

'Get behind your ball,' Desmonde would insist.

Field (irritated): 'It's behind all the way round!'

Desmonde would get annoyed; Field would be hurt. 'I wish I'd gone for my flute lesson with Miss Bollinger.'

The ball would eventually be driven off—to the injury of an off-stage voice. Field would observe: 'What a per-*for*mance!'

Field had the gift of making a large audience rock with laughter at simple bits of 'business' or the delivery of a straight line. Hancock often used to watch him in his earlier days. Now Hancock was approaching Field's class. For some years the debt to Field could be detected in his vocal delivery.

For Hancock's solo spot in *The Talk of the Town*, Simpson and Galton created the 'Crooner' sketch. Inspired by the antics of such singers as Johnny Ray, who would sob his way through lyrics like 'The Little White Cloud That Cried', it became a regular part of Hancock's stage act, persisting to the 1960s when most of the audience could only dimly remember such apparitions.

A photograph of the period shows him dressed in a long, loose jacket with lapels down to his waist and pockets nearly a foot square, trousers with the waist well up round his rib-cage, a string tie and thick crêpe-soled shoes. The suit was a delicate shade of pale blue.

The stooge was dressed exactly the same.

Here is a version of 'The Crooner' as it appeared in the later stage act.

HANCOCK: One hit record, that's all you need. That's how these Americans do it. They come over here and do a forty-five minute act. One song. The rest of the time they chat to the pianist, telling him how good he is. Then the pianist tells *him* how good *he* is. And there you are—forty-five minutes. So I've got myself a good lad on the jo'—got his own vamping chart. He's a life member of the Royal

26

Houston Rogers

'Knees up Mother Brown'—the original 'Crooner' sketch from The Talk of the Town

Horticultural Society. Ladies and gentlemen—I'd like to introduce now my pianist, composer, arranger and brother-in-law—Sam.

(Pianist comes down to stand facing Hancock.)

HANCOCK: Sam, it's great, great having you here, son. (*Hits pianist.*) And I wanna tell you that I'm pleased, nay, proud, to have the honour, the *hon*our, of working with you, Sam. (*Hits pianist.*) And I want you to know, Sam, that wherever I go, then surely you'll go, Sam.

(Hits pianist. Pianist eyes Hancock for a moment, then stamps very hard on his foot. Hancock hobbles away, then with a hurt toe sticking up, he moves towards pianist, rushes at him, but then stops, puts his arm around him, and smiles at audience.)

HANCOCK: He was only kidding. (Ooooh!) (*Pushes pianist off.*) How Frank Sinatra does an hour and a half in these boots I'll never know. I've got toes like globe artichokes. It's a pleasure to get off one foot onto the other. Now I'd like to sing you a little toon, a toon which we recorded over there and would like to bring over here from over there to over here, our latest record which should have been a hit but they forgot to drill a hole in the middle, a little toon . . .

ORCHESTRA: KNEES UP MOTHER BROWN.

(Hancock does tremendous high kicks, etc.)

HANCOCK: Oh, it's ridiculous. A man of my build and calibre, leaping about like a porpoise, spending half me life three feet off the ground. I think I'll have to get myself a violin and a few jokes.

After Hancock finished at the Adelphi, he made comparatively few stage appearances because television, requiring as it did a week's work for each show, did not allow him enough time. Apart from a tour of the Mediterranean entertaining the troops in 1958, he made only a few appearances until after his break with the BBC.

While he was building up his stage popularity he was also becoming widely known on radio, from an inauspicious start as a solo comedian to wide popularity in *Hancock's Half-Hour*, which by the time he finally left the Adelphi was beginning its third series. In order to trace his broadcasting career we must go back a few years.

3. Radio, 1941–54

Hancock made his first radio broadcast in the days when he was still learning his trade from George Fairweather. He was noticed by BBC producer Leslie Bridgmont, who offered him a spot in a programme called *À La Carte—a mixed menu of light fare* at 11 a.m. on June 6th 1941 on the Forces Programme (the wartime precursor of the BBC Light Programme). The programme was broadcast from Bristol, and was not, as has sometimes been suggested, an amateur 'talent' show—all the other artists had broadcast before in similar programmes. He was billed in *Radio Times* simply as 'Tony J. Hancock' and appeared with 'Hubert', Compton Evans and Ray Monelle, and Al Durrant's Swing Quintet.

He did not broadcast again until after the war. His first date was for television, on November 1st 1948; and then on January 9th 1949 he appeared in radio's *Variety Bandbox*. It was a disaster. He performed his concert party act, including the Hunchback of Notre Dame, which would have been a mistake in sound only, even if he hadn't developed a severe attack of nerves and mumbled his way through the routine.

It was with some reluctance that the BBC allowed him to appear again, on March 27th. He did rather better this time, acting out a passionate scene between Captain Chipperfield Scott of the Fourteenth Gurkhas and his sweetheart Linda Goosebody. ' "Linda, kiss me . . ." "No Charles, I can't . . ." "Linda, please . . ." "No, Charles, I can't . . ." "Why not ? . . ." "You're still on your horse" . . . "I wouldn't have come if I'd known this was going to happen, I'd have stayed in and bottled some jam . . ." '

He made numerous appearances in *Variety Bandbox* during 1950 and 1951, as well as a few *Workers' Playtimes* and other variety broadcasts. He also appeared in several radio programmes produced from the West of England by Duncan Wood, who subsequently produced all the television *Hancock's Half-Hours*.

His variety material was mostly written by Larry Stephens, an ex-commando who wrote many radio scripts, including collaborating with Spike Milligan on *The Goon Show*. Hancock usually told some unlikely story, acting the parts where necessary, and generally finishing up with a commercial announcement extolling the virtues of Milkie Wilkie Silkie Baby Food. On November 12th 1950, in *Variety Bandbox*, he told the story of Secret Agent Hancock, dropped from an aeroplane over Ruritania.

HANCOCK: It is dank, dark, and dismal, and he wishes he'd never

	volunteered. He wishes he was safe home in bed. And, most of all, he wishes he had a parachute. Luckily, beneath him is a hayrick. Unluckily, in the hayrick is a pitchfork. Luckily, he misses the pitchfork.
ORCHESTRA:	CRASH ON DRUMS.
HANCOCK:	Unluckily, he misses the hayrick. Hancock picks himself up, but after fifty yards finds himself too heavy, and puts himself down again. He arrives in the capital, where a great crowd of peasants are appealing to the Archduke for lower taxes. He turns them down, but they are starving. They appeal to him, again and again, they appeal.
ORCHESTRA:	(CRIES OF 'HOWZAT?!', etc., etc.)
HANCOCK:	Not out! . . . NO! (*to audience*) Oh, isn't it sickening! Never mind—back to work—nose to the grindstone . . . BZZZZZZ!—OO-o-oh! Where was I! Oh, yes . . .
	On he goes, and comes to the Palace. A great mob is surging around the Palace. The one-and-nines are standing only, and the place is littered with peanuts. Just above the town he spies a great castle, and takes out his field-glasses, the better to espy it. (*Repeats as for 'Twenty Questions'*)* The better to espy it. High up in the tower, he sees a tiny window, and a little midget woman. He is enraptured by her loveliness, he is amazed by her tinyness. He is looking through the wrong end of the field-glassisness.

And so on.

The money was not exactly rolling in. Around this time Phyllis Rounce, then his agent, wrote to the BBC to point out that his fee was not covering the cost of his script and the band parts, and could they up it? They raised it a few pounds—he was now showing a slight profit on broadcasts.

Variety Bandbox had picked up many of its best acts from the Nuffield Centre. Among these were Frankie Howerd and Derek Roy, who eventually found themselves topping the bill alternately as a regular booking. Howerd would start insulting Roy, and, a week later, Roy would return the insult.

At this time the Assistant Head of Variety Department was Jim Davidson, who had been a colonel in charge of the Australian equivalent of ENSA during the war. He decided to give Derek Roy his own show, which started on Thursday 2nd of August 1951 under the title *Happy-Go-*

---

* This radio quiz used a 'mystery voice', unheard by the panel, to identify the object to be guessed for the listeners; in each case the object was mentioned twice, the second time very slowly and clearly.

Lucky.

There seems to be a theatrical curse on shows with the word 'happy' in the title. There has hardly ever been a successful show, or film, with such a title, and *Happy-Go-Lucky* was no exception.

Jim Davidson was good at giving young artists and writers their heads, and *Happy-Go-Lucky* was filled with young talent. Because Davidson was an Australian there was a strong Australian contingent in the writing team, which varied from week to week, including Laurie Wyman, John Law, and Derek Roy's wife, Rona Ricardo. Much of Roy's material was patterned on American comedy shows; there was also a sequence each week in which a couple from the audience celebrated their wedding anniversary by doing a short sketch with Roy; and a self-contained comedy sketch each week starring Hancock. This was called 'The Eager Beavers', and featured Hancock as 'Mr Ponsonby', the scoutmaster of a troop of scouts played by Peter Butterworth, Graham Stark and Bill Kerr. Hancock knew Stark from the Gang Show days; Bill Kerr was an Australian comic whose pessimistic act on *Variety Bandbox* had made his catch-phrase 'I'm only here for four minutes' widely known.

The curse on *Happy* started to work rapidly. The cast hated the orchestra, the orchestra hated the choir, and everybody hated the writers. Hancock hated the 'Eager Beavers' sketches. They were direly written, by Australians Ralph Peterson and E. K. Smith.

About this time, two young men in a TB sanatorium, who had been keeping themselves occupied by writing, sent a trial script to Gale Pedrick at the BBC. Much to their surprise, he invited them to start contributing jokes to bolster up the rapidly sinking *Happy-Go-Lucky*. On October 1st 1951 they contributed 'additional material' for the first time. Their names were Alan Simpson and Ray Galton.

The producer of *Happy-Go-Lucky* was Roy Speer, described by Dennis Main Wilson as 'an English Gentleman'. He was not really tough enough to cope with the state that this programme was rapidly getting into. During the recording session on October 28th the nervous strain caught up with him and he collapsed.

The following week Dennis Main Wilson was brought in to take over. Main Wilson had come into the BBC at the age of twenty-three in 1947, having worked briefly for the BBC German Service before the war, and, after spending the war in the Royal Armoured Corps, had been seconded to the Propaganda Service of the Central Commission in Germany; after which he became Head of Light Entertainment for Nordwestdeutscher Rundfunk in Hamburg. He was offered a fairly high salary to go back into the BBC German Service, but he had set his sights on Variety. He was called 'an ungrateful young man' and given a supernumary post in charge of auditions. He subsequently became a

31

BBC Publicity
Dennis Main Wilson

radio producer, and later produced *Hancock's Half-Hour* for four series before transferring to BBC Television, where he is still at large. His main characteristics as a producer were—and still are—a tremendous nervous energy, a refusal to accept second best, and an ability to overwork his staff to a degree that is exceeded only by the amount he overworks himself. He has never been afraid to speak—or write—his mind if he thought that his programme was being obstructed in any way, as is testified by a number of lively (and frequently impolite) memos carefully locked away in the BBC's files.

He took one look at the next week's script for *Happy-Go-Lucky* and fired the writers. The script was re-written by Galton and Simpson, with Rona Ricardo and uncredited contributions from Roy and Main Wilson. Unfortunately he was contractually unable to get rid of the 'Eager Beavers' sketch, and Hancock, Stark, and Benny Hill (replacing Butterworth) fought their way through another turgid nine minutes.

The following week the 'Eager Beavers' sketch was entirely on the subject of sea-sickness. It was tasteless and embarrassing. Hancock and Stark went to Main Wilson and begged him to throw the sketch out. Main Wilson deliberately over-ran the final rehearsal by six minutes, so that something would *have* to be cut, and 'in the circumstances' removed the 'Eager Beavers' sketch.

As a result he and Hancock always got on very well; they became professional colleagues, and friends, as far as Hancock ever became friends with anyone.

Happy-Go-Lucky ran to one more episode, and was thankfully interred.

Rather happier than *Happy-Go-Lucky* was Hancock's association with *Educating Archie*. Peter Brough, like Edgar Bergen in the USA, had achieved the apparently impossible by becoming a popular

32

ventriloquist—on radio. He and his dummy, Archie Andrews, worked with a number of artists who later became famous—among them Dick Emery, Max Bygraves, Harry Secombe, and a young singer called Julie Andrews.

The scripts for *Educating Archie* were by Eric Sykes and Sid Colin. Hancock appeared throughout the second series, which started on August 8th 1951, as Archie's tutor, and doubled as a character who appeared in the first section of each programme in a variety of poses—such as a hairdresser, or, in this example broadcast on October 19th 1951, a cinema manager.

BROUGH: Well, tell me—what are you showing today?

HANCOCK: Today? Oh, it's a wonderful picture, absolutely brand new and all. Yes, there's one terrific scene where the girl is stranded on the ice. You should 'ear me accompany it on the pee-anno. I go *mad*.

ARCHIE: On the piano? You mean it's a *silent* picture?

HANCOCK: Of course it is—you don't think I'd bother with them new-fangled talkies, do you? Just a silly fad   like the motor car.

ARCHIE: Yes, yes—I suppose you're right—talking pictures will never replace the old-fashioned horse, will they?

HANCOCK: Oh, you're so right—nor will the motor car replace the back row of the cinema   I mean—hahaha . . .

BROUGH: Well now, tell me—what have you got on besides the film? I hear you said something about a stage show—is that right?

HANCOCK: Oh yes, a smashing stage show—oh, we've got a comedian here this week—laugh!—oh dear—oh, he's terrific, really worth seeing, he is.

Educating Archie—
*Hancock as the tutor
with Archie Andrews
and Peter Brough*

33

ARCHIE:	And when does he go on?
HANCOCK:	Just as soon as I can get round the back and change into me funny 'at. Well are you coming in or aren't you—the rest of the queue went in hours ago.
BROUGH:	All right, then—two one-and-threes, please.
HANCOCK:	Right you are, I'll just—where's the boy? Where's he gone?
ARCHIE:	I'm in here—in the pay-box. I'm just getting the tickets—I thought I'd save you the trouble.
HANCOCK:	That's very nice of you—I—just a minute—what have you got there in your hand?
ARCHIE:	This? It's a roll of tickets—I'm tearing them in half for you.
HANCOCK:	But—wait—put it down—put it down at once!
ARCHIE:	What's the matter? I might just as well tear them all in half—after all you'll have to do it sooner or later.
HANCOCK:	But you can't—put it down, I say.
ARCHIE:	Why?
HANCOCK:	That isn't a roll of tickets—it's the big picture.
ARCHIE:	Oh dear—come on, Brough—let's go over to the other cinema, quick, the audience is just coming out.
HANCOCK:	No—come back—oh, me entertainments—me Lillian Gish!—me business!—Oh, flippin' kids!

'Flippin' kids' rapidly became a national catch-phrase, and Hancock found himself widely popular for the first time.

In his other character, as Archie's tutor, he frequently worked with Hattie Jacques who made an excellent foil for him as the over-amorous Agatha Dinglebody.

At this stage, Hancock's voice was still a long way from the more natural delivery he eventually adopted when he arrived in East Cheam. It is very much a 'funny professor' voice, high pitched and with the throat muscles kept tight. If the existing recording from *Educating Archie* were used in a quiz, most present-day Hancock fans would be unable to identify him correctly.

As we have seen, *Educating Archie* led to his first appearance in the West End theatre, in *Archie Andrews' Christmas Party*.

Both Hancock and Max Bygraves rose to their first popularity as a result of *Educating Archie*. One night, Dennis Main Wilson and his current girl friend were driving home with Hancock and Cicely, in their separate cars. The two large cars drew up at a petrol station, and Hancock got out. 'Fill 'em up,' he told the assistant.

'Good heavens!' said the assistant, 'look who it is! Wait till I tell the missus I've seen you—she'll never believe me! We're great fans of yours—we never miss *Educating Archie*.'

'That's very nice of you,' said Hancock. He felt in his pocket and brought out two sixpences and a few odd coppers. Turning to Main Wilson, he said 'Have you got any cash?'

'No,' said Main Wilson.

Hancock said to the assistant: 'I'm afraid we have a little financial problem here.'

'I wouldn't dream of taking your money,' said the assistant. 'It's a pleasure to serve you. Anyway, how are things, Max?'

There was a silence while Hancock resorted to his 'frog face'. Main Wilson smothered a laugh and drove away as quickly as possible.

Hancock never really liked working with Archie Andrews—the sight of the dummy hanging up behind the door in Brough's dressing room apparently gave him occasional nightmares years after—and he also had visions of himself being permanently type-cast as Archie Andrews' tutor; so he left when the series ended on January 25th 1952.

He started to make appearances in *Calling All Forces*, a Variety programme aimed at British Forces stationed around the country and in Germany. There was also a large civilian audience, and gradually the emphasis of the show moved away from the Forces, as it went through various permutations of title—*Forces All-Star Bill, All-Star Bill* and *Star Bill*.

After a couple of isolated appearances, Hancock joined Charlie Chester as co compère of *Calling All Forces* on April 14th 1952, staying until the end of the series on July 28th. The scripts for the first ten programmes were written by Bob Monkhouse and Denis Goodwin, after which Alan Simpson and Ray Galton took over, writing specifically for Hancock for the first time.

Hancock and Chester, apart from doing solo material and working together, would also do a sketch with the main guest; and it was in these sketches that Hancock began to have opportunities to react to the guests. Slowly, Galton and Simpson were able to build up the idea of him as a reaction comic.

It was at this time that Hancock almost got his own half-hour series, two years before *Hancock's Half-Hour* actually started. On June 29th 1952 Hancock took part in *Hullo There*, a Saturday morning programme for children produced by Lionel Gamlin. Apparently everybody connected with the programme advised him that his 'métier' was non-audience comedy. Strange advice, to a comic whose performances and timing depended on the 'feedback' from the audience to gain the maximum effect. Comedy shows done in a studio without an audience have been few and far between, and generally have been quietly satirical, such as *In All Directions* (with Peter Ustinov and Peter Jones) or *Just Fancy* (Eric Barker and Deryck Guyler). Anyhow, the idea took root. Hancock and Larry Stephens thought about it, and came up with a suggestion which they put to producer Peter Eton. Eton put in an official memo on the subject on July 8th. Hancock was to be an estate agent and local councillor, a bachelor who lived with his aunt in a semi-detached villa in a South Coast seaside resort. The aunt would be anxious for Hancock to marry into the 'county set', but Hancock would prefer the local girls. There would be a loud-mouthed garage proprietor to whom Hancock could react, and Hancock himself would be pompous and blundering, but likeable. There would be no audience, no orchestra and no singers.

Stephens was given the go-ahead to provide a sample script. The title decided upon was 'Welcome to Whelkham'. Eton took Hancock to Seaford in Sussex, which fitted the description of the mythical Whelkham exactly.

But the programme came to nothing. Eton was at that time a Drama producer (he was later to transfer to Variety Department, where he took *The Goon Show* over from Dennis Main Wilson), and was told that, as a Drama producer, he could not produce what was in effect a Variety show. The idea fizzled out.

Perhaps it is just as well. Hancock was probably not yet really developed enough as a comic to carry a half-hour series, and the format proposed would have been rather self-limiting.

Hancock celebrated November 5th 1952 by starring in *The Guy Fawkes Show—a musical-comedy travesty of history* written by Jimmy Grafton, who at the time was closely associated with the Goons. It was produced by Dennis Main Wilson, and featured Joy Nichols, Max Bygraves, Wilbur Evans, Graham Stark, and an unbilled contribution from Jimmy Edwards.

On January 6th 1953 he returned on a regular basis in the second series of *Forces All-Star Bill*. The scripts were by Simpson and Galton, who were by now beginning to develop their writing style. The producer for the first half of the series was Dennis Main Wilson.

Main Wilson wanted to do the series from what had once been the Paris Cinema, and was now a BBC studio, but this was already booked on Sundays for *Take It From Here*. On the suggestion of Peter Sellers, he contacted Bertie Ray, Sellers' uncle and manager of the Garrick Theatre, which at that time was owned by Jack Buchanan, who was currently away in Hollywood filming *The Band Wagon*. With Ray's help, the series took over the Garrick every Sunday. After the Saturday evening performance, the theatre staff struck the set, and the BBC engineers set up the portable outside broadcast equipment. The control cubicle was in the saloon bar, behind the stalls. The equipment, the cumbersome wartime OBA/8 gear, was not really flexible enough for Main Wilson's needs. He demanded facilities for adding varying amounts of artificial reverberation on each four-channel mixing section.

36

This was supposed to be impossible, but he got it. The studio manager, Keith Fell, who worked regularly with Main Wilson, got an excellent sound from the orchestra, choir, and cast.

There is something about the Garrick auditorium which is particularly conducive to laughter; and the theatre is much more comfortable than the average BBC studio, which meant that the audience would be more relaxed. It was also a much larger audience— about 800—than was usual for this type of programme. In the early days of ITMA, the producer, Francis Worsley, had conducted experiments to find the optimum size of audience. He tried performing the show in the studio at Bangor (where Variety Department had been evacuated) with an audience of 200; he tried it in a cinema in Llandudno with an audience of 2000; and he tried it with no audience at all. He found that the large audience slowed the programme down too much, and that no audience at all gave a sense of emptiness. As a result, 200 had tended to be the standard size for a studio audience ever since. But ITMA, of course, was an extremely fast-paced show—the fastest ever broadcast, and that without benefit of pre-recording or editing. Hancock's delivery was slowing down, and in this he was helped by the larger audience. Gradually he was refining his timing.

There was some difficulty in providing Hancock with a 'girl friend'. In the first six shows he was partnered by Joan Heal, but she was not entirely satisfactory. Main Wilson and Hancock had a most enjoyable time interviewing attractive young ladies before deciding on Geraldine McEwan, who stayed with Hancock until the end of 1953 in these shows. His other partner was his regular sidekick Graham Stark.

Hancock was the star (although he would insist 'The *show* is the star'). There was a variety of guests, and the compère changed weekly, giving Hancock a chance to react to various types of artists. The first week, the compère was Ted Ray.

EFFECTS: THUDS OF LUGGAGE BEING BROUGHT IN

HANCOCK (*Off mic, calling*): All right now, bring me luggage over here. Mind how you go with me trinkets. Be careful with that big crate—there's a fortune in glassware in it. Look out!

EFFECTS: TERRIFIC CRASH OF CRATE FALLING TOGETHER WITH TINKLING OF GLASS

HANCOCK: Fools! Ruined! There was tuppence on that one, fourpence on that one, tuppence here, threepence there . . .

RAY: Here, just a minute, just a minute, what's the meaning of this? Who *are* you?

HANCOCK: Stand back, Dad, the comic's arrived. Just let me announce myself. Hang out the flags, raise a cheer, queue up girls, Hancock's here!

37

(APPLAUSE)

RAY: Look, what do you mean by coming in here and interrupting the programme? I don't know *you*.

HANCOCK: You don't know me? Ray, my merry little moron, *I* am one of the famous stars of *London Laughs*.

RAY (*realizing*): Why yes, of course, Vera—you've had your hair cut!

HANCOCK: Yes, I had to, it was getting in me eyes, and . . . ha! ha! ha! ha! Oh my word yes, highly comical that was. Yes, old Hancock's taken a liking to you. Now belt up before he takes a sledge hammer to you.

From the seventh show Main Wilson was replaced by Alistair Scott-Johnston. *Forces All-Star Bill* came to an end on May 26th 1953 and was replaced on June 7th by *Star Bill*. The regular comedy team was still Hancock, Stark, and Geraldine McEwan, and the producer was Alistair Scott-Johnston again.

Simpson and Galton were beginning to develop the Hancock character, and also to develop relationships between him and the others. This dialogue between Hancock and Geraldine McEwan comes from the 3rd show, broadcast on June 21st.

HANCOCK: Any moment now I'm expecting to see the door open, and to see a beautiful young girl come in and walk over to me, put her arm round my neck, raise her head to mine, take a deep breath and say in a voice throbbing with passion . . .

GERALDINE (*approaching*): Anthony, you've been drinking again.

HANCOCK: Geraldine!
(APPLAUSE)

HANCOCK: Hallo, Geraldine. Well, how did you like our little outing to Splithead?

GERALDINE: Don't you mean Spithead?

HANCOCK: No. Somebody bashed me over the bonce with a bottle of Vodka.

GERALDINE: Well, I thought it was wonderful, Tony.

HANCOCK: I know, I saw you. Disgusting. Making eyes at all those Russian sailors.

GERALDINE: Well, at least they were safe.

HANCOCK: What do you mean?

GERALDINE: They were the only sailors down there who know the meaning of the word 'No'!

HANCOCK: Ah, but what a magnificent spectacle it was—the ships lit up all night . . .

GERALDINE: . . . and you lit up all day. Honestly, Anthony, I was ashamed of you. What an exhibition you made of

	yourself—floating on your back behind the procession and shouting out 'Put some more water in the bath, Mrs Higgins, me boats are running aground.'
HANCOCK:	Yes, but I . . .
GERALDINE:	And as for what you did during the firework display, well really.
HANCOCK:	What do you mean?
GERALDINE (*disdainful*):	Sticking a sparkler in each ear, doing handsprings along the deck and saying 'Look, everyone, I'm a Catherine Wheel'. There's no doubt about it, Anthony, you really must try to improve your manners.
HANCOCK:	Improve them? My manners are impeccable. Didn't I help the Admiral of the Fleet's wife off with her fur coat?
GERALDINE:	Yes, that's true. We had a postcard from her this morning. She wants to know if she can have it back now.
HANCOCK:	She can have her fur coat back, but I'm keeping her rings.
GERALDINE:	How did you get her rings?
HANCOCK:	I shook hands with her, didn't I?

As can be seen, the Hancock character of this period was something of a fly boy, dishonest, and untrustworthy. It would be some time yet before the seedy gentility of East Cheam would replace this. But the scriptwriting techniques that would later make *Hancock's Half-Hour* such a landmark of comedy were already beginning to appear. Hancock's over-fertile imagination was beginning to be featured—this same imagination which in later programmes would lead him to deceive himself (though nobody else) that he could captain a ship, or pilot an aircraft.

Another technique, later to become familiar in *Hancock's Half-Hour*, was that of having the others discuss his latest odd behaviour before his entrance. In this example Hancock has evidently been preparing himself for the arrival of the guest in the broadcast of July 26th 1953.

GERALDINE:	Graham—have you seen Tony?
STARK:	Yes, but I'll get over it.
GERALDINE:	No, seriously—he's wearing a ten-gallon hat, a check shirt, boots and spurs and a holster.
STARK:	Don't worry—we all go through that phase . . .
GERALDINE:	Yes, but he has a six-gun as well.
STARK:	He'll be all right when he's run out of caps.
GERALDINE:	Shhh—here he is.
HANCOCK:	Howdy folks—mighty fine . . . have a ceegar . . . where's the chow . . . (*ordinary voice*) Well, how do I look—authentic?

STARK:	Not quite authentic—more psychopathic.
HANCOCK:	Look—Gene Autrey hat, Gene Autrey shirt—Gene Autrey six-guns—Gene Autrey gun-belt.
GERALDINE:	I know—Gene Autrey's our Guest.
HANCOCK:	Oh, you've told them—I wanted to keep it a surprise.
STARK:	If you're wearing all Gene Autrey clobber, what's he wearing—a Tony Hancock loincloth?
HANCOCK:	You ain't seen nothin' yet—watch this . . . (*Whistles*) Here boy.
EFFECTS:	HORSE COMING ON
GERALDINE:	Oh, isn't he a dear.
EFFECTS:	PAT, PAT. BODY OF HORSE FALLING. NEIGH
HANCOCK:	What do you want to pat him for?
GERALDINE:	Well . . . I only . . .
HANCOCK:	Never mind. Help me lift him up.

Hancock left *Star Bill* after the broadcast of August 2nd, and was replaced by Alfred Marks. He appeared as special guest in the last of the series, on October 25th 1953.

Meanwhile Hancock, Main Wilson, Simpson and Galton had been cooking up ideas for a half-hour series. It was the natural next step for any comedian to break away from variety to appear in a show of his own. Simpson and Galton wanted to do a straight-through half-hour situation comedy, with no musical interludes, and deliberately avoiding catch-phrases and funny voices. They put a programme suggestion to the Head of Variety on May 1st 1953. He was at first not particularly keen but in the end, and after some discussion, permission was given for the series to begin in November 1954.

The contract came through just before Hancock started in the second series of *Star Bill*, which ran for ten weeks from February 28th 1954. It was a particularly happy series. Once again Galton and Simpson wrote the scripts, and Main Wilson produced. With the certainty of their own half-hour series to come, they let themselves go and produced a highly successful show.

Main Wilson remembers sitting his his control cubicle behind the stalls in the Garrick Theatre, looking at the stage past row upon row of an audience literally rocking with laughter. Ted Ray, the guest on the second programme, said 'It's the nearest thing to a first night at the Palladium I've ever known.'

Main Wilson had considerable difficulties casting women to play opposite Hancock. Most women found that Galton and Simpson did not write particularly well for them, and left of their own accord. Main Wilson has found that it is always difficult to cast women in broad comedy—women can't really be coarse enough, and as a nation, he says,

BBC Publicity
Moira Lister and Graham Stark in a publicity pose with Hancock

we tend to be polite to women. Hancock's new female foil was Moira Lister, a thirty-one-year-old South African leading lady and character actress with considerable film experience. She came over as a strong personality, and was the best female partner Hancock had until, much later, Hattie Jacques joined the cast of *Hancock's Half-Hour*—but she, of course, was not playing a girl friend.

The weekend work at the Garrick continued as before. One day, a message came to Main Wilson that a strange man in evening dress and a top hat was wandering round back-stage, and should they throw him out? Main Wilson went to investigate. It was Jack Buchanan, standing in the wings watching the rehearsal. 'It *is* my theatre,' he said. There was a pause. 'I do walk-ons, you know!' he added. And so, on March 14th, Hancock played opposite his most famous guest yet.

HANCOCK: Ah, good evening, Mr Buchanan
BUCHANAN: Good heavens—a coal sack with legs.

41

HANCOCK (*icy*): This is my dinner jacket.

BUCHANAN: Yes—half of it's still on there.

HANCOCK: Ha! Ha! Oh my word, two on the trot, eh? (*on mic.*) Don't worry, Hancock lovers, your favourite boy is about to cope with this obstreperous 'Erbert. (*Aloud*) Any more of those and I'll flatten him with one of me broadsides.

BUCHANAN: We're not going to do the boomps-a-daisy?

HANCOCK: Ha! Ha! Three nil and we've only just kicked off. I wonder what the Comedian's Year Book has to say about this. Ah, here we are—Chapter 3: 'Crushing retorts to Flash Harrys who are coming it'. (*Mumbles to himself*) Ha! Ha! That's a good one. This'll have him. Right. Go. Mr Buchanan—do you like sweets?

BUCHANAN: Why—yes.

HANCOCK: Then how would you like a gob-stopper?

BUCHANAN: I'd love one. Where is it?

HANCOCK: On the end of me fist. Hello!

MOIRA: Now Tony, behave yourself—that's no way to talk to our guest.

HANCOCK (*hurt*): Well—he comes on here dressed up like a dog's dinner and tries to make old Hancock look a right Toby Jug. Who is he, anyway? Look at him—Fred Astaire with skin.

MOIRA: I'm sorry about this, Jack—you see, he's jealous. He hates anybody who's better looking than he is.

BUCHANAN: So?

MOIRA: He hasn't got a friend in the world.

This series also saw the development of a character called Higgins, who was honoured by a billing in *Radio Times* from programme five onwards, but who never actually spoke—he was always off-stage, having instructions shouted at him by Hancock. In this sketch, from the fourth show, broadcast on March 21st 1954, Stark and Lister play an elderly couple arriving at Hancock's seaside boarding house.

STARK: Do you mean to say, sir, that you run this place by yourself?

HANCOCK: By myself? Oh, my word, no—I couldn't possibly run this gigantic establishment on me tod. No—I got 'Iggins.

MOIRA: Who's Higgins?

HANCOCK: 'Iggins? Oh, he's me staff. Yes. He's been with the hotel many years, has 'Iggins—a bit old now, you know, a bit past it—he was posted here during the war—Chief of Invasion Defence Forces, he was—oh, a very responsible job. It was 'Iggins who saved England.

STARK:	How?
HANCOCK:	Who do you think lit the beacons when the Armada come? Now then—I expect you want to see your rooms. Are you fully insured?
STARK:	Of course we are.
HANCOCK:	Yes, well we'll take a chance on the lift, then. Oh yes we've got all the mod. cons. here, you know—usual offices—that's it, pile in, close the gates. That's it, right—now we'll be up there in no time. I'll just get it started. I have to shout up the lift shaft to the engineer. Pardon me. (*Shouts, off*) 'Iggins! Second floor! That's right—ready?—Pull! Good lad!— 'eave, 'Iggins—Oh, well done—we made five foot on that one—oh—we're dropping! Dig your heels in, 'Iggins, lad—that's it—well done—another two foot—that'll do it—Fool! Don't let go—we haven't got out yet! Hold it— there! (*To mic.*) Swipe me, I'll have that cable round his neck before the day's out, I will. There we are—all out— here are your rooms. There we are.
STARK:	Oh, I say! Oh dear—I suppose you call this the blue room, what?
HANCOCK:	Blue room? Oh my word! 'Iggins—have you been writing on the wall again? I do apologize, madam—I assure you this is the finest room in Seaview Hotel.
STARK:	Seaview? You're quite sure we shall be able to *see* the sea?
HANCOCK:	See it? Six o'clock every night we're *in* it!
MOIRA:	You mean, when the tide's in, the sea comes right up to the hotel?
HANCOCK:	Right up to it—oh, it goes past it—oh, very handy. We can serve drinks all day if we like, we're outside the three-mile limit. Of course, we've had to fix up a lighthouse on the roof, you know—well, I say lighthouse, that's boasting a bit—I've got 'Iggins walking round in circles with a candle tied on his bonce.
STARK:	Tell me, has the sea always been as close as this?
HANCOCK:	Oh my word, no—when I first come here we was four-and-a-half miles inland. There was a whole town between us and the sea. All gone over the years, you know—the sea's claimed it.
STARK:	Erosion, I suppose.
HANCOCK:	No, no—it just wore away.

The series came to a rousing end on May 2nd. On a growing wave of popularity and optimism, on the gales of laughter from the audience in the Garrick Theatre, Hancock was now ready for his Half-Hours. The long haul through *Variety Bandbox* and *Workers' Playtime* and the dismal music-halls up and down the country was over. He had done a popular revue in the West End, a Royal Variety Performance and was shortly to open in another smash hit stage revue. He had sung his last soppy song in Pantomime and compèred his last variety broadcast. Ahead of him stretched his own radio series, with writers and a producer who understood him and a cast who were perfect foils for his increasingly subtle style of comedy.

He had arrived.

4. Radio, 1954–56

Simpson and Galton did not, as has sometimes been suggested, invent the half-hour radio situation comedy. Indeed they have never claimed that they did. Several programmes had adopted the format of half an hour without musical interludes and telling a continuous story, by the time *Hancock's Half-Hour* started. *Life with the Lyons*, with Ben Lyon and Bebe Daniels Lyon, had been running for several years; and *A Life of Bliss*, written by Godfrey Harrison and using a cast of actors rather than comedians, had been running since 1953. Both were domestic comedies, rather sheltered and cosy in their approach. *A Life of Bliss* was extremely skilfully written, avoiding jokes as such and relying entirely on the confusion of the central character, a shy young bachelor. *Life with the Lyons* relied much more on actual jokes, and was firmly in the tradition of American domestic comedies.

Ted Ray had his own half-hour series, *Ray's A Laugh*, which had started out in the traditional BBC Variety format of three separate sequences with intervening musical numbers; one of the sequences was a short domestic sketch with Ray's radio 'wife', Kitty Bluett. This was later expanded into a straight-through half-hour, with no music. Again, this was basically a domestic situation comedy series, but with more outlandish characters appearing regularly to do sections of the show with Ray, and not necessarily carrying the plot forward. This show was as a result poised somewhere between pure domestic situation comedy and shows of the *ITMA* and *Goon Show* type, where a thin plot-line was filled out by a succession of characters revolving round a central comedian.

What Simpson and Galton did was to break situation comedy away from the domestic surroundings of the other shows, and to build a firm plot-line round their central character and his friends. They intended that there should be no catch-phrases and no funny voices—two of the basic props of comedy scriptwriters—but neither they nor Hancock were yet quite experienced enough to manage without such aids altogether. There is also an air of unreality about many of the shows—although this is really only noticeable when they are listened to with hindsight, in the context of the later programmes.

A tremendous amount of preparation has to go into a new series. Simpson, Galton, Hancock and Main Wilson put considerable thought into their format, and how they would develop their situations. Firstly they had to build up a strong cast. A girl friend was needed for Hancock. This seems a little odd in the light of the later development of the character, who would never be able to attract women; but it was more or less traditional at that time that comedians would have 'girl friends'; this went back to the American variety shows, where the guest was often a girl, and the resident comic would spend most of the programme trying to date her. Moira Lister made a good choice, having been with Hancock for the final series of *Star Bill*. Again, her strong personality enabled her to stand up well to him; she was always trying to 'take him in hand', though one sometimes wondered what she saw in such an unsuccessful and often shady character.

Hancock's other friend was played by Bill Kerr, who had been one of the Scouts in the *Eager Beavers* sketches in *Happy-Go-Lucky*. Simpson and Galton visualized him as a fast-talking American-type Australian; in these early shows he is in fact brighter than Hancock, and it was only later that he evolved into a sort of Stan Laurel-like character, of rather lower intelligence.

One of the aspects of Hancock's radio personality that Simpson and Galton wanted to play up was his gullibility, so they needed a confidence trickster who could fleece him in some way each week. They saw just the actor they wanted playing one of the crooks in the film *The Lavender Hill Mob*, and had to go back to see the film again in order to find out his name. It was Sidney James.

James was born in Johannesburg in May 1915; he had qualified as a diamond polisher, but soon got bored with it, and after the Second World War he came to England, where he took up acting. His highly individual features made him a gift to film directors needing to cast petty criminals or taxi drivers, and he appeared in minor parts in many films. As it happened, Hancock had recently worked with James in a film called *Orders Are Orders*. Later James became closely identified with Hancock—he made an ideal foil for him in the television series; but in these early radio programmes it is really Kerr who is Hancock's sidekick, and James who scores off Hancock; in the later radio programmes James became more a friend of Hancock's (though a highly shady one) and Kerr, by now much more stupid, became the butt of many of Hancock's funniest remarks. Kerr was also billed above James in the *Radio Times* for the first three series, after which the billing favoured James.

Main Wilson needed one more regular voice, to play the succession of lower-middle-class bureaucrats with whom Hancock was expected to get involved. He rang round various theatrical agents without success, until one of them suggested that Main Wilson should go to see an actor—not on the agent's books—who was appearing as the Dauphin in Shaw's *Saint Joan* at the Arts Theatre. It was the twenty-eight-year-old Kenneth Williams.

Main Wilson went to see a performance. He was not disappointed— Williams imbued the Dauphin with comedy, sadness, and towards the end, a malevolence that deeply impressed Main Wilson. He remembers his first meeting with Kenneth Williams extremely vividly: 'I go backstage—and I'm going to do this young man the biggest favour he's ever had in his life—and I'm told, "Oh, he's very busy—you'll have to wait". So I go round the corner to the bar . . . and this tall, elegant, Irving-Garrick-type actor laddie comes in, and *booms* at me—"Well, what do you want?"

'So I said—"I'm a BBC Producer"—Williams said "Mmm—I don't like the wireless . . ."

'So I bought him a large light ale . . . and he said, "Well, what's it all about?"

'So I said, "We've got this great idea for a great show"—and *I* am trying to *placate* him!

'We were half-way through this—and Ken Williams collapsed into a fit of giggles, and said "I don't care, I'll do it—what is it?"

'He took me in for about half-an-hour . . . a very powerful personality, of enormous warmth.'

They had their cast.

One decision that had to be made in choosing the cast was whether to carry over Hancock's friend Graham Stark from *Star Bill*. It was Main Wilson who decided against this, partly because Stark's voice was a little too similar to Hancock's at this time. Stark was disappointed, and probably Hancock was a little embarrassed about it; unfortunately it dampened their friendship.

Considerable care was taken over the music. Simpson, Galton and Main Wilson put their heads together and worked out a large number of possible situations for which linking music would be required. Stanley Black was to have composed the music, but became ill shortly before the recording session, and Wally Stott took over the job. He hurriedly composed opening and closing signature tunes, playout music, and nineteen link pieces, with durations ranging from seven seconds to one minute fifteen seconds. They had titles (for easy reference behind-the-scenes, not for on-air use) like 'Back to Tony's—Sad', 'Back to Tony's—Happy', 'Hancock going downstairs', 'Hancock going upstairs', and 'Hancock Rumbled—All Scarper'. They were all based on the signature tune; a jaunty, optimistic piece, scored for tuba with a light orchestral accompaniment, which has gone into radio history:

In those days it was possible, under Section 'D' of the BBC's agreement with the Musician's Union, to hire musicians for pre-recordings of signature tunes and incidental music on an 'all rights', or once-for-all basis. The fees paid covered the recording session, after which the musicians expected no further payments no matter how many times the recordings were used. This of course applied only to incidental music; concert broadcasts were much more tightly controlled by the Union, for obvious reasons; and even under today's more flexible agreement any musical performance may only be broadcast twice, with an additional 'repeat' fee being payable for the second transmission.

The music was recorded on October 29th by the Augmented BBC Revue Orchestra conducted by Harry Rabinowitz; the orchestra consisted of five violins, two violas, a 'cello, a guitar (doubling electric guitar), a trumpet, a trombone, a flute (doubling piccolo), harp, tuba and drums. The tuba, featured as the musical representation of Hancock himself, was played by Jim Powell.

The first edition of *Hancock's Half-Hour* was recorded on October 30th 1954, and broadcast at 8 p.m. on November 2nd. The opening of the show demonstrates careful planning by Simpson and Galton, who were already giving Hancock the chance to show his timing in pauses, a technique for which he would become famous later on.

GRAMS: 'HANCOCK OPENING'
ANNOUNCER (*over music*): We present Tony Hancock with Moira Lister, Bill Kerr and Sidney James in . . .
GRAMS: 'HANCOCK OPENING'
HANCOCK (*all excited—breath*): 'Hancock's Half-Hour'
GRAMS: 'HANCOCK OPENING'
ANNOUNCER: Yes—this is the first night of the lad's new radio series. Such occasions are usually marked by a *small* celebration

of some sort, but Tony Hancock is really doing it in style—*he* is going to throw a cocktail and dinner party. So let's go over to Tony's flat in the English quarter of London's West End, where he and Bill Kerr are making the arrangements.

GRAMS: 'HANCOCK OPENING'
CROSSFADE TO

EFFECTS: TYPEWRITER CLACKING—VERY SLOW AND DELIBERATE—ONE FINGER

HANCOCK: Hurry up, Kerr. Haven't you finished typing out those invitations yet?

BILL: Don't rush me, don't rush me.

EFFECTS: TYPEWRITER CONTINUES SLOW CLACKING. DING OF BELL. CARRIAGE SLIDES BACK. SLIGHT PAUSE. SLOW CLACKING AGAIN

HANCOCK: It might help if you took the gloves off.

BILL: My hands are cold.

EFFECTS: MORE SLOW CLACKING. SEVEN KEYS STRUCK

BILL: Anyway, what's wrong with typing in gloves?

EFFECTS: MORE SLOW CLACKING. SIX KEYS STRUCK

BILL: I *like* typing in gloves.

EFFECTS: MORE SLOW CLACKING. FIVE KEYS STRUCK

BILL: Lots of people type in gloves.

EFFECTS: MORE SLOW CLACKING. FOUR KEYS STRUCK

HANCOCK: Not in boxing gloves.

BILL: Now quit flapping. I'm nearly finished.

HANCOCK: I should think so. Sixty-five invitations to be done. You've taken five hours over it.

EFFECTS: FIVE MORE CLACKS—LAST TWO FAST AND FINAL

BILL: There you are—finished.

HANCOCK: Good—that's one done. Let's see now—let's have a look at it. (*Reads*) 'Dear sir or . . . or . . .'

BILL: Madam.

HANCOCK: Oh yes! Yes—it's the first time I've seen it spelt that way—M, percentage, five eighths, question mark, A, semicolon, M.

BILL: Look, Tub—I only *hit* the keys—after that they're on their own. Now read the rest of it.

HANCOCK (*reads*): 'You are cordially invited to a dinner party to celebrate the first programme of my new radio series, x, x,

48

	x, x, x . . .'
BILL:	I was chasing a fly across the paper.
HANCOCK:	And the smudge?
BILL:	He didn't quite make it.
HANCOCK:	Ha ha—well done. Where are we? (*Reads*) 'Dinner will be served at 8.30 sharp. Dress optional. Bring your own wife'. Yes, that should be all right.
BILL:	Look, I think the whole idea's screwy. What do you want to throw a dinner party for, anyway?
HANCOCK:	Diplomacy. Get 'em all on my side—the National newspapers—the BBC. I'm inviting all the radio critics and the high BBC officials.
BILL:	How high?
HANCOCK:	By the time they leave here it'll be coming out of their ears.

Hancock sends the invitations off in envelopes marked OHMS ('Old Hancock's Mail Swindle'). Moira arrives, and points out that the flat is no fit place to hold a dinner party. Bill knows a friend who can hire Hancock a place—'Smooth-Talking Sidney'—'As honest as the day is long'. Hancock: 'That's not much of a reference in November.'

They go round to see Sid. They are met at the door by Coatsleeve Charlie ('sniff, sniff'), played by Gerald Campion. Charlie was to have been a regular character but Galton and Simpson decided he had already worn out his welcome.

Sid is most impressed by Moira. 'Permit me to shake your hand.' Hancock: 'You won't find her hand round there.' A bargain is struck, and Sid hires out a posh flat in Park Lane to Hancock. As soon as the others have gone, Sid sends a telegram to the owner of the flat telling him to leave for Scotland immediately.

Hancock, Moira and Bill get into the flat with the aid of a crowbar thoughtfully provided by Sid. They look round. It is magnificent, palatial. Hancock wanders into an adjacent room, and immediately lets out a cry of panic: 'Help—me feet—they're gone'. Moira: 'Tony, you're standing on the carpet.'

The preparations for the party get under way. Hancock shouts instructions to his French Chef: ''Iggins!—half past seven, lad—give the ox another turn on the spit.'

Sid and Charlie volunteer to act as butlers. The first guests arrive, and the party gets under way. Hancock takes time off for a chat with a character played by Alan Simpson; this was to become a regular spot, with Hancock telling a tall story and Simpson always agreeing with him.

The party continues. ''Iggins!—gut another sturgeon.' Sid and Charlie make their way round the guests picking pockets. Gradually the

49

guests get more and more drunk on Hancock's bath-tub gin. They have just lit a fire on the table and started throwing things out of the windows when the owner of the flat, Lord Bayswater (Kenneth Williams) arrives. He is naturally annoyed 'Do you realize who I am?' Hancock: 'I'm afraid your mime wasn't very helpful.'

Realizing that the game is up, Hancock and the others scarper. As they leave, Lord Bayswater demands to know Hancock's name.

Next morning, there is no radio column in the paper—but the 'Stop Press' carries the announcement that sixty-five hooligans have been arrested for housebreaking, and that the police are still looking for a little fat man by the name of Ted Ray.

The listeners' reaction to the show was not particularly enthusiastic, and adverse comments were made on the quality of the script; but there were also favourable comments, and as the series progressed the reactions became more and more favourable.

The show was also taken by the BBC Transcription Services, who issue various BBC programmes for use by overseas radio stations, so that from the beginning *Hancock's Half-Hour* reached a wide audience, particularly in Australia, New Zealand, and South Africa. Not all of the shows were considered suitable for an overseas audience; from the forty-eight shows in the first three series, Transcription Services issued twenty-three.

Kenneth Williams appeared in most of the programmes in the first series, and a few other artists appeared in minor rôles, including Dora Bryan, Peter Sellers, and Canadian Paul Carpenter (better known at the

BBC Publicity
Hancock rejecting yet another of Bill Kerr's schemes

time as 'Jeff Arnold' in *Riders of the Range*).

The basic format of most of the plots was that Hancock would need something done, and that Bill would know just the man to do it—Sid James. Hancock would start by refusing to have anything further to do with Sid. 'He's a twister—do you know, last week he sold me two tickets to see a West End show . . . it wasn't till I got inside and bought me programme I found out it was the one I'm in!' But Bill would persuade him; and once Sid started talking, Hancock would be hopelessly lost.

The thirteenth programme, 'A House on the Cliff', provides a particularly complicated example of a Sid James fiddle. Hancock has bought some land from Sid to build a house on. Sid insists that any building on his land must be done by a company nominated by him—in fact, his own. Then the complications start:

SID: Now, let's get down to details. I suggest we build the house on the beach, *underneath* the cliff. It'll shelter it nicely. All right? (*General agreement.*) Now that should provide you with a very comfortable little home, right up to eight o'clock at night.

BILL: Well, what happens then?

SID: Then you move out.

HANCOCK: Why?

SID: The tide comes in.

MOIRA: And *where* do we move to?

SID: Into the other house.

HANCOCK: Oh, I see. The other house.

SID: The one we've had built on the cliff top.

HANCOCK: Oh, that old thing! Whose idea was it, building that one?

SID: Mine.

HANCOCK: Oh yes, of course, yes. You're the man who owns the building company, aren't you.

SID: 'sright. Mind you, I'm only doing it for your own good.

MOIRA: Of course.

SID: I mean, you don't want to stay in that one on the beach all night and drown, do you.

BILL: No, of course not.

SID: Well then, you've got to have another one built on the cliff top, haven't you.

HANCOCK: Yes, I suppose we have.

SID: Well shut up, then.

HANCOCK: Just a minute—I can't afford to buy two lots of furniture.

SID: You don't have to. You take it with you when you go. Now look—you start moving the furniture at four o'clock in the afternoon, so when the tide comes in at eight o'clock, you

	just have time to nip back down and lock all the doors.
HANCOCK:	Why?
SID:	To stop the sea getting in.
HANCOCK:	Well, if the sea can't get in, why can't I stay down there?
SID:	What, and leave all the furniture out on the cliff top all night?
HANCOCK:	Of course, I hadn't thought of that.
MOIRA:	Now look, just a minute—why can't we just build *one* house, on the cliff top?
SID:	Well, you can do, but then where are you going to live during the day?
HANCOCK:	Where are we going to live during the day. Well, it's obvious, we just ... he's right, you know! He's right! (*Tragically*) We've got nowhere to live during the day! Homeless! Tramping the moors waiting for night to come so we can go home! He's dead right!
MOIRA:	Tony, don't be so silly, he's *not* right. I know plenty of people who manage perfectly well with *one* house. We'll build it on the cliff top. We don't want the one down on the beach.
HANCOCK:	Don't want it? I've paid seven thousand quid for that house. I'm not knocking it down for you or anybody.
MOIRA:	It's not built yet!
HANCOCK:	That's no excuse! It's my home—just because you don't like it, I'm supposed to knock it down and have nowhere to live during the day!
MOIRA:	You can live in the one on the cliff top all the time!
HANCOCK:	Then who's going to live in the one down on the beach?
MOIRA:	Nobody!
HANCOCK:	You expect me to leave it down there empty, after all the money I've paid for it?

Moira and Bill try to persuade Hancock that he is being twisted, but Hancock is adamant.

HANCOCK:	We're having two houses built and that is that.
SID:	Good. Now there's just one point about the house on the cliff top. If the weather gets rough, and the sea undermines the bottom of the cliff, the house might collapse.
HANCOCK:	Oh dear.
SID:	But you've got nothing to worry about. I'm going to take precautions.
HANCOCK:	Good lad, Sid, my pal.
SID:	I'm going to build you another house, two miles inland.

52

HANCOCK: Yes, of course, no point in taking chances.

MOIRA: But, Tony . . .

HANCOCK: Quiet! The man's saved me life again.

BILL: So now we've got *three* houses! One underwater twice a day, one liable to collapse any minute, and one—there's nothing wrong with the third one, is there?

SID: Not a thing. Perfectly good house.

MOIRA: Then let's just settle for that one. Forget about the others, eh?

HANCOCK: Don't be ridiculous, Moira, the only reason we're building this one is because the other two aren't safe! If you don't build 'em, there's no point in building this one—the reason's gone.

MOIRA: Yours isn't doing so good, either, is it.

Sid's master plan also includes an elevator between the first and second houses, and a railway between the second and third. Total cost— £144,000.

The series ended on February 15th 1955. All concerned were quite pleased with themselves, but aware that they had not made a particularly big impression with the public, despite some favourable comments; so they were delighted when the BBC asked them to do another series almost immediately, to start only two months later on April 19th. Even better, the shows would have repeats on Sunday afternoons.

Then complications set in. On April 4th George Black Ltd, who had Hancock under contract for his appearances at the Adelphi Theatre in *The Talk of the Town*, wrote to Kavanagh Productions Ltd, who were now representing Hancock. They felt themselves unable to authorize Hancock to appear in the new radio series. A dispute began between George Black's and the BBC as to the exact legal position, but in the end permission was obtained for the series to go ahead.

Then, only a few days before the first recording session, came Hancock's collapse at the Adelphi. Suffering from nervous strain and a high temperature, he left the theatre before the final number in the first evening performance. (Dickie Henderson Jr took over for second house.) Main Wilson arrived at the theatre shortly afterwards, only to be told by the stage door keeper that Hancock had gone. After the show finished, Main Wilson and Jimmy Edwards scoured the West End pubs and drinking clubs looking for him, without success.

When Main Wilson got home a friend of his, a Superintendent in Scotland Yard's Special Branch to whom he happened to have given two tickets for the recording, rang him and said 'What is Hancock doing on the last plane to Rome?' Hancock turned up in Positano.

Hurried negotiations took place. George Black Ltd promptly

53

rescinded the permission they had given for Hancock to broadcast, on the grounds that the Adelphi audiences would be upset if he were to be heard on radio when at the same time he was not fit enough to appear in *The Talk of the Town*. On April 15th the BBC decided officially that a replacement must be found, even though there was a slight possibility that Hancock might return and be willing to do the broadcast. Main Wilson rang his friend from the *Goon Show* days, Jimmy Grafton, and said 'Help!'

Grafton was (and still is) Harry Secombe's agent, and Secombe agreed to cover for Hancock. The first show was recorded on April 17th, and transmitted on April 19th. It began with the rather incongruous announcement: 'We present *Hancock's Half-Hour* starring Harry Secombe, Bill Kerr, Sidney James . . .'

Andrée Melly was the new girl friend, Moira Lister having left, and the first script tells how Hancock and Bill, intending to holiday in Southend, finish up in Paris, where they meet Andrée, who comes back with them. (As a result of this, Andrée has a strong French accent, which Galton and Simpson came to regret by the end of the series.)

Harry Secombe, already well known as a solo comedian, was in the difficult position of having to stand in for a completely different type of comic. Despite his bubbling exterior, Secombe was often a very nervous performer, but his four years in *The Goon Show* had given him experience of getting out of any tricky situation by using funny voices, giggling infectiously, and blowing raspberries. As a consequence, the programme sounded more like a *Goon Show*. There had been no opportunity to re-write the script, and Secombe just took over Hancock's part, though under his own name, not as Hancock.

As the second show approached, there was still no sign of Hancock; Jimmy Grafton was reluctant to let Secombe continue doing a show that was so far outside his normal comedy style, but, out of friendship for Hancock, Secombe covered the next two programmes. The scripts were altered so that, in Hancock's absence, Bill was staying (as a slightly unwelcome guest) with Secombe; Andrée was also there, having been smuggled in from France. During these two programmes, Secombe became more confident and gave excellent performances. Main Wilson wonders whether Secombe might not have made a first-class actor-comedian as well as the effervescent Neddie Seagoon he is so well known for. Hancock returned for the fourth programme. (He did not return to the Adelphi for several weeks, but George Black's allowed him to broadcast in the meantime.)

In this programme, Andrée has attached herself to Hancock as originally intended. She and Bill persuade him that he ought to thank Harry Secombe for standing-in in his absence. They go to Swansea, eventually finding Secombe, who appears once more as a guest, down a coal mine. Hancock swears that he will never again miss a show so that someone has to stand in for him—and promptly gets an attack of lumbago. As Bill and Andrée look after him, Secombe sets out for London—to cover the *next* radio show.

The sixth programme, 'The Chef That Died of Shame' is something of an oddity. The usual signature tune was abandoned, and the cast stepped out of their normal characters to enact the story of the rise and fall of a pie-stall cook—the story, in fact, of the ubiquitous 'Iggins, played by Hancock. The programme makes chilling listening today, because the downfall of the cook, who has risen to be a Haute Cuisine chef, is through drink; and the programme ends with the now alcoholic 'Iggins back at his pie-stall. There was no conscious prophecy in the writing—at this time Hancock, though fond of his beer, was not drinking much more than many other people in show business, and it was not in any way affecting his work: neither he nor Simpson and Galton had the slightest inkling of what was to come some years later.

In the eighth programme of the series, 'The Rail Strike', broadcast on June 7th 1955, Hancock, Sid and Bill take advantage of the current national rail strike to run their own unlikely train to Brighton. In fact, the train, consisting as it does of a pram, two bathtubs, a wheelchair, a four-poster bed and a pie-stall, all hauled by 'The Rocket' (stolen from the Science Museum), is perhaps just a little *too* unlikely.

The programme is principally interesting for the first of many encounters between Hancock and a character played by Kenneth Williams, generally indicated in the scripts as 'Ken (snide)'. This new addition to the gallery of Williams's portrayals became extremely popular in the fourth series, and it will be more convenient to refer to him as Snide, although he is never actually addressed by this name in the shows.

This voice, still in the early stages of its development, appears in one or two shows earlier in the second series—in 'The Holiday Camp' he masquerades as Edwardian Fred (usually a deeper, Cockney voice), but 'The Rail Strike' marks the first appearance of the character in his proper form. He makes himself a nuisance to Andrée while she is waiting for Hancock's train to start from Clapham Junction, and then annoys Hancock during the journey to Brighton.

Another passenger on the train is Alan Simpson, in his regular appearance as the little man who listens to Hancock's tall stories. A storm has blown up, and Hancock is boasting to Simpson (whose interjections are given in brackets in the following transcript) about his previous experience in storms.

'Of course, this isn't the first time I've been out in a storm. (Isn't it?) No. This is nothing to what I'm used to. (No?) I've been in storms when it's rained so much even the fish were swimming about in raincoats.

(Really.) The storm I remember most . . . (Yes?) the one that'll really have you interested, the one that had me worried, (Yes) happened when I was in the Caribbean. (Get away!) I was fishing for whales, I was just winding me rod in, to see how big the whale was. (Yes.) 'Course, if they're under twenty ton, I throw them back, you know. (Well, of course.) Anyway, I was winding me rod in, when it struck, the whirlwind. Well this whirlwind centred right over my boat and it sucked us right up in the air. (Did it really?) There I was, two hundred feet up in the air on top of a waterspout! (Oh dear!) Still sitting in me boat. (Yes.) Well, I stopped rowing. (Did you, yes.) Well, there's not much point when you're in the air, I always say. (No.) I usually do if I'm in a predicament of that type. (Yes, when you're in the air.) I stopped rowing. Well, as suddenly as it started, it stopped—you can guess what happened. (What?) Splash. (You were in the water.) That's right. (Dear oh dear.) There I was, floundering about, almost drowning, (Yes) nearly given up, I had, when suddenly, the whaling fleet saw me. (Did they?) Thank you. I waved and shouted, and they steamed towards me at full pelt. (Yes?) Ooh, I *was* relieved. (Wonderful, I bet you were.) Ooh, it was a weight off my mind I don't mind telling—I was relieved. I thought I'd had it. (Did you?) I thought I'd had it. I can't tell you how pleased I was to see them. They came nearer, all the crew rushing about, exciting,—they got within, oh, about twenty yards of me, and—do you know what they did? (What?) They harpooned me!'

The following week, in 'The TV Set', Snide made an appearance in a scene which firmly established him as one of the most irritating inhabitants of Hancock's radio world. These scenes became immensely popular in the later series, and Snide's entrance line could always be relied on to get a round of applause. In this show, Hancock has bought a kit for making a TV set, and has managed to get it working. He, Sid, Bill and Andrée have just settled down to watch a play they particularly want to see when there is a ring at the front door bell.

HANCOCK: Yes?
SNIDE: Good evening.
HANCOCK: Oh, cor blimey, it's him.
SNIDE: I'm your next door neighbour.
HANCOCK: Well, make the most of it, I'm moving tomorrow.
SNIDE: I've just come round to borrow a pint of milk. My Tibby hasn't had anything to drink all day.
HANCOCK: Well, I'm very sorry to hear it, I—
SNIDE: 'Course, he only gets fed when I come home from work, you see . . . and he does like the top off the milk . . .
HANCOCK: Yes, well look, here's a quart. Must go.
SNIDE: You haven't got any fish as well, have you? Any old little

56

	bits'll do, he's not fussy—cod fillet, bit of plaice, anything like that. Nice cat, he is.
HANCOCK:	Yes I've seen him, digging up me rhubarb. Now look I must go, it's been very nice . . .
SNIDE:	Oooooooohhh! You've got a telly!
HANCOCK:	Yes, we're watching the play, so if you don't mind . . .
SNIDE:	You don't mind if I step inside for a minute and watch it, do you?
HANCOCK:	Well, I . . .
SNIDE:	Thanks. Good evening all.
OMNES:	(GOOD EVENINGS)
SNIDE:	I'll sit here, shall I?
HANCOCK:	No, well, that's my seat you see, and . . .
SNIDE:	Oh, dear.
HANCOCK:	What?
SNIDE:	You haven't bought one of *those* sets, have you?
HANCOCK:	Well, yes, . . . and we're trying to watch the play, you see . . .
SNIDE:	You've bought trouble there, you have.
HANCOCK:	Yes, well . . .
SNIDE:	I'll give it three weeks and you'll need a new tube.
HANCOCK:	Yes, well it's going all right at the moment, so if you'll keep quiet we can all watch the play, eh?
SNIDE:	Have you had any trouble with the valves yet?
HANCOCK:	No.
SNIDE:	You will. They go in bunches. Cost you a fortune. (*Laughs*)
HANCOCK:	Yes, well let's see if they last to the end of the play, shall we . . . I've been waiting all week to see this and—
SNIDE:	You've got it too bright, you know.
HANCOCK:	Oh cor . . .
SNIDE:	Of course, it's nothing to do with me, but quite frankly, I think you've bought a lot of rubbish there.
SID:	Oi . . . pimples.
SNIDE:	Are you talking to me?
SID:	Yes—and if you keep on, I'll probably be the last person to do so.

Despite the funny voice, this is comedy of character rather than jokes.

It was a happy team. Hancock never saw the script before the morning of the recording, although he could have had it two days earlier if he had wished; instinctively he knew that he should not spend too much time on the script, or it would go sour on him. He would read it through with the others on the Sunday morning. Ray Galton remembers: 'He was a great interpreter of lines. You could go through a script on the first read-through, the first time he'd seen it, and every line would be right on the nail—the timing, the delivery, the rhythm.' Alan Simpson adds: 'Even if he didn't understand it he would deliver it perfectly.' It was a facility he never lost. He was also a generous giver-away of his own best lines— he would say 'Can't we give that one to Sid, he'd do it much better than me.'

The only problem during the series—apart from the fraught start— had been in finding a suitable recording venue. The Paris Cinema was, again, booked for *Take It From Here*. Main Wilson tried doing a lunchtime matinée at the Camden Theatre (like The Paris, in exclusive use as a BBC studio) but got a rather unsuitable audience—'Too many housewives'. Then he tried recording late in the evening at the Paris, after *TIFH* had finished. This resulted in a number of show-business 'mates' turning up from the nearby theatres, with the result that there was too much laughter, which sounded rather false. The problem was solved in the next series by recording at the Fortune Theatre, which was available for the usual mid-evening recording time.

With the third series the programme began to settle into the style of the later, more famous shows. Hancock was now firmly established at 23 Railway Cuttings, after a few variations of the address in the earlier series, but the ownership of the property varied from week to week to suit the requirements of the story. Sometimes it was a council house, sometimes there was a private landlord, and on a few occasions Hancock owned the house. Later on Hancock's ownership became the rule rather than the exception. A few changes were made to the characters—Andrée lost her French accent, Snide became fully established as a regular pest, and Alan Simpson's dialogues with Hancock were dropped because they were beginning to get in the way of plot development.

On October 12th 1955 the signature tune was re-recorded in a slightly different version, together with eleven more links and a different playout. On October 19th the series began with the saga of a pet dog, bought for Andrée, which grows rapidly and takes over the house. The show is well written and performed, and very funny; heard today in the context of the later shows it is noticeable that the cast perform at the frenetic pitch then normal in comedy programmes—it was not until the later series that they felt really able to relax and lower the pace. Hancock is still using the tight-throated and pitched-up delivery, a remnant from his days in *Educating Archie*, and Bill is still the fast-talking character. During this series they both slowed their delivery and dropped the pitch of their voices, though only slightly—it was in the next series that they adopted the more familiar style.

One of the less desirable traits of the BBC Variety Department at this time was a tendency to attempt to eat its young. Having given a new show every sort of encouragement, including the best technical and production staff, the hierarchy would then start sniping, particularly at any manifestations of 'controversy' or 'bad taste'. The more popular the programme was, the heavier the sniping was likely to be. The programme which suffered most from this was of course *The Goon Show*, which found itself in danger of summary execution at frequent intervals, but *Hancock's Half-Hour* had a certain amount of difficulty too. During the first series Main Wilson had made loud complaints that the budget did not allow him to hire as many extra voices as he would like (this was one reason why Galton and Simpson appeared in many shows reading odd lines), and expressed annoyance at a ban on guest stars. During the second series someone in Administration suddenly woke up, noticed that Main Wilson was consistently staying well inside his financial allocation, and suggested that the allocation should therefore be reduced. This danger having been averted, sniping started at the programmes themselves.

The sixth programme of the third series was a skit on the current film *Blackboard Jungle*, and dealt with the difficulties of a young schoolmaster in a school full of juvenile delinquents. Several complaining letters were sent on to Main Wilson, who pointed out that two of the letters came from one man who had also been bombarding the newspapers on the subject, and that the rest were, judging by the handwriting, from neurotics. He also defended the programme's right to be controversial.

In November, complaints were made about the over-enthusiasm of the studio audiences. Main Wilson had found himself, for the first time in his career, having to ask his Studio Manager to hold down the volume of the laughter from what he described as 'hysterical fans'. There was also a growing tendency to applaud jokes, which Main Wilson found irritating as it slowed down the action.

The eighteenth programme, 'The Greyhound Track', broadcast on February 15th 1956, is one of the best from this series, skillfully written (although a little far-fetched compared with programmes in later series), and performed with enthusiasm by all concerned—with the possible exception of Andrée Melly, who has so few lines that she is really rather superfluous. She had found that the gradually changing style of the programme left her with less and less to do, and asked to leave at the end of the series.

The scene is, for once, not Railway Cuttings but Hancock's country retreat—or as Bill points out 'It's more than a retreat—it's a mass surrender'. Apart from the dilapidated condition of the house, the furniture has no legs, leaving them all sitting round like Japanese Warlords. 'It's like the "House of Bamboo" in here some nights.' Hancock decides to have the place renovated. The workmen do an excellent job—but Mayor Sidney James has his eye on the land, where he wants to build a greyhound racing stadium.

59

BBC Publicity
Bill Kerr, Hancock, and master criminal Sidney James

Sid approaches Hancock, showing him the plans for the stadium but representing them as plans for a housing estate. Hancock's suspicions are lulled by explanations that the track is for the residents to exercise their dogs, that the traps are in fact bicycle sheds, and that the architect's name is Harry Tote. Hancock still refuses to sell, so Sid tries another ploy. Discovering that an old public footpath runs right through Hancock's house, he puts up signs encouraging people to use it. Hancock's puzzlement at the string of intruders making their way through his living room turns to fury when one of them turns out to be Snide. Snide is hiking—'I've been walking for hours and I'm 'iking all over'. He has come all the way from next door but one—and, being hungry, immediately invites himself to join in Hancock's dinner. Hancock's temper deteriorates even further when Snide puts up his tent in the hall. Snide, however, is sensitive to other people's feelings— 'You're trying to get rid of me, aren't you—I can tell'. He says Hancock only has to tell him, and he'll go. Hancock: 'Get out!' Snide: 'You don't mean that'.

However, Snide makes a sudden disappearance—on the handlebars of a motor-bicycle which happens to be passing through. Things go from bad to worse; Sid tells the Royal Tank corps that the footpath is a short cut—Hancock finishes up on Salisbury Plain with a gun barrel stuck up his pyjama leg. Defeated, he agrees to sell the house—but demands a flat in Harry Tote's new housing estate.

When the greyhound track opens, it is observed that only five dogs are racing—and that there is a bottle of milk outside the sixth trap. Inside it, Hancock is planning to have the decorators in, but is disturbed by his noisy neighbours—'They keep barking—it's that rabbit again!'

The final show, 'The Test Match', positively sparkled with guest stars from the world of cricket—Godfrey Evans, Frank Tyson, Colin Cowdrey, and commentator John Arlott. The actual match is part of a dream sequence which occupied most of the show—Simpson and Galton were coming to rely on dreams and fantasies when they wanted to write a script which would otherwise jar with the gradually increasing reality of the programme. Sid being the manager of the MCC, and having bet heavily on England to lose, has made Hancock the Captain. Evans, Tyson and Cowdrey object to his incompetent methods of play, but are over-ruled. To cap it all the Umpire is, of course, Snide—'You destructive devil—you deliberately knocked those little bits of wood down'.

The whole series was a resounding success, and achieved excellent listening figures. *Hancock's Half-Hour* was now firmly established as one of the leading comedy programmes on radio.

5. Radio, 1956–59

When the third series ended on February 29th 1956 Hancock had been out of the show at the Adelphi Theatre for three months. He was, however, still under contract to Jack Hylton for stage performances. Hylton took the view that Hancock was also under contract for all other appearances as well, and a wrangle developed as to Hancock's exact position. BBC Television wanted to give Hancock his own series; Radio wanted to do another series of twenty programmes. Hylton decided that he wanted Hancock for a series on the new Independent Television network instead of another stage show. He wanted Galton and Simpson to write the series, as they were obviously the most suitable writers for Hancock, but they were under an exclusive long-term contract to the BBC. Hylton wrote to the BBC claiming that he had exclusive rights in

Hancock, but that he would allow him to do the twenty sound and six television programmes for the BBC provided that Simpson and Galton were allowed to write the ITV series. Simpson and Galton had agreed to write the BBC Television series in March, before going on to write a new radio series for Bernard Braden, to which they were already committed. In view of the pressure on them, and their exclusive contract, the BBC refused to release them for the ITV series. The possibility of Hancock being allowed by Hylton to do the next radio series remained in dispute. Hancock, muttering that a man had a right to earn a living, consulted a lawyer, as a result of whose advice Jack Adams, Hancock's agent at Kavanagh Productions, wrote to the BBC suggesting that Hylton's hold on Hancock was not as exclusive as Hylton would like to think.

In the end, it was agreed that Hancock should do two series of six programmes each for Hylton, on either side of the BBC-TV series, and that Hylton would have to find other writers. The BBC series, originally scheduled for the end of May, was postponed to the beginning of July as a result of the disagreements.

The radio series was planned to start in October, after the BBC-TV series had finished. Now another snag appeared. The musical links, planned with so much care and skillfully integrated into the programme, were an essential part of the show's style. The original set of recordings had now been in use for three series, and it occurred to one of the musicians involved that he was getting no money for the repeated use of his performance, for which he had been paid an 'all rights' fee. The Musician's Union had recently had a head-on collision with the BBC, culminating in a total strike in February, on general conditions and payments; now they raised the specific matter of the 'all rights' use of incidental music.

The outcome was that, although opening and closing signature tunes could still be recorded on the same basis as before, incidental music had to be bought for use on the first programme, and attracted a 50% repeat fee on all subsequent appearances. This of course placed a considerable strain on the programme budget. Main Wilson was most upset: 'I don't get a repeat fee, and I work a seven-day week'. He was even more upset when the heads of his department decided that the use of special linking music was now too expensive a luxury, and instructed him to use 'funny links' from the mood-music library. These records differ from commercial gramophone records in that they do not count as 'needle-time', i.e. the amount of broadcasting time which can be filled by gramophone records, which is closely controlled by the Musician's Union. Mood-music records are much cheaper to use than specially recorded music, but in 1956 much of the repertoire was rather dated, and anyone who has ever heard the ham-fisted humorous links on these records will understand why Main Wilson lost his temper and dictated a pungent memo running to six pages.

Hancock's Half-Hour kept its special music. Wally Stott re-scored the links for a reduced orchestra (which, incidentally, turned out to be more suitable for the programme as it settled into its new style) and a new set of recordings was made. The old discs were ceremonially destroyed in order that no-one in the Musician's Union should have any fear of their re-surfacing at some later date.

Other programmes caught in this argument were not so lucky. The last series of *Ray's A Laugh* lost the battle, and had to rely on mood-music records—which may be one of the reasons why it *was* the last.

The characterizations had changed noticeably with the early shows in this series. Hancock, after only two or three weeks, was using the voice which he is remembered for—not his natural speaking voice, which was rather more diffident, but a good deal more natural than the remnants of the funny voice from *Educating Archie*. Kerr was more relaxed, and his characterization was slowly becoming more stupid, so that Hancock could score off him. James was much the same, but his characterization deepened during the series, and he became more of a friend, though a dubious one, instead of merely the crook who 'fleeced' Hancock. From this series James was billed above Kerr.

The fifth programme saw the arrival of a new character, played by Hattie Jacques. Instead of giving Hancock another girl friend, Galton and Simpson decided to cast Jacques as an aggressive and incompetent secretary. Named Griselda Pugh, she descended upon Railway Cuttings in answer to an advertisement and, threatening Hancock with her umbrella if he dared to criticize, joined the entourage. At first she came in to cook Hancock's breakfast (and eat most of it—her size and appetite gave the writers many opportunities for gags); but later on she came to 'live in'.

Moira and Andrée had both at various times been established as 'living in' with Hancock. Surprisingly, there seem to have been no complaints on that score from listeners in that less liberated period (not that there was ever any question of Hancock actually sleeping with them); but no listener could possibly object to the presence of Miss Pugh. Hancock, however, frequently did.

Her original characterization was extremely aggressive, but this softened fairly rapidly, and though she had no patience with Hancock's foibles, she was liable to show sudden streaks of sentimentality. In the eighth programme, Sid abruptly falls in love with her, but, under-standably, is nervous about expressing his feelings to her. Hancock, always willing to prove himself a man of the world, is giving Sid a demonstration of how to propose to her, when she comes in, overhears Hancock, and assumes that *he* is proposing to her. Hancock finds himself overwhelmed in her sudden passion for him, and gets more and

63

Popperfoto
Hancock with Alan Simpson (left) and Ray Galton

more panic-stricken as she relentlessly makes arrangements for the wedding. But she emerges from the ceremony distraught, and turns to Sid for comfort. Hancock emerges arguing with the registrar. It seems that there has been a muddle, and that Hancock is married to the registrar. The registrar is, needless to say, Snide.

After this, there are frequent hints that Sid and Miss Pugh are having some sort of relationship, but life at Railway Cuttings goes on with Miss Pugh doing the cooking (and eating) and Bill just hanging about.

Gradually, the scripts were becoming more and more realistic. Simpson and Galton were shedding the standard tricks of the comedy scriptwriters—such as scenes which did not contribute to the story, and skits on current films (always an easy way of finding a plot). They were moving towards a style which would surround Hancock with reality rather than the fantasy world in which radio comedy had existed up to then; and their plots became less and less complicated as the characterizations became deeper. Eventually the plots would, on occasion, disappear altogether.

Once during this period Simpson and Galton's relationship with Hancock became a trifle strained. Generally they got on well with him—although most writers will agree that their performers tend to treat them as slightly socially inferior, and this was true in Hancock's case. He was rather in awe of them, these two young men who seemed to know him better than he did himself, and who could put in his mouth the words that fitted his comic style perfectly. The final rift between them was a long way off, but it was foreshadowed in an incident during this series. Hancock was having a weight problem, and was in hospital on a strict diet. Once a week they let him out to do the show, then back to the hospital and the carrot juice. This would make anyone irritable. Hancock complained to Main Wilson that there had been too many programmes where he finished up in a doss-house, or in jail, or at the labour exchange. 'You tell Alan and Ray, either they write me *up* where I *belong*, or I get Eric Sykes.' This outburst was more the result of starvation than anything else, but it had a grain of truth in it. Hancock saw his character as going *up* the social scale; Galton and Simpson, quite unconsciously, were writing *down* the social scale, perhaps moving towards 1962 when Harold and Albert Steptoe would argue their way round the junk-yard.

With the fourth series came some of the shows which have gone into radio history, partly as a result of being issued on gramophone records. 'The Diary' is remembered for the 'Test Pilot' sequence, and 'The Wild Man of the Woods' was—and is still—available complete. The range of ideas was widening—fewer shows depended entirely on some complicated fiddle by Sid. However, one event that was a gift to Sid—and the writers—was the introduction (as a result of the Suez crisis) of petrol rationing, announced on November 20th and implemented on December 17th 1956. In the programme of December 9th Sid and his cronies throw a party to celebrate the return of rationing and promptly set about siphoning petrol from cars and hi-jacking tankers, with the unsuspecting Hancock in charge of a petrol station. All goes well until someone hi-jacks a beer tanker by mistake. The appearance of petrol with a head on it causes confusion, until Hancock decides that the answer is to observe normal licensing hours.

Many other programmes contain remarks about the rationing, although overseas listeners will be unaware of them as Transcription Services would remove them on principle as being too confusing—and 'dating' the programme. Petrol rationing ended on May 14th 1957, by which time the series had ended, so Sid was unable to react to its removal.

It has already been remarked that one major characteristic of the Hancock persona is his gullibility. In the thirteenth programme of the series it emerges that he is also extremely superstitious. The show begins with announcer Robin Boyle stating that, as this is the thirteenth programme, the series has passed the halfway mark. Hancock is alarmed. 'That's it then—I'm not moving a muscle till I've got me gear—my rabbit's foot, my Cornish Pisky, my alligator's tooth . . . and me bottle of coloured sand from the Isle of Wight.' He refuses to go ahead with the programme. Boyle is sceptical. 'This is ridiculous—there are three or four dozen people all over the country tuned in waiting for the programme to begin.' Hancock is adamant, and quotes an old Cornish saying: ' "When the moon is in the quarter, don't do nothing that you didn't oughter"—if that's good enough for Jon Pertwee it's good enough for me'. Boyle retaliates with an old BBC saying: ' "If the show does not go out, the artist's contract's up the spout".'

Hancock is not to be persuaded, and goes home, where he retires straight to bed for fear of the 'little people'. He demands that Bill should draw a circle round his bed, and sprinkle the floor with salt. Bill sarcastically offers to fetch him a unicorn, or a one-horned goat, or something. Hancock is not amused. 'Don't be ridiculous—one-horned goat! Do you take me for an idiot?' This gets a reaction from the audience, and Hancock breaks off to deal with them. 'Nobody asked you lot—I'm speaking to my friend here.' He then points out to Bill that you never use goats when there's an 'R' in the month.

Bill and Miss Pugh discuss the situation. Hancock, it appears, has joined 'The East Cheam Mystics', a local crank society. Miss Pugh goes up to his room to remonstrate with him. He tries to justify his behaviour—'I'm not falling by the wayside like Harry Perkins did—oh, that poor wretch—walked under a ladder and crossed his knife and fork on the plate when he'd finished his dinner. Tragic, it was, he died the very next day.' Miss Pugh is touched. 'How old was he?' 'Ninety-seven.'

Bill comes in, whistling cheerfully. Hancock is most upset. 'Stop whistling! You've done it now, haven't you—whistling on a Tuesday when the year ends in seven—you fool! Bring the cat up here and make him walk in the room backwards, it's our only hope.' Bill has brought up a telegram from the BBC—if Hancock won't do the show they will cancel the rest of the series and sue him for breach of contract. Hancock decides that he had better go to see the head of his Mystic society—the Head Druid, who alone has the power to lift the curse that will follow on his doing the thirteenth show—for a substantial fee.

The Head Druid is, of course, Sid. At first he doesn't realize the seriousness of the situation, and offers Hancock some more frogs at ten bob each. Hancock, however, has a bath full of frogs at home. 'Gave old Bill quite a turn when he came home after a heavy night last week.' Hancock asks whether thirteen can't be a lucky number, just for once—a suggestion Sid complies with when he realizes that no radio series means no money. However, a special ceremony at Stonehenge is required, to propitiate the 'little people'—at a cost of £100.

The ceremony consists of Hancock placing his money on the sacrifical altar at Stonehenge, and counting to 1000 with his eyes closed while Sid makes off with the cash. He has got to twenty-four when he is interrupted.

SNIDE: Good evening!
HANCOCK: Twenty-five, twenty-six, twenty-seven . . .
SNIDE: No, stop messin' about, I'm talking to you.
HANCOCK: Twenty-eight, twenty-nine—
SNIDE: Thirty, thirty-one . . .
HANCOCK: I know, I know—thirty, thirty-one, thirty-two—
SNIDE: What's the matter, can't you get to sleep?
HANCOCK: Hop it! Thirty-three, thirty-four, thirty-five—
SNIDE: You'll drop off much quicker if you imagine they're jumping over backwards.
HANCOCK: I'm not trying to get to sleep. Thirty-six, thirty-seven, thirty-eight, thirty-nine, forty . . .
SNIDE: Well that's our fingers and toes finished, what are you going to do now?
HANCOCK: I can count without fingers and toes! Forty- . . . oh, why don't you go away?
SNIDE: You can't lay here on the sacrificial stone all night.
HANCOCK: Why don't mind your own business. Who are you?
SNIDE: I'm the Stonehenge Police Force.
HANCOCK: I didn't know there *was* a Stonehenge Police Force.
SNIDE: Ooh, yes—it's our job to see the stones are kept safe.
HANCOCK: What do you mean, 'safe'—there's nothing that could happen to these!
SNIDE: No, but there might be if we didn't take 'em home every night.
HANCOCK: Take 'em home?
SNIDE: Yes—on me bike. Then I bring 'em back in the morning, and we set 'em up again before the sightseers arrive.
HANCOCK: All on your own?
SNIDE: Well, there was two of us—me and Superintendent Spooner.
HANCOCK: Where's he?
SNIDE: He's under here somewhere. One of the stones fell on him.
HANCOCK: Oh, charming, charming! Have you reported it?
SNIDE: No, he knows.

Hancock explains that he is a Sub-Druid from East Cheam waiting for the 'little people' to come and take his money away. Snide: 'I think

I'd better get a couple of big people to come and take you away.' Protesting loudly, Hancock is carted off to jail. The next morning Bill comes to bail him out—only to find the terrified Hancock trying to ward off evil influences—in Cell Thirteen.

Snide was by now immensely popular, but Hancock was beginning to be irritated by him. It was not so much that Snide got most of the laughs in his sequences—Main Wilson remembers Hancock saying 'the show is the thing, it doesn't matter who gets the laughs'—but that Snide was tending to overbalance the programme, which was otherwise becoming more and more realistic. Hancock also found it irritating for Snide to be able to get an easy laugh on a catch-phrase, such as 'Good Evening' or 'Stop messing about' (which actually gets a round of applause in the example quoted above).

After the end of the fourth series, Snide was not used again, though Kenneth Williams stayed in the show to do pompous judges and incompetent policemen. The 'snide' voice re-appeared in 1964 in *Round the Horne*, as one of the gallery of strange characters that Williams played as a foil to Kenneth Horne.

During this series, Hancock made a departure from his usual sphere of activity by appearing in a 'straight' radio play. Broadcast on New Year's Eve 1956, this was a ninety-minute adaptation of *The Man Who Could Work Miracles*, made by Main Wilson from the screenplay written by H. G. Wells for the 1936 film, which was in turn based on Wells' own short story. Hancock played George McWhirter Fotheringay, an ordinary man who suddenly finds that he has been given the power to perform miracles. He starts cautiously, with what are in effect party tricks, but gradually becomes more ambitious. Local interfering busybodies try to influence him when they discover his abilities, and after some confusion he assembles all the Heads of State, Churchmen, and professors in the world to advise him. Since they cannot agree, he rashly orders the world to stop turning until they do. Inertia causes everything and everybody on the earth's surface to be flung off into space, and Fotheringay decides that he will order time to go back to the moment when he found he had the gift, and that he should no longer have it. Hancock gave an excellent performance, with a cast including Warren Mitchell, Hattie Jacques, Fred Yule, Deryck Guyler, Miriam Karlin, Charles Lloyd Pack, Alfie Bass and Kenneth Williams. Main Wilson produced, and the only jarring note was the use of the 'Hancock Theme' in the incidental music, since the story was, after all, supposed to be about Fotheringay and not Hancock.

The fourth series ended on February 24th 1957, and eleven months elapsed before the next radio series started, on January 21st 1958. Dennis Main Wilson had by now left for Television, so a new producer was needed. Charles Maxwell was suggested, then Pat Dixon (who actually produced the first show of the series), before the job finally went to Tom Ronald.

Some uncertainty was expressed by Variety Department as to whether Galton and Simpson would be able to write both for radio and television, but there was really no question of Hancock having any other scriptwriters. Many famous shows come from this series—'The Publicity Photograph', 'The Unexploded Bomb', 'Hancock's Car', 'Hancock's War' and 'The Threatening Letters' among them. The performances and the writing were by now excellent, with the cast giving increasingly deep characterizations; many of the shows still have plots which are physically impossible, but the more unlikely flights of fancy had been eliminated, and several programmes are perfectly possible—not even particularly unlikely, but brilliantly observed bits of real life.

'Hancock's Car', broadcast on April 1st 1958, tells the story of a clash with bureaucracy that is not all that far removed from possibility, while throwing some light on the home life of 23 Railway Cuttings. Sid and Bill are unwillingly helping Hancock to clean his car—a daily ritual. Sid cannot understand what all the fuss is about—he hasn't cleaned *his* car for three years. Hancock points out that this is only so that any witnesses won't be able to tell what colour it was. 'It's a disgrace, your car is—you have to feel along the door to find where the handle is.' One of the reasons that Hancock's car gets dirty is that the drivers of the passing trains make a game of blowing smoke and heaving lumps of coal at it.

After three-and-a-half hours of continuous rubbing the car is gleaming. Sid doesn't like the colour scheme.

HANCOCK: Don't like the colour scheme? Orange and heliotrope? Very voguey, that is.

SID: I think it's the tartan hood that spoils it.

HANCOCK: You've got no taste, have you. You've got to have something bright for the hood to balance up with the pink-wall tyres.

SID: All you want is a couple of plants in there, and it'll look like a travelling coffee bar. Is it clean enough for you?

HANCOCK: It'll do for now. We'll have another three hours on it tomorrow. Bill—have you finished the underneath? Where is he?

SID: His legs are poking out the other side.

HANCOCK: I'll bet he's asleep. I've a good mind to jump on his ankles. I'd love to see him spring up and hit his head on the big end. Or, shall I start the engine up? His ear'ole's right by the end of the exhaust pipe. No, no, no, no, no,—ha ha!—no, no, no! Hang on, hang on—(*shouts*) Pull your legs in,

69

	there's a bus coming!
BILL:	What—where—what—(*bonk!*) Ow! Ow!
HANCOCK (*laughs*):	Oh dear—I did enjoy that! I bet his knees felt that! He didn't half fetch them a whack on that running board. . . . My running board! If you've damaged that running board you will have the benefit of my starting handle across your nose.
BILL:	I haven't hurt your running board.
MISS PUGH:	Coo-ee! Dinner's ready!
HANCOCK:	We'd better go in now, otherwise she'll eat it all. Put a barrage balloon over the car in case it rains, William.
MISS PUGH:	You must all be very hungry after all that work you've done—I've made a nice big dishful of cauliflower cheese.
HANCOCK:	Oh—I don't like cauliflower cheese.
BILL:	Neither do I.
SID:	Neither do I.
MISS PUGH (*innocently*):	Don't you really?
HANCOCK:	You *know* we don't like cauliflower cheese! You've always known it!
MISS PUGH:	Oh, well, never mind—I'll just have to eat it all myself.
HANCOCK:	You planned that! You made it on purpose—you're always doing that! You've made a list of everything we don't like, and you deliberately go and make dirty great binfuls of it. Ooh, you gannet!
MISS PUGH:	You can have bread and dripping.
HANCOCK:	Thank you very much indeed. The perfect Sunday dinner—roast bread and dripping. Most appetising—the height of luxury. Draw the curtains—I don't want the neighbours looking in and seeing a man of my calibre eating bread and dripping.
SID:	Turn it up, Grizzly, you must have something else in there.
MISS PUGH:	No—there's no more.
HANCOCK:	She's hidden it all! She buries it somewhere—she's like something out of Armand and Michaela Denis. She drags it all off to her lair and stands guard over it.
MISS PUGH:	The car looks nice.
HANCOCK:	Don't change the subject. Bread and dripping!
BILL:	I'm hungry after all that work—I think I'll *have* some cauliflower cheese.
SID:	Yes, I might as well, too.
MISS PUGH:	But you don't like it! You said you didn't like it—you told me you didn't!
HANCOCK:	Aha! That's frightened her! She didn't expect that! I'll

70

have some too! Ha ha ha! It's worth making yourself ill just to see her face! Drops two inches every spoonful we take! Where's me blindfold—I can't look at it *and* eat it.

The doorbell rings; Miss Pugh answers it and announces that it is a policeman (Kenneth Williams). Sid chokes and has to be patted on the back. However, the constable is not after Sid—it appears that Hancock's car is causing an obstruction. 'Move it!' The council want to re-surface the road—and Hancock's car hasn't been moved for ten years. Sid is not pleased about this—'Do you mean to tell me you've had us cleaning that car every day and you never use it?' Hancock: 'Well, I get in the driving seat sometimes, and I turn the wheel, and a bit of "vroom vroom, vroom vroom!" and pretend, and that—but if you mean actually moving, no.' The policeman points out that the road has been re-surfaced eight times since the war—all except the bit Hancock's car is standing on, which as a result is now eight inches lower than the rest of the road. Hancock still refuses to co-operate.

HANCOCK: . . . so if you will kindly take your helmet off the teapot I shall bid you good day.

POLICEMAN: Very well. I shall have to make a report, and no doubt you will be hearing from the magistrate's court within the next few days.

HANCOCK: Good! And I shall answer any charge in person! I am willing to defend my civil liberties, whatever you try to do to me. I'm not frightened! Use your rubber hoses—and your lights in the face—and all smoking while I haven't got one, see if I care! And it's no use trying to come round to tow it away because I'm taking the wheels off! . . . That showed him. They've met their match in me. Now, let's finish me dinner. I bet he thought . . . Where's me cauliflower cheese gone? Who has had my cauli- . . . it's her, she's woofed it—she's like greased lightning—I only took me eyes off it for thirty seconds. I bet it never touched the sides on its way down. Stone me, no wonder the dustmen don't bother to call here. All they get is ashes. Oh, spread me some bread and dripping.

The case goes to court. Hancock makes an impassioned speech, and is fined forty shillings. He protests, and the fine goes up to forty-five shillings, then fifty shillings, then fifty-five shillings: 'Will you allow me to get on with the next case, or will you go on for the three pounds? Oh—and one other thing—move it!'
After further altercations with the police, during which Hancock

instructs Bill to lie down in the road in front of the car, a compromise is reached; the police will move Hancock's car, the Council will re-surface the road, and the police will put the car back where it was. This has been done, and Hancock is congratulating himself, when a train goes by. Once again the driver slings lumps of coal at the car—this time with devastating accuracy. Hancock realises that this is because the car is now eight inches higher up—they have more to aim at. He decides to stop the trains, and orders Bill to be tied across the railway line. Bill protests, but Hancock is not to be stopped. 'Look, it won't hurt, Bill, you just lay in front of the train—we'll see who gives in first. We're not going to take this lying down—well, I mean *you* are . . .'

However, the most significant programme of the fifth series, in terms of the show's future development, was 'Sunday Afternoon at Home', broadcast on April 22nd 1958. This is one of the best known of all Hancock's broadcasts, because it was issued in Spring 1960 on a gramophone record (albeit with a few minor cuts) and has been continuously available ever since. The script was a deliberate experiment—there was no plot to speak of, and much use was made of long pauses. The programme sounds less innovatory when heard today, but at the time 'dead air' (i.e. silence) was considered the cardinal sin in broadcasting (except on Third Programme) and everyone thought that Simpson and Galton must have gone mad to fill a programme with so many long silences.

Hancock, Sid, Bill, and Miss Pugh are stuck at home on a Sunday afternoon with nothing to do. The gramophone is broken, nobody can play the piano (which in any case is locked), and the television doesn't work. Miss Pugh suggests that Hancock could do a few odd jobs. Hancock refuses—'I'm not mending your bed again'. He spends some time seeing imaginary faces in the wallpaper pattern. Miss Pugh decides to knit a sweater. Hancock thinks that this will solve the unemployment problem in the wool industry. Then the man next door (Kenneth Williams) calls. He is bored too, and treats the others to a recital of animal impressions, which goes on for some hours. Hancock: 'That's six hundred animals you've done and we haven't touched Africa yet'. At midnight he finally goes, and Hancock wakes up the others. They decide that next Sunday they really must *do* something—but nobody can suggest what.

The show is a brilliant example of technique, with every line delivered in the best possible vocal tone by all concerned, and with the pauses perfectly judged. It is one of the finest comedy programmes ever broadcast.

Not all the reaction to it was favourable, however, and Tom Ronald found himself having to defend the programme's suitability. A man in Bristol wrote to the Director General, complaining that the programme was a subtle attack on the day of rest and worship which implied that it ought to be a day of entertainment no different from the other days of the week. The Fourth Commandment, the writer said, could not be broken with impunity. Tom Ronald wrote to the Assistant Head of Light Entertainment that, as a Roman Catholic, he did not consider that the injunction to 'keep the Sabbath Day holy' was violated by this programme, which was specifically about a wet Sunday *afternoon* rather than the morning, when one might still go to church.

At the end of the series Hattie Jacques left to have a baby, but returned for a Christmas Special, recorded on December 7th 1958 and broadcast on Christmas day; and two recording sessions in which four of the shows from the previous two series were re-made for Transcription Services, incorporating amendments in the scripts which would remove topical references, and so on. Neither session went particularly well— the audiences were not as good as usual, and Hancock seemed irritated by the re-emergence of Snide in two of the programmes; in the second session he insisted on reversing the order in which the programmes were to be recorded, with the result that the better script was done second instead of first, when it would have warmed up the audience. It is a pity that in all four cases only the Transcription Services re-make still exists, the originals having long since been destroyed.

The sixth, and final, radio series was scheduled to begin transmissions at the end of September. Since this would have clashed with the fifth TV series, the shows had to be recorded in advance, during June. Simpson and Galton wrote two shows a week—twice their normal rate. Hancock, who was now firmly established on television, was reluctant to do this radio series, and claimed that he only undertook it because he thought Galton and Simpson 'needed the money'. He was also afraid that the series could not be up to the previous standard, as it was done in a hurry. In fact the series is excellent. Galton and Simpson deliberately applied the 'no-plot' technique that they had pioneered in 'Sunday Afternoon at Home', and spent long sequences developing the characters of Sid, Bill, and Hancock. Hattie Jacques was no longer in the programmes, and, after the first two, Kenneth Williams left as he felt that he was not getting enough to do. The various minor characters were now being played by straight actors, so that the situations in which the lead characters found themselves became increasingly realistic.

The programmes were re-arranged into an order which would provide a better balance when transmitted, and the series began on September 29th 1959. A Christmas Special, without Bill Kerr who was in Australia, was recorded on December 6th and included in the series.

The first programme, both as recorded and as transmitted, was 'The Smugglers'. It includes an interesting demonstration of Bill's mental processes, which by now had become very peculiar—a long way from the fast-talking character of the first two series.

Hancock, Sid and Bill are returning from a continental holiday, and are approaching Dover on the cross-Channel ferry. Sid is worrying because he is carrying a large consignment of smuggled watches, and is trying to tell Hancock about this, but in terms of an imaginary friend of his who is trying to get business secrets into the country past some villains (including the police) who are trying to steal them. Hancock, however, is not really listening. He plans to go on to Clacton on a bird-picking-up trip, and is trying to persuade Bill that they should pretend to be French.

HANCOCK: Avez-vous un cigarette, mon ami?

BILL: What?

HANCOCK: Avez-vous . . . look, you're supposed to be French. Oh, you're going to let us down, I can see this.

BILL: Oh, yes, yes . . . no, j'ai haven't got pas un cigarette.

HANCOCK: Isn't that marvellous! Supposing these girls speak French? I know, I've got it—I'll do the chatting. Now, our background—must have a watertight background, we don't want any slip-ups—we've got to organize this like MI5 did during the war, so that we really live the part. What are you pulling those faces for?

BILL: I'm trying to look French.

HANCOCK: I think I'll go with Sid. Sid—how do you fancy Clacton?

SID (*still worrying*):   How far is it from Dover?

HANCOCK: Oh, never mind. Now look, Bill, you're Pierre LaValle, you're twenty-five years old, your father is the Grand Duke of Roquefort, your mother is Baroness DuBarry, your family owns vineyards in the south of France, and you were born in . . . er . . . let's see now . . . born in—

BILL: Wagga Wagga.

HANCOCK: You're useless. Can't you grasp even the simplest fundamentals of bird-deceiving? Name me one Frenchman who was born in Wagga Wagga.

BILL: Well, I'll admit it's difficult.

SID: Here—how long do you think it would take to learn how to swim?

HANCOCK: Well how do I know?

SID: This friend of mine, could he have some lessons on board ship and learn how to swim in, say, forty-five minutes?

HANCOCK: I don't know—bring him here, I'll see what I can do.

SID: Can't you teach me, and I'll pass it on to him?

HANCOCK: No I can't.

BILL: Felix Frankovitch.

HANCOCK:	Pardon?
BILL:	Felix Frankovitch—he was born in Wagga Wagga, and he was French. Oh, no he wasn't—he was a Yugoslavian.
HANCOCK:	Well, what are you talking about, then?
BILL:	Well, can't we be Yugoslavians?
HANCOCK:	No we can't! Yugoslavians just aren't in vogue with women at the moment.
BILL:	Yes, but I was . . .
HANCOCK:	Do you want to go to Clacton or not?
BILL:	Yes.
HANCOCK:	All right then.
BILL:	I been thinking.
HANCOCK:	What.
BILL:	If Sid's friend can't swim, why doesn't he wait until it's dark before he jumps overboard?
HANCOCK:	Why?
BILL:	Well, then nobody'll be able to see that he can't swim.
HANCOCK:	Go on.
BILL:	That's it.
HANCOCK:	That's what?
BILL:	That's what I been thinking about.
HANCOCK:	What difference does it makes when he jumps overboard, it's not going to stop him drowning, is it?
BILL:	Oh; no.
HANCOCK:	Well, what are you talking about then?
BILL:	Well, he said he doesn't want anybody to see him. . . .
HANCOCK:	But if he were drowning he'd be grateful for people to see him!
BILL:	Ah—but he didn't mention that, did he.
HANCOCK:	He doesn't *care* if people can see that he can't swim! He just wants to go ashore without anybody seeing him!
BILL:	That's what *I* said, why doesn't he jump over at night-time?
HANCOCK:	*Because he can't swim!*
BILL:	Exactly! Now if he's going to drown anyway, he might as well do it at night-time, so that the people he doesn't want to see him won't see him, and will wonder what's happened to him. . . . Well, at least it would be a sort of moral victory, wouldn't it? . . . I mean, they'll be at Dover waiting for him for years, and all the time, he'll be under the water safely drowned; that way the laugh would be on them, won't it . . . I'm sorry I spoke, I'm sure.
HANCOCK:	And so am I mate. I've been sitting here boggling. I haven't the slightest idea what you're talking about. How *does* your

75

	mind work? This fascinates me—when you get an idea, what happens to it?
BILL:	Well, I . . .
HANCOCK:	I hadn't finished, had I? Look, you get an idea; now, what happens to it while it is en route to your mouth? It goes through a sort of threshing machine, doesn't it? It gets chewed up into little pieces, and gets thrown out, willy-nilly.
BILL:	Well, we've all got our own methods, haven't we.
HANCOCK:	That's the most unsatisfactory explanation I've ever heard about anything!

The series contains a high proportion of classic shows. 'The Childhood Sweetheart', 'Sid's Mystery Tours', 'Hancock in Hospital' and 'The Christmas Club' are all fairly well known as a result of repeats, but some of the less well known shows are also excellent. 'The Last Bus Home' sees Hancock, Sid and Bill stranded in a thunderstorm; 'The Picnic' sees them taking a day out in Hancock's car (now actually moving!) with three unwilling girls and a hundred and forty plum jam sandwiches; and the fact that Madame Tussaud's embarked on a waxwork of Hancock in April 1959 inspired a show in which Sid decides that they can make their own waxwork.

There was still a little behind-the-scenes sniping. At the start of the series Tom Ronald had to fight the battle about the use of 'funny links' from the mood-music library all over again. He was more restrained in his language than Main Wilson had been in 1956, but he won his point.

The eleventh of the series, 'The Poetry Society', is remarkable in having no incidental music, the action being continuous through the show. Hancock's entrance is greeted by raucous laughter from Sid and Bill—he is apparently wearing a blue and white striped stocking cap, a home-woven vegetable fibre shirt, canvas trousers, and fisherman's rope sandals. He has joined an avant-garde cultural group—or as Sid puts it, 'another load of layabouts'. Hancock is indignant. 'We are not layabouts—we are artists, mush!' They intend to set the world to rights—'Culture, mate—that's where the hope of the world lies—and a more cultural mob than us you wouldn't find outside the Chelsea Embankment.' Bill wakes up. 'Can I join?' Hancock is contemptuous. 'No you can't—this isn't a ping-pong and darts club.'

Sid wants to know what else this group does. 'Some of us make pots and jugs—then there's Adelaide—she's very good on the raffia mats—then there's Percy and his Welsh bedspreads—and some of us paint, and sculpt—and the rest of us lie in bed, thinking.' Hancock, of course, is one of the lie-ers in bed, thinking.

Bill is very anxious to join—even as caretaker. Hancock is firm. 'No—

we'd be conscious of you—it'd put us right off our contemplating.' He is also firm that they should both be out of the house by seven o'clock, as tonight is the group's night for poetry reading. Hancock has invited them round, as he is the only one in the group who has a house. Sid wants to know where the others live. 'Ten of them live in a basement under the pet shop—seven live on a boat on the canal—and the other fifteen of them live with them.'

A knock on the door heralds the arrival of the group; Hancock persuades Sid and Bill to stay in the hope that they might come to a better appreciation of his new friends.

The group enters; its leader, Gregory, announces that he is 'definitely getting turquoise vibwations'. Sid is more inclined to blame any vibrations on the trains going by. Gregory is surprised to find Hancock actually *living* with such people—Sid starts to get annoyed.

Hancock introduces Sid to Greta (played by Fenella Fielding in her best languid purr). Bill immediately tries to date her—she finds him 'an intriguing little savage'. Hancock compliments her on being 'the weirdest looking one here tonight'.

Hancock invites the group to sit down—only to be told that chairs are 'a symbol of unproductive work, the furnishings of a decadent society'. The Handbook of the group apparently states that 'members should adopt postures in keeping with the intellect of the individual, without sacrificing the mood of the work—we are thus irrevocably united as a Group in relationship to the poem being read'.

The first poem is by Gregory, and is entitled 'Tin Can'. Hancock decides to lean up against the fireplace with one arm up, suggesting the lid's been opened. Gregory reads his poem.

'TIN CAN, by Gwegowy.

Splish, Splash, Splonk . . .
Wooden shoes, red socks,
Coffins, tombstones, and tranquilizers.
Aspirins and driving tests, jet planes and skeletons,
Frog singing to egg-timer;
Calendars and candles upside-down
Plastic apples on coconut trees . . .
Splish, Splash, Splonk.'

Hancock is overwhelmed. 'Marvellous—I haven't heard anything like that since "The Road to Mandalay".'

The next poem is to be by Rupert. Bill has adopted a pose in readiness for it. Hancock is not amused—'Very funny—now come out of the sideboard before I clout you one.'

Rupert is sending his poem to UNESCO for translation into eighty-four languages, but is going to read it in English for the moment. Sid observes that if it's anything like the other one it won't really matter. Gregory and Sid come near to blows, until Greta intervenes—'Oh for goodness sake, be quiet—all this quarrelling is interfering with my perceptive aura'. Hancock: 'You see, you've upset Greta now—her perceptive aura's gone for a burton'.

Rupert's poem, 'Blank Detail', consists of the line 'Straw in the wind' read five times, followed by 'Fly, Fly, Fly'.

Bill suddenly comes to life. 'Can I read my poem now?' Hancock: 'I somehow don't think the sort of poems you write will be suitable for this gathering. We are not interested in young ladies from various parts of the country'.

Bill's poem, however, is abstract. Hancock is still disbelieving. 'One has to be sympathetic with the symbolism of existence to turn out that sort of stuff. Get back in the sideboard.'

Greta, however prevails upon Hancock to allow Bill to read his poem:

'INCANDESCENCE, by William.

Hic, Hack, Hoc!
Rinky-tinky on purple grass.
Shafts of light—hobnailed boots
Tramping down the bamboo that grows
Upwards, downwards, sideways into the concrete cosmos.
Life is mauve
I am orange
Hic, Hack, Hoc!'

This effort is greeted by a round of applause from the studio audience, and contempt from Hancock. 'What a load of rubbish! You buffoon! "Rinky tinky on purple grass!" What *does* that mean! I have never heard such unadulterated codswallop in all my life.'

Gregory is furious. 'How *dare* you speak to a genius like that? In a few bwilliantly conceived lines he's summed up the human capacity for suffering and its struggle for survival.' Hancock is still unimpressed. 'My aura of perception didn't even wobble.'

Greta concurs with Gregory in praising the poem, and they insist that Bill should become the leader of the group. Hancock, growing desperate, reads them his poem:

'THE ASHTRAY, by Anthony.

Steel rods of reason through my head!
Salmon jumping, where jump I?
Camels on fire—and spotted clouds.
Striped horses prance the meadow wild
And rush on to drink at life's fountains deep.
Life is cream, I am puce . . .
Ching, Chang, Cholla!'

Gregory is not fooled, and demands an explanation of the poem's meaning. Hancock flounders. 'What does it mean? Well, I should have thought that was obvious! It's a plea for the . . . well, it's more of an outcry against the . . . er . . . it's an outcry against the licensing laws. You take, for a start, the camels on fire under the spotted clouds. In that I've summed up the whole situation in the Gobi desert. And "life's fountains deep" . . . well, it's a plea for more water-holes! That's why the camels are on fire—they're gasping, they haven't had a drop to drink since they left Kabul.' 'And "Ching, Chang Cholla"?' 'Well, they're the drivers, you won't get any change out of them.'

Challenged by Hancock to explain Bill's masterpiece, Greta says that William has told them that 'life is a fraud—that we are merely insects existing on the tail of a turtle'. Hancock is puzzled. '*Did* you tell them that?' Bill is taking no chances—'Well, you heard the poem—I thought it would have been obvious'.

Mysteriously, Sid also upholds the artistic claims of Bill's poem, and, with his support, Bill is invested as leader of the group. Hancock is bewildered by Sid's change of position—until he realizes that Sid has been reading the group's Rule Book. 'The leader of the group receives from levies from the other members a remuneration of no less than £500 per year, so that he may be exempted from the need to work, and may spend all his time on contemplation and intellectual pursuits.' It also emerges that the leader may choose his own lieutenant, who gets £350 per year. Sid is, of course, after this—and has produced his own abstract poem to back up his claim:

'LIMBO, by Sidney.

Mauve world, green me
Black him, purple her
Yellow us, pink you.
Lead pipes—fortune made.
Six to four, coming second
Green country, Blue Harringay and White City;
Hic, Haec, Hoc!'

Gregory is overcome—'I can't take any more—all this sensuous excitement in one evening!' And Sid is immediately installed as Bill's lieutenant.

Hancock, now panicking, offers them another poem: 'Jake was a coward, a great big fellow with a turned-up nose . . .'

He is told to get out, and retaliates with another panic-stricken piece of verse:

> 'It's a funny old world we live in
> But the world's not entirely to blame
> It's the rich what gets the pleasure
> And the poor what gets the blame'.

They throw him out, now reciting 'There's a green-eyed yellow idol to the south of Katmandu . . .' He hammers on the door. 'What about our aims for improving the world? "It was pouring with snow on the equator, and the icebergs were melting fast . . ." I can't be bothered with them. I'll go down to the coffee-house—there's bound to be another movement started up since yesterday. I'll start one of me own! How did that poem of Sid's go, now? . . . "Mauve world, green me, black him, purple her" . . . that's it—that'll get'em. A breakaway group! We'll be anti-everything! The new intellectual movement to shake the world! . . . Or shall I go to the pictures? Yes, I might as well, I think that's more my hammer, really—Cab!'

This is one of the best of the radio *Hancock's Half-Hours*, suitably barbed at the expense of pseudo-intellectuals—a target Simpson and Galton were to return to a few months later in the film *The Rebel*. The regular team is augmented by Fenella Fielding, Fraser Kerr and Warren Mitchell.

The series ended on December 29th 1959. With it, Hancock's radio performances also ended—with the exception of *'Ancock's Anthology* in 1964, which was a collection of readings and gramophone records. All his other radio appearances were interviews. There were two attempts to interest him in radio plays. He was offered the lead part in *Mr Biedermann and the Fire-Raisers* by Max Frisch, but he was uninterested, and in the end the play was broadcast on June 26th 1961 with Edward Chapman in the lead. Then in December 1963 he was offered the part of Bérenger in Ionesco's *The Killer*, but again he showed no interest, and the play was broadcast on March 6th 1964 with Eric Barker.

But at the time the last radio series ended, Hancock was the highest-ranking star on television. To trace his rise in this medium we must back-track to 1948, and return once again to the Windmill Theatre.

6. T.V., 1948–59

The performances by Hancock and Derek Scott at the Windmill led to a television audition, on August 14th 1948. They did the concert party routine, with the comic, the tenor, the impressionist, the amateur talent competition winner, and a parody of the Western Brothers. The report on them was favourable, and led to an appearance in a programme called *New to You*, at three-o'clock in the afternoon on November 1st 1948. There was no immediate follow-up to this, and Hancock's next television appearance was with *Flotsam's Follies*, on February 20th 1950. He appeared in a sketch called 'The Conjuror', with four supporting players.

Another long wait followed, although he was of course establishing himself on radio, which at this time was still by far the more important medium—few homes had television sets.

Then in May and June 1951, he made five appearances in *Kaleidoscope*, a regular hour-long magazine programme best remembered for 'Puzzle Corner', in which viewers were invited to identify well-known objects from unusual photographs of them. Hancock appeared in five editions, in a series of sketches each running about six minutes. He played the lead part, George Knight, who was described as a 'would-be rescuer of damsels in distress'. The sketches, under the title 'Fools Rush In', were written by Godfrey Harrison. They represent Hancock's first appearances on television in specifically situation comedy, and though they bear little resemblance to the later Hancock character, they are well written and give him good opportunities for reacting to the confusing situations into which he has precipitated himself. In one sketch he rashly takes over the job of a hotel receptionist so that she can go and meet her boy friend, and gets himself into a state of total confusion with the telephone switchboard, an irate colonel and a confused foreigner. In another, he sits at a restaurant table with a husband and wife who are arguing and unwisely joins in the conversation with them. This idea re-emerged eleven years later in another Godfrey Harrison script for Hancock, 'The Girl', part of the 1963 ATV series, where Hancock and a girl he is interested in are forced to share a table with a husband and wife.

Then on August 1st 1951 he appeared in the first of a series called *The Lighter Side—a humorous slant on current affairs*. It was again written by Godfrey Harrison. This first programme was on the subject of food, and Hancock appeared as a Civil Servant, thus for once representing the bureaucracy that he normally found himself in opposition to.

But now his radio career really began to take flight, with *Happy-Go-*

Lucky and *Educating Archie*, both of which started a few days after this broadcast, and Hancock made no more television appearances for nearly three years.

The contractual wrangles that took place at the end of the third radio series have already been detailed in the previous chapter. When the dust had settled, Hylton had obtained Hancock's services for two series of six programmes for Independent Television, although he had failed to persuade the BBC to release Simpson and Galton to write the shows.

The first series started on April 27th 1956; the regular cast included June Whitfield, Clive Dunn and John Vere, with a dance group called The Teenagers; the series was directed by Kenneth Carter and written by Eric Sykes, with the collaboration of Larry Stephens on the first two. The programmes consisted of several sketches, sometimes quite separate, and sometimes linked by a slender narrative. Each show finished with a dance number, after which Hancock and Whitfield would do a parody of that type of dancing. The shows are very ambitious, with a fair amount of music and singing, but suffer from under-rehearsal—particularly the second show, which has one or two minor clangers, such as a stagehand appearing in shot. The later shows are rather better in this respect, although the whole series is marred by some very clumsy sound mixing.

There are several very successful sequences. The first show includes a coffee-bar sketch, based on an idea of Hancock's, in which the potted plants decorating the bar suddenly start growing, and choke him. The plants themselves were rather under-rehearsed, and did not perform quite as intended (although later stories—told by Hancock—that they developed a will of their own and started to strangle unsuspecting actors too early in the sketch, are pure invention). In the same show, a skit on *A Streetcar Named Desire* has another brilliant demonstration of Hancock's ability to be funny while doing nothing; June Whitfield launches into a long speech and Hancock gets progressively more irritated as he waits for her to finish. 'You built that up a bit, didn't you?' he says when she finally does. The second show, despite the very rough presentation of some of its sketches, ends with an excellent sequence in which Hancock, as a Balinese dancer, has to mime a little story told off-screen by June Whitfield. The story is repetitive, and he has to keep on miming a banana tree, a butterfly, a pool, ('which is made of water'), and various other aspects of the narrative; once again, the expression on Hancock's face is the whole joke.

The fourth show includes a particularly interesting sketch, in which Hancock is the owner, commissionaire, cloakroom attendant, head waiter, chef, and cabaret of a tatty nightclub. This would appear to be the origin of the idea which many years later was developed into the ABC-TV series *Hancock's*—the original sketch even includes a 'gypsy

82

fiddler' routine which was extended into a full-length sketch in the later series.

In the final show, Hancock begins by auctioning off the scripts, the dancers, and some of the props. This sequence provides the funniest moment in the whole series—and probably an unscripted one. For no better reason than that he has a gavel in his hand, Hancock suddenly launches into an imitation of a Punch and Judy show, with his arms folded, muttering 'that's the way to do it', and flopping around on the auctioneer's counter. It is hysterically funny, and one wonders why he then thought it necessary to explain it to the audience.

Despite the difficulties which are all too apparent earlier in the series, and which are only partially resolved by the end, Hancock and June Whitfield give excellent performances, really making the most of their material. John Vere gives strong support, but Clive Dunn seems none too happy in the items where he is given a straight rôle, and only comes to life when he is allowed to play one of his cantankerous elderly characters.

Meanwhile, preparations were going ahead for the first BBC-TV series. The Controller of Light Programme gave permission for use of the title *Hancock's Half-Hour* and the Wally Stott signature tune, with the proviso that it should be made clear in the publicity that the TV series was not just a re-make of the radio programmes. The producer chosen was Duncan Wood, who had worked with Hancock on several of his early radio appearances from the West of England. Wood, Galton, Simpson, and Hancock appeared in an afternoon programme called *House Magazine* on July 1st 1956, as a trailer for the TV series, which began on July 6th.

The first decision that had to be made was how many of the cast of the radio series could be successfully transferred to television. Galton and Simpson, although inexperienced at television writing, realized that they would not be able to get through the same amount of material in a TV script as in a radio script, and also that there were too many regular characters in the radio series. It has been suggested that Hancock 'closed the door' on Bill Kerr and refused to have him in the TV shows, but in fact the decision not to carry him or Andrée Melly over was entirely made by Simpson and Galton. They realized that they could only afford one foil to Hancock, and James was the obvious choice.

The style of writing was very little changed. Ray Galton says: 'Everybody told us that we must change, because television *is* visual, and actors had to be *seen* to be moving about. They were all obsessed by moving about. But most of our scripts were dialogue anyway, so instead of saying "pick up that bucket", we'd say "pick that up". That was our concession to television.'

The first script was not entirely successful, as they were still finding their feet in the new medium. In fact, they deliberately included a lot of visual material, but it was not very effective, and they soon reverted to their usual style, with considerable success.

In the first show, announcer Peter Haigh introduces the first of the new series, and we then see a husband and wife watching the programme in their living room. They react adversely to Hancock, who is apparently able to hear them, and who gets increasingly annoyed. Eventually he leaves the TV studio, bursts into the living room and smashes their set. We next see him in hospital with his leg in plaster—it appears that the husband was a heavyweight wrestler. Sid insists that the show must continue, and the television cameras are brought into the hospital, where Hancock unwillingly takes part in a sketch about Lord Nelson from his bed. During this, the nurse comes in, insists that visiting time is over, and gives Hancock a sleeping tablet which effectively brings the sketch to a halt. When he wakes up, he thinks he is still in the Nelson sketch, to the alarm of the patient in the next bed.

The subsequent shows in the series were rather more successful, and in fact, despite the prohibition on such re-makes by the Controller of Light Programme, include re-makes of 'The Bequest' and 'The Chef that Died of Shame'. In the latter case, Simpson and Galton had written a script called 'The Diplomat', but it was felt to be too near the knuckle in view of the Suez crisis, then in full swing, and as the writers were away, the radio script of 'The Chef . . .' was hurriedly re-worked.

There was also a special show—the fifth of the series—from the National Radio Show at Earl's Court, which included a sketch purporting to show how Hancock and Sid first met—Sid being in the process of burgling Hancock's house.

Television is, of course, a vastly more complex medium than radio, and it was at this time further enlivened by the fact that most programmes were broadcast 'live'. It was possible to record programmes in advance on film, but the technical quality obtained was considerably inferior to a live broadcast, and the use of telerecording was discouraged. Even if a programme was recorded in advance, it was not normally practicable to edit the film, and so all programmes had to be arranged so that it was possible for them to be performed continuously. If one looks at TV scripts from this period—the early *Quatermass* serials, for example—what is most noticeable about them is that each scene starts with one or two minutes of chatter from minor characters in order to allow the main characters time to get from one part of the studio to another. The same applied in *Hancock's Half-Hour*. Hancock would often find himself performing a scene with a change of clothing on underneath the clothes he was supposed to be wearing, and then having to rush off, get the top set of clothes off, and re-appear in the next scene without being visibly out of breath.

There was also no possibility of retrieving mistakes. Fluffed lines, bits of 'business' going wrong, the complicated camera arrangements coming adrift—these were all part of the normal risks of television at this time. Disasters on-air were not uncommon. The viewers were prepared to accept that television gave them immediacy—that what they saw was happening *now*, and this excitement with what was still a new idea enabled them to be tolerant of accidents. Later, when the pre-filmed American series such as *Bilko* appeared, the viewers came to expect perfection.

On top of the nervous strains imposed on any performer by this system, Hancock had the additional difficulty that he was a 'slow study', that is, he found it very hard to memorize his lines. The shows were done on a six-day-a-week basis—rehearse for five days in a rehearsal room, rehearse and perform in the studio on the day of transmission, have one day off, then start again. After several weeks of this Hancock would naturally enough be getting into a nervous state. As time went on, he resorted more and more to alcohol to release the tension, as he had done at the Adelphi Theatre. He was not alone in doing this—many people involved with television are heavy drinkers because of the nervous strain involved—and he never at this stage allowed it to affect his work. It was not until the 1960s that this happened; all through his period with BBC Television he confined his drinking to after hours.

Considerable planning and care went into the shows. It became necessary to bring to life the sitting room at 23 Railway Cuttings. Duncan Wood and designer Roy Oxley worked out the set that lasted until the end of the sixth series, with minor variations. Wood says: 'The important thing in designing, from a television point of view, is that you have to make up your mind—for example, if you're going to have an ordinary sitting room—which wall you want the door in, and which wall you want the window in, where the stairs are going to be, and where other rooms are in relation to that. You have to imagine the actors in a sort of limbo-land, and you imagine, before you even start rehearsal, the kind of camera shots you want to take. And having done that, you

BBC Publicity
Duncan Wood, producer of all the BBC Television Hancock's Half-Hours

virtually build the scenery round the limbo-land; and then you know that within certain limitations your camera work is going to be all right, and that you haven't got a set which you can't photograph.'

The set is part of television history. At audience left, the door, and to the right of that, a corner alcove. In the centre of the rear wall, the fireplace; and to the right of that, the window, with a view of the street. There is a table in the centre, and the décor usually includes a grandfather clock and a stuffed eagle. The right-hand wall sometimes has a door to the pantry, sometimes the back door, and sometimes no door at all. Simpson and Galton never bothered themselves over-much about consistency, and the room is sometimes on the first floor of a block of flats, and sometimes is on the ground floor of Hancock's own house. The hall outside the door on the left of the set also varies; the stairs are usually just outside the door, and the front door opposite it, but on at least one occasion the kitchen door is where the front door should be. This lack of consistency does not matter really, of course, and only becomes apparent when the existing telerecordings are seen over a short period of time.

The first BBC series, which consisted of only six programmes, ended on September 14th 1956. The second ITV series, also consisting of six programmes, but at fortnightly intervals, started on November 16th. Difficulties arose as the shows progressed, and the series was rather less successful than the first ITV one. The BBC was approached once again to allow Simpson and Galton to write for the series, and this time the Corporation, realizing that it would do their subsequent Hancock shows no good if his image were spoilt by an unsuccessful ITV series, allowed Simpson and Galton to contribute provided that they were uncredited. They wrote the last two shows.

On Janaury 18th 1957 Hancock appeared with Irene Handl and John Deverill in Alan Melville's series for the BBC, *A–Z : the ABC of Show Business*. It was, of course, 'H' that week. Hancock performed for the first time the budgerigar sketch by Galton and Simpson, which subsequently reappeared in *Christmas Night with the Stars* in 1958. Hancock is the budgerigar, and has very definite opinions about his owner.

IRENE: What a naughty Mummy—been away so long at that naughty Whist Drive.

HANCOCK: Naughty Whist Drive! More like naughty Bricklayer's Arms. Gets on your nerves. Stuck here all day long: nothing to eat: not a bit of millet since Tuesday—it's not good enough. It's not right. How can I stop me feathers dropping out without me nourishment. I'm not the bird I was. If I knew his number I'd have Peter Scott round. Here

	she is—say nothing.
IRENE:	Beauty—look what Mummy's got here—has she got Beauty's din-din . . . lovely din-din—look . . .
HANCOCK:	Well come on, then, poke it through—stop playing about.
IRENE:	Look, Beauty, nicey-nicey . . . all gone!
HANCOCK:	I know how to eat it, just poke it through. She does carry on so—if she ever leaves that door open I'm off. Sparrows or no sparrows, I'll take me chance.

A second BBC series of six programmes was arranged. By now Hancock was really getting into his stride on television, and the programmes were attaining an increasingly high standard. The first series had been done in Studio 'G' at Lime Grove, which had started life as one of the Gaumont-British film studios before the war. It was a long, narrow studio, so that the audience was spread out along the longer dimension, four rows deep and about ninety feet long. The sets were similarly strung out, and the cameras had to work perpetually at an angle because they couldn't get back far enough from the cast to do head-on shots. It was a relief to everybody when they moved to Riverside studios for the second and subsequent series—apart from anything else, the floors were smooth. At Lime Grove a camera tracking around on the floor was liable to look as if it was suffering from a minor earthquake.

The second series began on April 1st 1957 with 'The Alpine Holiday'. Sid James was absent from both this and the next show, the only two shows he missed until he parted with Hancock at the end of the sixth series.

'The Alpine Holiday' is the earliest TV *Hancock's Half-Hour* still to exist, on a telerecording originally made only for internal use, so that the success of the performance could be more easily judged by those involved in it (a fairly common procedure at this time when most programmes were live). In fact, it was repeated during the next series when a programme had to be postponed. The technical quality of the telerecording is not particularly good, but it makes interesting viewing, and stands up very well despite the fact that it is only Hancock's seventh TV Half-Hour.

The programme starts inside an airliner on its way to Switzerland. Hancock, dressed in full Alpine costume and carrying a bag and his skis, from which he refuses to be parted, gets himself jammed in the aisle with the amply-proportioned air hostess (Peggy Ann Clifford). After considerable effort and argument, they free themselves, and Hancock goes back to his seat. He is not welcomed by the passenger next to him (John Vere), particularly as Hancock insists on standing on Vere's lap in an attempt to put his skis on the luggage rack. Finally Hancock sits down, with his skis on his lap—and John Vere's lap—and the lap of the passenger on the other side of the aisle.

Hancock announces that he is going to Switzerland for the winter sports. 'Of course, I've learnt to ski in a department store in the West End, so I'm all right.' He tells John Vere that he is a very experienced traveller, and then tries to lower the window. John Vere explains about pressurized cabins: 'If the window opened, the plane would explode'. Hancock is not impressed. 'That's bad workmanship, old man.' He rhapsodizes about the joys of flying—and then panics when he cannot see the wings.

The air hostess helps to calm him, but Hancock is further upset by the appearance of the pilot (or, in Hancock's terminology, the driver). 'Why aren't you sitting in the cabin—steering?' The pilot calms him down, and points out the Alps to him, with the shadow of the plane on the snow. This merely starts Hancock off again. 'There are no wheels—where are the wheels? That's it, we're doomed—where are the boats?'

Having had this explained to him, he tries to re-assert his flying experience. 'You don't remember me, do you—Stick Hancock of the Flying Fools, 1916? I got the one over Potter's Bar, you know. I'll always remember it; it was a winter's morning when I spotted this cigar-like monster at Angels One Five. Only one thing to do—climb above him. I kicked the rudder, climbed up, got him in me sights; and what happened? You may well ask. Me twin Vickers jammed. Well, the Hun was throwing everything at me. Three on me tail, I was looping the loop at 120 miles an hour. Only one thing to do, I stepped out on the wing, controlling the plane with me feet. Grabbed the bombs out of the racks and threw them at him. Did me victory roll over Hendon Airport picking up handkerchiefs off the tarmac with me wingtips. Nerves of steel. Hundred-and-forty-four missions and never turned a hair.' He is asked to fasten his safety belt. 'What's the matter then? That's it, we're out of control, aren't we.'

As the pilot and air hostess attempt to calm him, we fade to film of the plane landing, and of the hotel.

The next sequence is set in the hotel lobby. Hancock approaches the hotel manager (Richard Wattis). 'I want complete rest and relaxation while I'm over here. I don't want people rushing about plaguing me for autographs. I want to be completely icognito, I don't want anybody to know I'm here.' The manager has never heard of Tony Hancock—until Hancock unwisely reminds him that he had stayed at the same hotel last year. 'Yes, here we are, Tony Hancock, yes. A little matter of four towels, a tea service, and an ashtray.' Hancock claims that these were just a few mementos of Switzerland. The manager is unconvinced. 'Do you think we might have a few mementos of England, such as seventy-eight pound notes to cover last year's bill?' Hancock reluctantly agrees to add it to this year's bill. He is told he'll have to share a room, and accepts this only when he realizes that this means he will only have to pay half price. He is given the key to Room 26; as he goes off he is approached by a girl asking for his autograph (Liz Fraser); having got it she turns to her friend—'There you are—I told you it wasn't Sabrina'.

An attractive French girl, Miss Dubois (June Whitfield) now enters, and is given the key to room 29 by the manager.

Hancock is seen going into his room; as he shuts the door, the 6, which is screwed on only at the bottom of the number, slips round so that the room number now reads 29.

Inside his room, Hancock is debating whether to have the bed near the door, in case of fire, or the one near the window, in case of an avalanche. Having decided on the bed by the door, because the bloke there gets his breakfast served first, Hancock discovers that the bed squeaks. He is underneath, investigating, when Miss Dubois enters, under the impression that she is in Room 29. Hancock's first view of her is her leg. 'Only half price for the room as well!' She sees him and orders him out from under 'her' bed. He tells her she will have to have the one by the window. 'And I hope you don't snore, I'm a very light sleeper.' She accuses him of being a Peeping Tim. He can't see what she is complaining about. 'It's nothing unusual for you Continental ladies. What? I've been to Boulogne.' A row develops; she starts throwing things at Hancock, and the manager arrives. He is not pleased. 'You Englishmen are all the same. Highly respectable all the year round and the moment you leave Dover harbour you're at it.'

Hancock is able to prove that it is fact his room, and the manager tactfully ushers Miss Dubois out—although he still retains considerable suspicion of Hancock. 'Ooh—you *naughty* Englishman.'

Hancock's real room-mate arrives. It is Snide—one of the few appearances by Kenneth Williams in a TV *Hancock's Half-Hour*, and the only one to survive in a telerecording. Hancock's immediate reaction is to try to throw him out again, but Snide manages to push his way in. 'Come on—stop messin' about.' Snide likes the room. 'I think we're going to get along very well, don't you?'—'No.'—'No, don't be like that.' Snide puts some photographs on his dresser.

HANCOCK: But they're all of you!
SNIDE: Yes—I haven't got anybody else.
HANCOCK: How sad.
SNIDE: I know—nobody likes me, I don't know what it is, I seem to get on people's nerves. They think I'm daft.
HANCOCK: I can't understand that.
SNIDE: I mean well.
HANCOCK: I'm sure you do.
SNIDE: People give me photographs, but when they get to know me

they ask for 'em back. Even me mother.

HANCOCK: Your mother? That's terrible—do you know, you've hit me right here now? No, you move me there, really. You really have me going, there. You poor wretch! Here, I'll tell you what—I've got a photograph of me here—you have that.

SNIDE: Ooh! *Thank* you! Ooh—I think you're nice! It just goes to show you there is some kindness left in the world after all. I shall treasure this. You don't know what this means to me. Ooh, I'll never forget you. Ain't you ugly!

HANCOCK (*grabs his photograph back*)

SNIDE: Ah—you've gone off me now, haven't you. You're like all the rest—you don't like me now.

HANCOCK (*bitterly*): No I don't.

SNIDE: Come, let's be chums—make up (*He extends his hand to Hancock with the little finger sticking out. Hancock folds it back into Snide's hand.*)

HANCOCK: No. I don't want you to speak to me again.

Undaunted, Snide reveals that he is the Yodelling Champion of East Dulwich, over for the Swiss Championships. Hancock has thawed by now, and listens in fascination to a brief lecture on the technique of yodelling.

Snide now demands to have the bed by the door—he can't have the bed by the window because he hasn't brought his halibut oil capsules with him. Snide rushes for the bed and sits on it—'You can't touch me—feet off the ground!' In the scramble which ensues the bed collapses. Hancock and Snide rush for the other bed; as they jump onto it the cover is drawn back and its occupant, who has been there unremarked throughout the scene, demands 'Do you mind being quiet, I want to get some sleep'.

After a couple of shots of the outside of the hotel, we see the room again. It is now dawn. Snide is walking up and down gargling. The man in the bed by the window is making vile noises on a ten-foot alpenhorn. Hancock is sitting on the floor wrapped in a blanket. 'I haven't had a wink of sleep all night. I thought he was going to smoke this when he first dragged it out.'

Hancock goes down to the foyer and complains to the manager that there are two maniacs in his room. The manager offers him Room 36. Hancock announces that he is going ski-ing. 'Mind the trees,' says the manager, sarcastically. 'I know where all the trees are,' says Hancock. 'I'm not a newcomer here.'

After some (stock) film of somebody ski-ing, and taking a spectacular fall, we return to the hotel foyer. Miss Dubois is complaining to the manager that her room is too near those idiots who yodel and blow

Alpine horns all night. The manager directs her to Room 39.

Hancock comes in, one ski still on his foot, but with the end split, and carrying the other, which is bent. He has a number of branches and twigs sticking to him. 'I wish to report a new tree on Slope 604. Carniverous, I fancy.'

He goes to his room—number 36—and the same accident with the number makes it appear to be Room 39 after he has shut the door. While he is searching underneath his bed for a button he has dropped, Miss Dubois comes into what she thinks is her room. A row develops. Enter the manager, this time with two policemen, who cart the protesting Hancock off. The manager and Miss Dubois gaze fondly into each other's eyes as we fade out.

We now see a close-up of Hancock, behind bars. He is musing on the advantages of solitary confinement—peace and quiet, no women—when the camera tracks back, revealing the occupants of the cells on either side. They are the Alpine horn player and Snide. The show ends with their cacophony, and Hancock protesting that he wants to go to Holloway.

The second series ended on June 10th 1957, and only three months later, on September 30th, the third series began. This was planned to run to thirteen programmes, but in fact only twelve were performed. On November 18th Hancock was down with Asian 'flu and was unable to appear, so the telerecording of 'The Alpine Holiday' was shown. The scheduled show was postponed for a week, which caused Wood some concern, as the script had been written for a guest star. They had booked Jack Hawkins, but nearly lost him when the show had to be postponed, as he was due to go to America on a promotion tour for *The Bridge on the River Kwai*. In the event, he was just able to appear, and flew to America the next day. In this show, Hawkins comes to Hancock for elocution lessons. Hancock teaches him to recite 'To be or not to be' in a very odd manner; but in the end Hawkins is unable to get any rôles under Hancock's tuition, and he becomes the leader of a rock-and-roll group.

With the eleventh programme of the series, 'There's an Airfield at the Bottom of my Garden', broadcast on December 16th 1957, the inherent risks of live broadcasting caught up with Hancock in a spectacular manner. The story of how a special set, intended to collapse at a crucial moment, started to fall apart too soon, leaving the cast desperately propping up the scenery, has been told in several places, always suggesting that the process took place throughout the show. In fact, the disaster lasts only about four minutes, in a scene about half-way through. (The programme was telerecorded, but never repeated because of the departures from the script.)

It is worth examining those four minutes in detail, if only to demonstrate what can happen when a live transmission goes wrong.

What follows is a transcript from the telerecording; dialogue which deviates from or is additional to the original script is shown in brackets, and the details in italics indicate what is actually happening, as the cast find themselves in an increasingly bewildering situation. The young man is Leslie Smith, the girl Paddy Edwards, and the Surveyor and his wife are Dick Emery and Esther MacPherson.

Hancock has been sold a house on the end of the runway of an RAF airfield. His attempts to make a good social impression come to nothing when a musical evening is ruined by the noise and vibration from the aircraft. He demands a refund from Sid, without success, then decides to try to sell the house himself, choosing a day when a thick fog has grounded all aircraft. The young couple have just decided that they will buy the house.

HANCOCK: Come along—where's that cheque-book now?
MAN: I left my pen at home.
HANCOCK: I've got a pen over here, that's all right. A. Hancock six thousand, there we are.

(The man prepares to write the cheque on the table in the centre of the room ; we hear the sound of aircraft, and as it starts the mantelpiece just behind the actors falls off, out-of-shot, but with a loud crash, and seven pages of script too early.)

GIRL: What's that noise?
HANCOCK: (What's that? Which one? Oh, that one, yes.) Probably the fridge starting up. (*To man*) A. Hancock, sixteenth of December.
GIRL: It sounds like an aeroplane getting ready to take off.
HANCOCK: It can't be that, madam, no, no, no, no—hang on (*rushes to the window*)—Stone me, the fog's lifted.
GIRL: Ooh, let's have a look at the view—is there a big garden?
HANCOCK: You can't see anything dear, I'm afraid . . .

(As the man goes to write the cheque on the table, it collapses—eight pages of script too early.)

HANCOCK: (*steering the girl away from the window, and also trying to guide her so that she doesn't fall over the mantelpiece*) (Oh well, we'll think of something else.)

(As the planes are heard to take off, the room starts to shake—as intended.)

MAN: What's happening? The room's shaking!

92

HANCOCK:	(Don't ask me mate, I only just got here!—Pardon?)
MAN:	The room's shaking!
GIRL:	(*jumping her cue—screams*)
HANCOCK:	(*restraining her*) (Hang on, hang on . . .) It must be you, you've got Asian 'flu or yellowjack or something. (*Trying to persuade the man to sign the cheque, with some difficulty as there is now no table*) Here we are, Hancock, Anthony Hancock.
GIRL:	(*screams*)
HANCOCK:	Oh, shut up—Come on now, hurry up and sign.
MAN:	Well, what was all that about, what happened?
HANCOCK:	(What happened? You may well ask!) It was you, sir—you were shaking like a leaf—are you drunk?
GIRL:	It wasn't him—it was the house shaking. I don't like it here, Bert, I'm frightened.
HANCOCK:	It's just an air tremor, Madam, it's Stromboli going off, it does occasionally, every thousand years. It's nothing to worry about.

(*The girl pulls back the curtains and looks out of the window.*)

GIRL:	There's an aerodrome out there—we're on the edge of an aerodrome!
HANCOCK:	That was their last flight—they're pulling out today.
GIRL:	We can't live here. Bert, it might fall down.
HANCOCK:	Please—there's nothing wrong with the place—five thousand.
MAN:	You twister—if you think we're buying this you're mistaken.
HANCOCK:	(*barring their exit*) Two thousand five hundred.
MAN:	Will you get out of our way, I'm leaving.
HANCOCK:	Seventeen-fifty and a packet of headache powders.
MAN:	Get out of my way.

(*The man and girl go out. Hancock calls after them.*)

HANCOCK:	Well name your own price then. (*Off-screen crash.*) Pick that gate up!

(*He shuts the door, turns and looks at the fallen table and tries not to burst out laughing. He goes over to the table and tries to get it to stand upright. Knocking from outside the door.*)

HANCOCK:	(Hang on!)

(*He struggles with the table . . .*)

HANCOCK:	(I'll do it if kills me!)

(. . . and finally gets it to stand upright ; but then finds that he can't let go or it will collapse again)

HANCOCK: Come in!

(He kicks the carpet straight, and makes a pose, still holding the table. The surveyor and his wife come in and bustle past Hancock.)

SURVEYOR: I've seen your advert, I haven't got long, I'd like to look the place over if I may . . .

HANCOCK: It's very nice, it's got panoramic scenery (I can't leave here, you see) it's got panoramic scenery . . .

SURVEYOR: Well I'm only interested in the house, you see, I'm a surveyor, I want a sound structure—have you got dry rot, woodworm?

HANCOCK: No, no, not a touch anywhere.

SURVEYOR: We'll soon see about that—the dry root and woodworm test, m'dear.

(They start jumping up and down heavily. Hancock reacts, still fighting with the table.)

HANCOCK: Have you gone raving mad?

SURVEYOR: It's a bit weak over here, isn't it.

(He and his wife start ripping up the floorboards)

SURVEYOR: Hullo, hullo—just as I thought, rotten right the way through. Five hundred off for that.

HANCOCK: Yes, all right, all right, yes.

SURVEYOR: Walls.

HANCOCK: There is nothing wrong with the walls, I promise you that *(moving away from the table, which is now standing by itself)* they're as sound as . . .

(He thumps the wall, and puts his fist through it.)

HANCOCK: Serving hatch. I must have papered over it.

SURVEYOR: Serving hatch? Through to the front garden!

HANCOCK: Yes, that's right. It's the milkman, he likes a cup of tea when he comes round.

SURVEYOR: *(Indicating where the mantelpiece should be, which he is supposed to tap so that it can fall down)* (No mantelpiece, eh?)

HANCOCK: *(laughing)* (No, no)—two hundred, then? Two hundred?

SURVEYOR: *(remembering that he has missed some lines)* (Yes, that's three hundred off for the wall, ain't it?)

HANCOCK: Yes!

SURVEYOR: (And two hundred for that.)

HANCOCK: Yes. I'm a reasonable man.

SURVEYOR: What about the wiring then?
HANCOCK: Oh, it's very good, I just had it put in. It's a lovely job—help yourself.

(The surveyor pulls the electric light switch. It comes away from the wall, followed by several yards of wiring with an assortment of lamps on it.)

HANCOCK: *(as the lamps come through)* That's the kitchen . . . that's the bathroom . . . oh, the lounge! . . . here—that's next door! Oh, that's the lot, anyway.
SURVEYOR: Well, we'll knock another seven hundred off for that.
HANCOCK: Yes.
SURVEYOR: *(trying to keep a straight face)* The furniture doesn't look too good, do it. *(He kicks the leg of the sideboard rather harder than he need, to make sure that it collapses as specified.)* Ah—woodworm!
HANCOCK: No, I've just had it treated.
SURVEYOR: You haven't.
HANCOCK: I have. *(He bangs on the table, which is supposed to collapse at this point. It doesn't. He kicks it, and it collapses on his foot, which, to judge from the expression on his face, he wasn't expecting.)*
(The surveyor and his wife break up more of the furniture : Hancock backs away and looks out of the window ; crossfade to film of jet bombers, followed by shots of collapsing buildings and a pile of rubble.)

The rest of the programme went as rehearsed—Hancock sells the rubble to Sid (omitting to tell him that the house has in fact collapsed), and Sid sells Hancock another house—in a valley about to be flooded by a new reservoir.

Hancock obviously found the incident funny as it happened (though probably in a nerve-racking sort of way) and often told the story afterwards—usually capping it with 'and as I stood there, my braces broke!' However, once was enough for that sort of occurrence, and the accident was one of the factors in the move away from live transmissions.

The final programme of the series, transmitted on December 23rd 1957, was really a variety show. Re-titled *Hancock's Forty Three Minutes : The East Cheam Repertory Company*, it was broadcast from the Television Theatre at Shepherd's Bush, and showed Hancock in a stand-up and compèring rôle—his least strong point. One of the most interesting items is a sketch in which Sid introduces a talented performer called 'Arnold' (played by John Vere). In the telerecording one can see something of Hancock's ability to be hilarious while doing nothing, which had rocked audiences at the Adelphi Theatre. In this case Arnold demonstrates paper-tearing (without bothering to make

95

patterns), spoon-playing (by banging two spoons together) and dancing on glass—plate glass. Hancock reacts to this situation by merely staring at the ceiling in the manner of one surrounded by buffoons and hoping that they will eventually go away. The programme also includes a performance of *The Three Musketeers*, with guest star John Gregson, in a manner which anticipates the Ernie Wise plays of fifteen years later. Gregson begins by doing 'To be or not to be' in the strange manner taught by Hancock to Jack Hawkins five weeks earlier. Hawkins had evidently been trying to show *some* profit from the debâcle.

Duncan Wood looked back over the series in an internal memo on December 31st. He thought that the last show was quite the worst, because Hancock was mediocre as a stand-up comic, and suggested that in future Hancock should be persuaded to stick to situation comedy. Wood also thought that the bout of Asian 'flu was a blessing in disguise, as it gave Hancock an opportunity for a week's rest, without which he might not have got to the end of the series. The strain on Hancock became a matter for some concern, and Wood suggested that four of the shows in the next series should be recorded in advance, and then placed at intervals of four shows as transmitted, so that Hancock would not have to do more than three weeks in succession.

Meanwhile Hancock made two television appearances outside his own series. On Christmas Day 1957 he appeared in *Pantomania*, a star-studded romp pre-recorded on December 17th, with a cast including Eamonn Andrews, Sam Costa, Kenneth Connor, Charlie Drake, Peter Haigh, Benny Hill, Cliff Michelmore, Ted Ray, Jack Payne, Huw Wheldon, Sylvia Peters and Jean Metcalfe. Hancock appeared as Aladdin and Robin Hood, with Sidney James as the Genie and Friar Tuck.

More important was Hancock's appearance in a serious play in the *World Theatre* series, broadcast live on February 2nd 1958. This was *The Government Inspector*, adapted from the play by Nicolai Gogol. Although the transmission was live, the play was telerecorded for use by Television Enterprises, who sell programmes to overseas broadcasting organizations in the same way that Transcription Services do for radio programmes. The recording still exists, and Hancock's performance in straight drama makes interesting viewing. He plays Hlestakov, a pretentious, penniless, out-of-work loafer, who is mistaken by the corrupt Mayor and Council of a Russian town for a Government Inspector sent to check on them. They placate him and shower him with gifts, much to his surprise, and it is only when he has gone that they discover their mistake. This production lost some of the sour bite of Gogol's original, but Hancock's performance stands up very well. The producer, Alan Bromley, wrote to Hancock congratulating him on his performance, saying that he thought Hancock had got more out of the

BBC Publicity
Hancock in costume for The Government Inspector

play than Alec Guinness or Danny Kaye.

A couple of other attempts were made to interest Hancock in drama as a result of this play, but they came to nothing. Eric Maschwitz wrote to Hancock suggesting a version of Molière's *Le Bourgeois Gentilhomme*, to be re-titled *The Gent*; and a suggestion was made that Hancock should appear as Sid Field, his hero from his early days. Hancock, however, was nervous about drama, and declined both offers.

The discussions about the possibility of pre-recording at least some of the forthcoming TV series continued. With the availability at the end of 1957 of the newly-developed 'stored-field' method of telerecording considerably improved quality was possible, although still not up to the standard of a live transmission, so that technical quality became less of an objection. It was, however, an expensive exercise, and although at one stage plans were made to pre-record the whole series, in the end the first four were recorded during November and December, live transmissions resuming with the fifth programme on January 23rd 1959.

Even though these first four shows were recorded in advance, they were still performed under the same conditions as a live broadcast, with the exception that in the event of a total disaster (the airfield incident was still fresh in Hancock's memory) the show could be started again—and extra time was allowed in case this should be necessary. In fact there appear to have been no snags, and the shows were highly successful.

97

Hancock's Half-Hour was by now one of the BBC's prestige programmes, and quite a lot of money was being spent on it. Already Hancock's own fee was high for the period (by the time he left the BBC in 1961 he was being paid an unprecedented £1000 a programme) and the standard of the supporting cast was getting higher all the time. The cast lists for the seven BBC Television series read like a *Who's Who in the Theatre*. What is particularly interesting is the number of actors who subsequently either had their own comedy series or played leading parts in other people's—they include Bill Fraser, Arthur Mullard, Hugh Lloyd, John Le Mesurier, Dick Emery, Warren Mitchell, William Mervyn, Frank Thornton, June Whitfield, and Patrick Cargill; while Andrew Faulds, who made several appearances in the early shows, went on to play an active part in that other long-running comedy show, the House of Commons. There were also a number of excellent comedy actors who appeared regularly in the shows, forming a sort of Hancock 'repertory company'; these included the diminutive Johnny Vyvyan, Alec Bregonzi, Mario Fabrizi, Robert Dorning, Tottie Truman Taylor, Elizabeth (Liz) Fraser, James Bulloch, Richard Statman, Gwenda Ewan, Paddy Edwards, Anne Marryott, and Patricia Hayes, who usually appeared as Hancock's awful charlady Mrs Cravatte.

This large budget, and Hancock's fee in particular, led to hopes being expressed by the Television heirarchy that the Americans would not find out how much money was being spent on *Hancock's Half-Hour*, as it might lead them to raise the price of their filmed series which, then as now, formed a staple part of British TV's diet.

The fourth series got off to a flying start with 'Ericson the Viking'. Hancock is worried about his new series—with good reason, Sid has persuaded him that they should make their own film series—a historical drama on the lines of *Robin Hood* and *Ivanhoe*. In flashback we see how they went about it. Sid's film studio is tatty in the extreme, and his idea of film-making is, to say the least, primitive.

SID:	Action! Enter the King of the Vikings.
HANCOCK:	Ho there.
SID:	Hold it! Shoot it—got it?
CAMERAMAN:	Yes.
SID:	Good boy—next shot: Left arm down a bit, right arm up a bit, Hold it—shoot it—got it?
CAMERAMAN:	Yes.
SID:	Good boy, next shot—Left arm down a bit, right leg up a bit, hold it—shoot it—got it?—That's lovely, Hancock, that's lovely boy, you're giving a lovely little performance here. Right—right leg forward a bit, right arm back a bit . . .

HANCOCK:	Wait a minute, wait a minute, correct me if I'm wrong, but didn't I hear a rumour a few years ago about movie cameras? You know, cameras with reels of film inside, so you can move about normally, and walk, and run, and have trains going by, and when you show it you can have everything moving about all over the place?
SID:	We ain't got one.
HANCOCK:	This is supposed to be a proper film studio—why haven't we got one?
SID:	We can't afford one.
HANCOCK:	But it's going to take four years to do it like this! How can you make a film taking all separate photographs?
SID:	You stick 'em all together, and you drill little holes along the edges.
HANCOCK:	Stick 'em all together and drill little holes—. . . he's right! I suppose it'll work, I don't see any reason why it shouldn't—of course it won't work! I'm sure Cecil B. DeMille doesn't approach it like that!

Sid is able to come up with a Mack Sennett Mark One movie camera—at a price—and filming continues.

Needless to say, Sid's film is a disaster, with half-a-dozen scruffy Vikings pursuing a like number of desultory Saxons across Hampstead Heath, onto the main road, across a zebra crossing and onto a bus. Hancock is aghast, but Sid persuades him to have another go—this time as King Canute.

The series progressed with a number of excellent shows, including 'The Set That Failed', in which Hancock and Sid, their TV set being out of order, try various ruses including joining a family who are so intent on the set that they think that the intruders are two more members of the family. This sequence is brilliantly played, with the cast moving about the room, laying the table, pouring the tea, talking among themselves, and never once taking their eyes off the screen. The point of the joke is blunted nowadays, when television is no longer a novelty.

On January 26th 1959 the final episode of Nigel Kneale's horror serial *Quatermass and the Pit*, which had kept the nation glued to its sets in suspense, was broadcast. Galton and Simpson, glad of a ready-made plot to help them in the difficult task of producing thirty scripts a year, seized on it and wrote a show in which Hancock, having just seen the final episode of *Quatermass and the Pit*, finds a strange object buried in his garden. No-one can convince him that it isn't a Martian cylinder, buried there since pre-historic times, and the plot continues in an exact parallel of the original serial.

The following week, while rehearsing 'The Italian Maid', Hancock

Professional protest-marchers Johnny Vyvyan (left) and Mario Fabrizi with James and Hancock in 'The Oak Tree' (broadcast 13.3.59)

objected to the script because it began with him doing the housework totally unappreciated by Sid. Hancock was afraid that the public would find overtones of homosexuality in the situation, and he demanded that the script be modified. (It is doubtful whether he need have worried. Eric Morecambe and Ernie Wise have done many sketches in which they are seen sharing a bed; so, for that matter, have Laurel and Hardy; and no-one seems ever to have imputed homosexuality to these comics.)

The technique of the show was developing all the time. Duncan Wood remembers: 'One of the things that Tony learnt about TV I think he learnt from Sid; and I learnt a lot from Sid. Sid was a very good technician, very experienced in films; he knew what a reaction shot was all about, and so Tony quickly twigged the reaction shot business. And so, I was having to break sentences down into half, so that Tony would say a line in close up, half the sentence, then cut to Sid for a reaction, and then back to Tony for the remainder of the sentence, and then back to Sid for the reaction. Of course, the net result of this was to double the camera rate—that whereas you used to shoot situation comedy on 150 shots in half-an-hour, you were now taking 250 to do the same amount of dialogue. Suddenly you were having to work at twice the capacity on camera routines, and this put pressure on the crews, and on everyone. It was one of the great revolutions, I think, reaction as against action.'

The last but one of the series, 'The Knighthood', shows Hancock playing Shakespeare in the style of Long John Silver. Complete with crutch and parrot, he performs extracts from *Julius Caesar, Romeo and Juliet*, and *Richard III* as he attempts to work his way to the Old Vic so as to be in line for the knighthood he thinks he deserves. Eventually he makes the Old Vic—as prompter, in a prompt box at centre stage front. Undeterred, he refuses to prompt Andrew Faulds, and swings the box round to face the audience, whom he treats to his impression of Punch and Judy.

Some of the telerecordings were shown to officials of CBS Television in New York. They liked the budgerigar sketch, which had been included in *Christmas Night with the Stars* and transmitted the day before the fourth series started, but were unenthusiastic about *Hancock's Half-Hour*—they complained that they could not understand Hancock. Duncan Wood thinks that what they really wanted was to buy the scripts and make their own shows, on the principle of 'anything you can do . . .', as American TV later did with *Steptoe and Son* (which became *Sanford and Son*) and *Till Death Us Do Part* (which became *All In The Family*).

However, there was an interest in Hancock, as in most British comedy, in Australia, New Zealand, Canada, and South Africa; and from the beginning of the next series BBC Television Enterprises made 16mm telerecordings of all the shows and sold them abroad. It is our great good fortune that they did so, because every one of those shows still exists as a result—the entire fifth, sixth and seventh series—twenty-six of the most brilliant comedy performances ever to be seen on television.

7. *T.V., 1959–60*

From the fifth series onwards *Hancock's Half-Hour* was able to take advantage of a major development in television—video tape recording. Telerecording, i.e. filming from a television screen by means of specially designed cameras onto 35mm and later 16mm film, had first been introduced in 1947, but the quality was so poor that considerable work had to be done in order to develop the 'suppressed-field' system in time for the Coronation in 1953. The telerecording of 'The Alpine Holiday' mentioned earlier would have been made using this system, and though the picture is reasonably acceptable it is not up to the standard that the original transmission would have attained—the definition is poor, and the general effect is rather smeary.

A television picture consists of a large number of horizontal lines—at that time 405—which are interlaced, that is to say all the odd-numbered lines are scanned first, then all the even-numbered ones. The suppressed-field system ignored the even-numbered lines, so that the picture in effect consisted of 203 lines, with consequent lack of detail. The next development was the 'stored-field' system, which 'held on to' the even-numbered lines, so that both halves of the interlaced picture could be accommodated. All this difficulty was caused by the fact that the film took a finite time to be moved from one frame to the next.

The quality of telerecordings was quite good by 1958, but despite this it was easy for even an untrained eye to spot that a programme was a recording and not live, with a consequent loss of the feeling of immediacy so important to TV. Also, film was extremely expensive, and took time to have processed. What every TV engineer dreamed of was a video equivalent to ordinary sound recording magnetic tape—cheap, easy to handle, flexible to edit, and to all intents and purposes indistinguishable from a 'live' transmission. The BBC research department set about inventing such a system, and on April 8th 1958 it was demonstrated to the press. It was unwieldy, using huge reels of $\frac{1}{2}$-inch-wide tape that travelled at 200 inches per second, and there was more than a touch of Heath Robinson about the whole device; but it worked, and although the pictures from it were still somewhat short of perfection it was given an on-air demonstration the following week in *Panorama*.

VERA, as it was called (Vision Electronic Recording Apparatus) had a short life, however. About the same time, the Ampex Corporation of America unveiled its new video tape system in California. This used two-inch-wide tape travelling at only 15 inches per second, achieving the high contact speed needed for television by means of rapidly rotating heads which scanned the tape sideways. The quality obtainable was excellent—under perfect conditions it was impossible for the viewers to tell whether a transmission was live or on tape. VERA was quietly retired, although it has been suggested that Ampex were at first reluctant to let the BBC have their machines, and that VERA provided a useful lever in persuading them. The first Ampex machine was installed at Lime Grove on October 1st 1958, closely followed by a second in January. By September 1959, when the fifth series of *Hancock's Half-Hour* started, there were four machines available. There was, of course, a considerable demand for them, and it is indicative of Hancock's pulling power that a mere Variety programme was able to command use of this new toy.

The big question was, could the tape be edited? Editing sound recording tape is simple—you cut it, removing the bit you don't want, or bringing two separate sections together, and join it up again, using a block to hold it steady, and sticking special adhesive tape onto the back. The only difficulty is knowing exactly *where* to cut for a smooth result. A television picture, however, as we have seen is not a continuously flowing signal like a sound recording. It consists of the 405 (or nowadays

102

625) separate lines that make up each frame of the moving picture, together with synchronizing pulses which keep the scanning spot on the television set in step with the scanning beam in the camera. If a video tape is not edited in *exactly* the right place, these synchronizing pulses will be upset, with the result that the picture on the TV set will hiccup, or even roll right over before settling down.

The engineers tended to the opinion that video tape could not be satisfactorily edited, for this reason. Duncan Wood and Hancock were however anxious to have the facility for editing their series. Wood got hold of a spare recording of a show called *On The Bright Side*, starring Stanley Baxter and Betty Marsden, which consisted of comedy sketches interspersed with dance routines to give the artists time to change for the next sketch. He spent a day editing out all the dance items, so that the show, from being forty-five minutes, became a twenty-five minute collection of continuous sketches. The result was quite satisfactory, and convinced the sceptics that video editing was practicable.

This new system was a tremendous help to *Hancock's Half-Hour*. The shows were now recorded in sections, usually of about five to eight minutes each, with breaks between so that the actors could get themselves sorted out for the next scene. It speeded up the presentation of the shows by enabling the removal of padding dialogue to cover the scene changes. In theory, if anything went wrong, it would only be necessary to go back to the beginning of the sequence, but naturally this was avoided where possible because the audience wouldn't laugh so much on the second performance. The edits were almost entirely done in the fade-outs between one scene and the next which were normal at that time so that the joins were made on what is called 'black level'; this provided a safety factor in case of picture rolling on some sets—it would be less noticeable if the screen was dark. There are a few edits actually on picture, but not many: the first show in the series, 'The Economy Drive', contains a complicated scene in a cafeteria which required six

Radio Times

Hancock and Sid at the end of 'The Economy Drive' (broadcast 25.9.59)

Radio Times

Rehearsing for the jury-room scene in 'Twelve Angry Men' (broadcast 16.10.59)

cameras, and a few picture edits allowed the sequence to be covered without cameras appearing in shot.

Every show in this series is excellent. The writing is brilliant, and Hancock's control of his facial expressions, and his reactions to the situations round him, are a joy to watch. Two of the scripts were published by André Deutsch in 1961—'The Economy Drive' and 'The Train Journey'; and the soundtrack of 'Twelve Angry Men', a neat parody of the film starring Henry Fonda, has been issued on a gramophone record.

'The Cruise', broadcast on October 30th 1959, for once takes Hancock and Sid away from 23 Railway Cuttings. They are on a Mediterranean cruise, enjoying the sun and sea-air. At least, Sid is. Hancock is still wearing his Homburg hat, his overcoat with the astrakhan collar, and is wrapped in a blanket. It is, as he points out, October: 'I always get into my heavy stuff on the first of October, and I don't get back into the light stuff until the first of May'. The fact that it is ninety-three degrees in the shade does not concern him. Furthermore, he complains that Sid promised him that he would be chased round the deck by the girls, whereas he hasn't had a sign of interest from anyone yet. He soon gets his wish. Sid goes off for a swim in the ship's pool, and Hancock finds himself the centre of unwelcome attentions from a large over-amorous lady, played by Hattie Jacques. He tries to get rid of her.

WOMAN: Hello—are you on your own?
HANCOCK: Yes, thank you.
WOMAN: Would you like me to sit with you and talk to you?
HANCOCK: No.
WOMAN: I've noticed you—you're always on your own, aren't you.
HANCOCK: Yes, thank you.
WOMAN: Don't join in anything, do you.
HANCOCK: I enjoy being on me own.
WOMAN: Are you an eccentric?
HANCOCK: No I'm not. Just leave me alone.
WOMAN: Do a lot of reading, don't you. You'll hurt your eyes, you will.
HANCOCK: I'll hurt yours in a minute.

She eventually leaves him, having made, as she imagines, an assignation under the lifeboat. Hancock goes back to his book—*Great Sea Mysteries*. Over-suggestive as always, he gets carried away reading about a shipwreck, and misunderstands an overheard conversation between a steward and rating about the leeks which are for dinner. Leaks! Hancock panics. Sid finds him scanning the horizon for icebergs. He panics still more when a sailor tips a bucket of slops over the side.

104

Baling out! Hancock buttonholes an officer and demands to see the Captain. He is told that the Captain is in bed. Further panic. 'We've got a bed-ridden invalid in charge of the boat!' Hancock stops a passing steward who has a tray of drinks. 'What's in those glasses?' Ice, he is told. 'Just as I thought! Small chunks of ice! That proves it—we've hit an iceberg. It's ripped open the side of the ship and they're down below, hacking away at it . . . and to try and keep it from the passengers they're putting it in the drinks! You cunning devil! Man the boats . . .'

Hancock's panic spreads to some of the other passengers. He is convinced that the Captain is in bed, strapped down. 'He's gone bonkers—it's the Caine Mutiny all over again. He'll be lying there in his bunk clicking those little steel ball bearings together . . . as soon as he starts asking about the strawberries we've had it!' Hancock is promising to have the Captain arrested when the Captain in fact appears (played by John Le Mesurier). He invites him up to the bridge to see that all is well. Hancock goes up, and Sid, always ready to take advantage of a situation, starts selling sweepstake tickets for the lifeboat.

On the bridge, Hancock demands to know where they are. After a few moments calculation, the Captain gives him an exact position. Hancock is unconvinced, and demands to know 'What about the hole in the bottom of the boat?' With some exasperation, the Captain relays this question over the 'phone to the Chief Engineer. Hancock overhears the apparently colourful answer. 'Haven't you *any* control over your men?' Assuming that a mutiny is afoot, he gets so carried away by the situation that he lapses into his Long John Silver impression. He is well into this when the ship's doctor arrives. In an attempt to calm him the doctor promises that Squire Trelawney is waiting in his cabin, and that they will go and find Benn Gunn. Convinced that he is in the hands of a maniac, Hancock is led away protesting.

Later, Hancock has been persuaded into more suitable clothing, and put in Sid's care. Sid has organized a fancy dress ball, which Hancock is supposed to be too ill to attend, but he and Sid reach a compromise whereby Hancock can go provided that he is back in his cabin by midnight, strapped down on his bunk, eye-rolling and screaming, so that Sid can offer a view of him as a prize.

So they go to the fancy dress ball, Hancock as the Lone Ranger (complete with mask) and Sid as Tonto. Immediately Hancock finds himself in difficulties with the over-amorous lady, who is dressed as Cleopatra. He gets away from her as the pianist plays a 'Paul Jones'. When the music stops Hancock is opposite an attractive young lady. He tries to persuade her out onto the deck, but it turns out that she is the amorous lady's daughter. Hancock is trapped again.

The Captain interrupts the dance to announce that the passenger who went beserk that afternoon has escaped from his cabin . . . Hancock is quickly identified, and is carted off protesting. He and Sid are put off the ship at Port Said.

They are flying back, when Hancock panics because the plane is in a cloudbank. He is calmed by the steward, who decides that he has been affected by the altitude, and arranges to have him put off at Zurich. Hancock: 'Zurich! You can't leave me up there—there's no atmosphere on it! Blokes with big heads and one eye in the middle of their foreheads—you wouldn't do that to me? . . .'

The series ended on November 27th 1959. Before the next series began three months later there was considerable discussion about the possibility of changing the recording method yet again. Hancock decided that he wanted to do the shows in very short takes—practically shot-by-shot—without an audience, and then to assemble the programme and run it to an audience, adding their laughter to the soundtrack.

He also apparently thought that this technique would enable him to get all his lines exactly right—under the existing system some of his lines came out slightly differently to the original text; but in fact these changes rarely mattered, and if he had done every line over and over again until the whole show was 100% word-perfect, the result would not have had the marvellous timing and delivery that was so important to the show. What Hancock wanted was, in effect, to adopt the techniques used to make films for the cinema. Duncan Wood thinks that he had failed to appreciate the essential differences between cinema and television: 'All precedents then indicated—and still do—that a comedy show of that nature, played without an audience present, totally alters its style, its performance, its timing; if you play something in front of an audience it gives you a kick, and it lifts you, and your timing goes along—and I always thought that Tony was better at timing in front of audience than without one.'

So Wood opposed the idea, as he thought that the results would be disastrous; the BBC were not happy about the idea because it would take eight hours to do each show instead of the usual one-and-a-half hours at maximum, and because the facilities for playing the show to an audience and adding their laughter to the soundtrack were just not available at that time. Some bright spark suggested the use of sound effects records of laughter, but this red herring was fortunately ignored. In the end the idea was totally squashed by Equity, the actors' union, who would not allow their members to work eight hours for a half-hour show; and one gets the impression that the BBC were rather glad to be able to present this to Hancock as their reason for refusing to adopt the idea. At any rate, Hancock accepted the fact that the next series would have to be done in the same manner as the previous one.

It seems on the face of it odd that such a skilled comic actor as

Hancock should want to adopt a system of working which would have been so disastrous. But Hancock's abilities were always entirely intuitive. He could always perform to a pitch of perfection that few other comedians have ever even approached, but he never had any idea how he did it. This, as time went on, worried him more and more. If he had been less intelligent—and Hancock, though never intellectual, was highly intelligent—he might have been content to leave well alone, and to accept that his talents were instinctive. Dennis Main Wilson says: 'I think, in his own private moments, he tried to examine himself, his inner persona or ego, to try to find out what actually made him the star that obviously he was . . . And in examining himself, he found nothing. I think this put the fear of God into him.' It was not that he was a shallow or empty person, but that he was looking for an intellectual reason for his abilities. He wanted to be in control of the gift of comedy which he had, whereas in fact it was in control of him.

In the context of all this, the interview with John Freeman in the series *Face to Face* is of particular interest. It was recorded on January 28th 1960, as part of a series of what nowadays would be known as interviews 'in-depth'. The subject was harshly lit, so that any emotions felt during the interview would show clearly, and Freeman pressed very

BBC Publicity
Hancock being sketched by Feliks Topolski for the caption card for Face to Face

hard in his questioning—much harder than had ever been done before in broadcast interviews.

After a discussion in general terms of Hancock's approach to comedy, Freeman asks about Hancock's religious beliefs. Hancock replies that he has no particular religion at the moment, and that he gave up the religious beliefs he had up to the time he was fourteen or fifteen. He does not go into detail about this, though pressed, and is plainly more nervous than at the beginning of the interview. He relaxes again as they discuss travel, and his reading, and politely declines to admit how much money he earns. Asked where he lives, he talks briefly about his home in Lingfield, and about his friends visiting him there. Again, although the words themselves are innocuous enough, he becomes uneasy and lights a cigarette to hide his nervousness. He admits to not sleeping well, and taking sleeping pills. They talk about his childhood—Freeman rather naïvely thinks that 'Anthony Aloysius St. John' are Hancock's actual Christian names, and is told that the correct names are 'Anthony John'. Hancock explains that he was at a public school but felt at fourteen that he was being forced into a mould. Freeman doubts that Hancock could have felt this at fourteen, but Hancock sticks to this and explains that he left school of his own accord at fifteen. During the following discussion of his early career Hancock seems quite relaxed, and also explains willingly something of his attitude to his work at the present. Asked about his health, he admits to collapsing while at the Adelphi Theatre, and explains some of the stresses involved. He is asked if he is happy; he persistently evades actually answering the question, and in fact becomes rather agitated and has some difficulty in framing a suitably evasive reply. Freeman pushes the point:

FREEMAN: Some of the newspaper writers who've tried to puzzle out what makes you tick have said that you're the 'angst-man', the anxiety-man—now have you any notion of what your anxiety is? Do you in fact get a kick out of your anxiety?

HANCOCK: Anxiety—would you explain that a bit more?

FREEMAN: Well, something appears to me, even at the end of this conversation, to be eating you. You say that your happiness is just ahead of you still, there's something troubling you about the world, I'd like to know what it is.

HANCOCK: I wouldn't expect happiness—I don't. I don't think that's possible.

Hancock goes on to say that he gets his happiness from his work, and from developing his work. Freeman sums up, rather cruelly:

FREEMAN: Tony Hancock, I wonder if you really get very much out of

108

BBC Publicity
Hancock in Face to Face

	your triumphs—you've got cars that you don't drive, you've got health which you tell me is a bit ropey . . .
HANCOCK:	I didn't tell you that.
FREEMAN:	Well, you find it difficult to learn your lines. You've got money that you can't really spend, you worry about your weight . . .
HANCOCK:	I spend the money, I do, I enjoy it.
FREEMAN:	Well, what I want to put to you, as a final question, is this— you could stop all this tomorrow if you wanted to; you're rich enough to coast along for the rest of your days— now . . .
HANCOCK:	Money is of no account in this.
FREEMAN:	Well, tell me why you go on, as a last answer.
HANCOCK:	Because it absolutely fascinates me, because I love it, and because it is my entire life.

There was some doubt expressed as to whether the interview should be shown, but Hancock had no objections to it, and it was transmitted on February 7th. Many viewers wrote in complaining about Freeman's interviewing methods, and he wrote a letter to the *Daily Telegraph* justifying his approach. The interview is for the most part not as harsh as what was then a new approach made it seem at the time, but there is no doubt that it made Hancock examine himself even more closely—this time in public—and once again he found nothing inside himself to explain his gift, or his compulsion to go on and on, always trying to develop, to refine his performances. He had no religious beliefs, which might have given him something to fall back on; and it may be that around this time his marriage with Cicely was beginning to show the first signs of strain. Certainly it is the questions about his religion and his home life that cause him to become most agitated in the interview, until the final probe into whether he is happy. The interview, then, can be seen as a contributory factor in the process of self-examination. If he could only have accepted whatever gifts he had without question, he might have had some chance to survive the stresses of his profession. As it was, in fear of the apparent emptiness inside him, it was inevitable that he should continue to use alcohol as a release from tension, and as a means of dulling the apprehension he felt at having to perform.

Whatever Hancock's inner fears and worries, there is no sign of them in the ten shows which make up the sixth series. As with the fifth, every show is excellent, the scripts brilliantly written, and Hancock gives superbly funny performances; every inflection of his voice, every tiny change of expression on that mobile face, contributing to some of the greatest comedy performances ever seen.

The series began on March 4th 1960 with 'The Cold', in which Hancock's hypochondria is exceeded only by that of his doctor, and continues with several well-remembered shows, including 'The Missing Page' and 'The Reunion Party', both of which have been published in a collection of scripts,* together with frame enlargements

* 'Hancock's Half-Hour', Woburn Press, 1974.

BBC Publicity
Hancock having his cold 'drawn off' by Mrs Cravatte (Patricia Hayes). ('The Cold', broadcast 4.3.60)

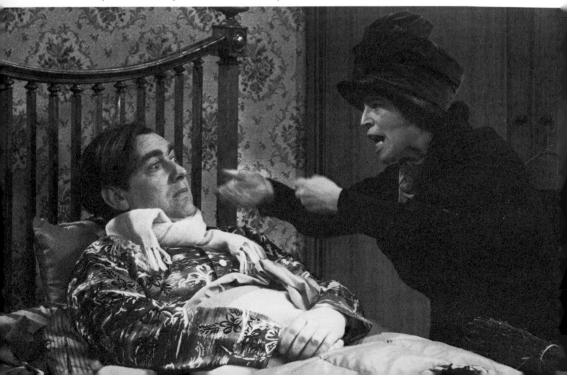

from the telerecordings. The frame enlargements give some idea of Hancock's performances, but, particularly in the sequence in 'The Missing Page' where he mimes the plot of a thriller (because he is in a library and therefore cannot talk), they can only give a sketchy idea of the brilliance of his mime. He manages to be the surprised lover, the erring wife, and the wronged husband all at once, and goes on to mime the murder of the lover, the arrest of the husband, and the passing of the death sentence. He is demonstrating the hanging when he realises that the librarian has been watching him for some time, and, now miming embarrassment, goes back to the business of selecting a book.

In the fifth show, 'Sid in Love', Hancock discovers that Sid has fallen in love with a bus conductress on a number 93 bus, and, being a man of the world, Hancock insists on helping Sid to meet her. It is unusual to see Sid heartsick and shy—but when Hancock's machinations cause chaos on the bus and the driver, coming round to investigate, turns out to be the clippie's husband, Sid's emotional involvement suddenly evaporates and he reverts to his old self—leaving Hancock to take the blame.

In the next show, broadcast on April 8th 1960, Hancock and Sid take up an unusual sideline—baby-sitting. The scene of the action is a plush modern house—contemporary paintings on the walls, expensive furniture, and every modern convenience. Mr and Mrs Frobisher ('Terence Alexander and Anabelle Lee) are awaiting the arrival of the baby-sitters they have booked from an agency, so that they can go out. The doorbell rings—it is Hancock and Sid. The Frobishers are a little alarmed, and just stand looking nonplussed.

Hancock: 'May we come in, or would you prefer to bring the baby out here?' Mrs Frobisher is uneasy—they have never had male baby-sitters before. Hancock tells her not worry. 'Just show us where the television set is and you can hop it.'

Mr Frobisher observes that they don't look like baby-sitters. This rather offends Hancock: 'Don't look like baby-sitters? Really, is that the remark of a scientific mind? What, pray, do baby-sitters look like? Did Rembrandt look like a musician? Of course she didn't.'

Mrs Frobisher wants to know whether Hancock and Sid have any qualifications. Hancock quotes his record as a member of the St John's Ambulance Brigade at the Chelsea Football Ground, 1945–49. If the baby's got any cartilage trouble, pulled muscles or knee ligaments they will have him right in no time. Mrs Frobisher demonstrates the baby alarm system—a two-way loudspeaker and microphone set-up so that the baby can be heard downstairs, and can be talked to from the downstairs microphone. Reluctantly the Frobishers leave.

Sid mutters that he doesn't like this baby-sitting lark. Hancock tells him not to be such a misery—here they are in a nice comfortable house,

111

using other people's electricity: 'When I think of those miserable evenings I've spent in that wallpapered damp rabbit-hutch in Railway Cuttings peering through the gloom at the shadowy flickerings of a worn-out nine-inch television set . . .' He admires the carpet. 'Doesn't it make a change to sit on a carpet without a floor-full of knot-holes staring up at you. And all these lovely plants here, hanging round the walls. And they're *meant* to be there—not like our place, forcing their way in from the outside.'

Hancock tries one of the chairs—a modern basket-work design rather like a large bowl. Sid thinks it is a dog-basket. Hancock insists that it is comfortable—and then has difficulty getting out of it.

Hancock thinks he hears something from upstairs, and goes over to the two-way system and yells 'Are you all right?' into the microphone. There is no answer. 'Yes, he's all right.'

Sid: 'He's nine months old—what do you expect—a detailed report?'

They look for the television set. It is nowhere to be seen, and Hancock is complaining that he has been defrauded when Sid discovers that it is hidden away and rolls out automatically upon operation of a remote control. Hancock is most amused and spends some time making the TV set roll in and out of its hiding place. Sid sniffs, moves around the room like a bloodhound, and finds the hidden drinks cabinet. 'I can always find it!' Hancock gets a good supply of food from the kitchen and they settle down to watch the television.

It is a Western. Hancock recognises one of the Indians: 'He used to be a detective in "M Squad" '. Sid thinks he is a real Indian. 'Of course he isn't—they can't get real Indians these days—they've all got big houses and oil wells.' Sid is trying to take the programme seriously; Hancock has seen most of the Indians before in other rôles. One of the characters has been pegged out as a victim for a whole army of ants. 'I've seen *them* before, too.' At the tense moment Sid is so involved that he covers his eyes, and Hancock so fed up with the rubbish that he switches the set off. An argument develops, with the set rolling backwards and forwards, on and off, which is only resolved when the remote control system breaks down. A shouting match ensues, which wakes the baby.

Hancock: 'Now look what you've done, you've woken him up—now you'll have to croon to him.'

Sid: 'I am not crooning to anybody'.

Hancock sings 'Go to sleep my baby' into the microphone, and the baby keeps on crying. Sid grabs the mike and shouts 'Belt up!' The baby does so. They discuss the modern paintings, which Sid doesn't like. The baby starts crying again. Hancock tells Sid not to start shouting at him again: 'Don't be cruel to him—there are other ways of stopping him.' He switches off the loudspeaker.

Sid now starts sympathising with the baby, and decides that it must be hungry. He picks up a roast turkey and a champagne bottle from the food trolley. 'Sidney, this is a baby, not a lion cub. Take a bottle of milk up to him. And not like that—don't you know anything? You can't just hold it like that and pour it into him.' Sid reluctantly goes upstairs to feed the baby. Hancock wanders round the room, lights a huge cigar, and does impressions into the mirror—Churchill, George Burns ('nothing like him!'), Groucho Marx.

We hear the baby crying, and Sid talking in baby-language to him. The baby won't stop crying, and Sid is getting worried. Hancock gives him instructions over the microphone. 'Now hear this, now hear this, Control Tower to bedroom. Place the bottle in his hand, shove the rubber thing in his mouth, and bring his legs up to support the other end of it.'

The baby pacified, they decide to have a nap. Hancock has some difficulty getting comfortable in the basket-work chair. He is just dropping off to sleep when he jerks awake: 'I was falling again'.

While they are asleep, two burglars creep in and completely empty the house of furniture—except for the chairs Hancock and Sid are in. When the Frobishers return they are naturally somewhat upset. Hancock tries to make excuses: 'It's the baby, the baby's been down here—I expect you'll find it all up in his room'. He tries to smooth over the awkwardness. 'No need for you to run us home, we'll make our own way, actually. It did come to thirty bob, but we'll make it a quid . . .' The police arrive—they have caught the burglars but the van skidded into the canal during the chase, and the furniture is all soaked. Sid offers to furnish the Frobisher's house while the furniture is drying out—and after a fade-out we see the room again, now furnished with the familiar trappings of 23 Railway Cuttings, including the grandfather clock and the stuffed eagle. Hancock and Sid, meanwhile, are trying to get to sleep—on the floor of their living room.

In the final show of the series, 'The Poison Pen Letters', broadcast on May 6th 1960, Hancock is most upset by a succession of unpleasant letters. The police are called in, and eventually investigation shows that Hancock himself is sending them—coming downstairs in his sleep and writing them with his left hand. Sid breaks the news to him.

HANCOCK: Sid! I'm bonkers!
SID: You're all right.
HANCOCK: Why, why?
SID: Well, you see, boy, you've been over-working—you're all strung up. Your nerves are like violin strings, and secretly, underneath it all, you don't like the life you've been living, so your subconscious mind has revolted. I mean, you're like everybody else, really—*you* don't like you either!

HANCOCK: It'll pass, Sid, won't it—I'll get better, won't I ?
SID: All you need is a bit of a rest, a long break.
HANCOCK: Yes, I suppose I have been flogging it a bit lately, haven't
           I—I'll move, that's it, I'll change me address, then me
           subconscious won't know where to write to me.

It was his last appearance with Sid. The series had been a
tremendous success, but Hancock was showing signs of strain behind
the scenes. Duncan Wood says: 'Tony really thought that he had come
to the point with the Homburg, and the astrakhan collar, and 23 Railway
Cuttings, where every conceivable permutation had been wrung out of
them. He also thought that possibly Ray and Alan would like a new
dimension in which to write; and in the back of his mind, although it
never became an overt statement, he thought that he and Sid were
becoming totally known as a double act. He felt that he was becoming
submerged in that double act, and that if he was going to go on one stage
further and junk Railway Cuttings, and junk that character with the
Homburg hat, then there was no way out but that Sid would have to go as
well, because he was part and parcel of the same thing.' Galton and
Simpson say that they could have gone on writing for Hancock and
James as long as necessary, but that they saw Hancock's point. They
benefitted from these changes, as it gave them a chance to explore new
fields.

Hancock has been the subject of more public criticism for his decision
to part with Sid James than for anything else he ever did. In the public
eye the 'lad from East Cheam' with his regular sidekick was firmly
established; and the viewing public are extremely resistant to change,
particularly if it affects their favourite programme. But Hancock felt, as
he had felt when he was Archie Andrews' tutor, that he was in a rut. He
needed to develop, to expand his characterization—and he still had
hopes of becoming an international star; leaving East Cheam was a
necessary part of this striving for international recognition.

James understood Hancock's reasoning, and although he was
naturally worried about his own future career, accepted it without
bitterness. The two men remained friends; and James need not have
been concerned about his future—he went on to stardom in the
seemingly endless succession of 'Carry On' films. The matter was
discussed, amicably enough, between all concerned; and it was agreed
that Galton and Simpson should write another series for Hancock and a
separate series for James (*Citizen James*), and that Duncan Wood should
produce both series.

Hancock was now, as far as his screen image was concerned, on his
own. A year elapsed before his next TV series; in that time he made a
serious bid for international stardom with his first major feature film.

8. 1961

Hancock had already made one feature film appearance, in 1954, in a very poor comedy called *Orders Are Orders* (see page 253). The presence of Raymond Huntley, Peter Sellers, Bill Fraser and Sidney James in the cast was not enough to save it; and Hancock often told the story of going to see the film one wet afternoon. He asked the cashier if there was any chance of a seat in the circle. 'A seat?—you can have the first fifteen rows,' she said. Hancock's performance as the bandmaster is the best thing in the film as he tries to weld his recalcitrant military band into shape.

Now he was set to break into films in a much bigger way, with *The Rebel*. Simpson and Galton wrote the screenplay, the director was Robert Day, and Frank Cordell wrote an attractive musical score. The story concerns an office worker with artistic leanings who goes to Paris and becomes the centre of the art world, more by accident than design. (See page 254 for a full plot synopsis.) The cast was impressive—George Sanders, Paul Massie, Dennis Price, Irene Handl (as Mrs Cravatte—a

Hancock and an irritated landlady (Irene Handl)—a still from The Rebel

change from Patricia Hayes), John Le Mesurier, Nanette Newman and Gregoire Aslan.

On the whole, the film is extremely good. Occasionally Hancock's timing is not allowed its full scope as the director makes use of opportunities for local colour and action, but there are many classic moments. The plot—involving Hancock in the longest performance he had yet given—hangs together well, and provides plenty of opportunity for him to explore the artistic pretensions of his character. A few 'in-jokes' are used—in one sequence Hancock appears once more in the budgerigar outfit which had appeared in *A–Z, Christmas Night with the Stars* and at the 1958 Royal Variety performance. It is his fancy dress for a ball on board the boat of his millionaire patron. Forced to abscond without time to change, he arrives at the airport and demands to fly to London.

The film was premièred at the Beirut Film Festival, and given a trade showing in London on January 27th 1961. It was an immediate critical and box-office success; a considerable achievement. Few British comedians have made such a spectacular success in their first significant film—even Peter Sellers took some time to become the international star he now is, and Morecambe and Wise, two of the foremost comics on British television, have never quite succeeded in coping with the completely different medium.

Galton and Simpson had tried to introduce a gag with Sid James— James would have made a brief appearance in a swimming pool—but Hancock would not allow this. His point was that James had been appearing without Hancock for years in films; now Hancock wanted to show that he could make his own mark in the cinema without having to rely on James.

On March 6th 1961 Hancock began a six-week theatrical tour in his own show, starting at Shrewsbury and taking in Newcastle, Southampton, Brighton, Bristol and Oxford. He was brilliantly funny. Everywhere he went he packed theatres and cinemas, and the audiences rocked with laughter. Seeing him today in the telerecordings, which are essentially more intimate performances, one tends to forget that he had tremendous projection on stage—he could dominate a huge theatre, and one reviewer commented that he received thunderous applause despite the fact that the audience had to adjust to what seemed like looking through the wrong end of a telescope.

After opening acts from the dancers and The Skylons, an aerial act, Hancock came on in the familiar Homburg hat and overcoat with the astrakhan collar and after some introductory remarks, removed them to disclose a juggler's costume. He then went on to introduce his 'brothers'—Les Ward (six foot something) and Johnny Vyvyan (five foot nothing). Vyvyan, who was a long-standing friend of Hancock's as

116

Hancock in budgerigar disguise once again, in The Rebel

well as a regular stooge, also appeared in many episodes of *Hancock's Half-Hour*. The three then went on to give a monumentally incompetent demonstration of juggling; this routine still exists in *Hancock's Forty-Three Minutes*, the Christmas show from the third television series. Hancock, Vyvyan, Albert and Les Ward and Alec Bregonzi also appeared in a sketch called 'Open-Air Theatre', with Hancock as a grandiloquent Shakespearean actor and Vyvyan as an unimpressed park keeper. The first half finished with 'The Crooner', from the Adelphi days, with Vyvyan as the stooge. In the second half Hancock did his old act, with all the usual impressions.

Preparations went ahead for his new television series, his seventh for BBC Television. The programmes were 25 minutes in length instead of half-an-hour (there appear to have been some hopes of selling them to America, where the commercial breaks would necessitate the programmes being shorter than the overall slot), and the series was re-titled *Hancock*. Six programmes were planned, starting recording three weeks ahead of transmission, and using studio 4 in the BBC's gleaming new Television Centre at White City, which had opened the previous year.

Simpson and Galton decided to begin the series by taking Hancock at his word. He wanted to be alone—alone he should be; and they wrote a twenty-five minute solo performance, taking place entirely in Hancock's new bedsitter in Earl's Court. Hancock plays the whole show unsupported apart from newsreader Michael Aspel, who is seen (but not clearly) on Hancock's television, as are a few moments of some obscure Western series. Hancock liked the idea—it would prove whether he could stand up on his own—and applied himself to the difficult task of preparing the performance.

Once again Duncan Wood and his designer, this time Malcolm Goulding, put a tremendous amount of care into the design of the set. It was most important that, as Hancock wandered about it—looking out of the window, talking to himself in the bathroom mirror, or just lying on his bed, the cameras should be able to get good close-ups of him—a considerable problem in logistics. They solved it elegantly.

The pattern of recording was the same as before—rehearse for five days without cameras, then go into the studio on the morning of recording for camera rehearsals. Wood was reluctant to keep Hancock on his feet for twelve hours, and suggested that a different technique be used for rehearsing this one show. Alec Bregonzi, who had appeared in many of the television shows, and was a good friend of Hancock's, was engaged as stand-in. Wood did not ask him to learn Hancock's lines—it would hardly have been fair to ask him to impersonate Hancock in front of a studio camera crew—but he learnt all the moves. Hancock sat in the front row of the audience stalls with a cup of coffee and a monitor set, and watched as Wood ran through the show with Bregonzi, without

118

dialogue, but with all the camera shots. It took about two hours, during which Hancock made various suggestions for angles and close-ups, so that he could make the best of each situation. They broke for lunch, and at two o'clock they came back and did a perfect run-through with Hancock. Wood says: 'It was one of the most successful camera rehearsals I've ever had in my life!' As a result, when it came to the recording, Hancock knew every shot, and how he would look. The performance was a brilliant success.

The next show to be recorded was 'The Lift', although the order was altered for transmission, so that 'The Lift' became number four, and 'The Bowmans', number four as recorded, became number two as transmitted. In 'The Lift', Galton and Simpson followed up a principle they had already explored in 1959 in 'The Train Journey'—the claustrophobic situation of a group of people trapped in a confined space with Hancock at his most irritating. In this case the confined space is a lift in Television Centre. True life was stretched a little to allow the presence of a lift operator (Hugh Lloyd) whereas in fact the lifts are automatic; Hancock is the ninth person to enter the lift, which is only supposed to carry eight. He refuses to leave, and of course half-way down the lift sticks. The passengers are forced to spend the night trapped in the lift, with Hancock trying to entertain them, organize them, and calm the more hysterical ones.

Radio Times
Hancock trapped in 'The Lift' (broadcast 16.6.61) ; with (left to right) Hugh Lloyd, Jack Watling, Diana King, Colin Gordon, John Le Mesurier, Noel Howlett, Jose Reed (behind Hancock) and Charles Lloyd Pack

The third programme, both as transmitted and recorded, was the famous 'Radio Ham'. Hancock is seen operating an amateur radio station (although his procedure is very odd—he never says 'over' and appears able to hold two-way conversations with the other operators—a piece of dramatic licence necessary to keep the show going at a reasonable pace). He has a rather disjointed conversation with an operator in Tokyo, eliciting the information that 'it is are raining not'. He makes a move in an over-the-air game of chess with 'HBX Belgrade', and continues a card game with 'B 45 Malaya'. Then he picks up a distress call—a small motor yacht is sinking somewhere in the Atlantic Ocean, and the yachtsman (Andrew Faulds) is putting out a 'Mayday' call. Hancock's incompetence, and interference from his neighbours who object to the noise, conspire to prevent him being able to take down the boat's position, and then, just as he is set to go again, the set blows up. (Actually it blows up rather feebly, and one suspects that the special effects failed to work as planned.) Hancock gets the police to bring him some more valves, but by this time the Tokyo operator has located the boat and arranged a rescue.

The programme is very funny, although it has a slight edge on it because the situation is perhaps just a bit *too* real. The Radio Society of Great Britain, which represents radio amateurs, were not amused, however. Their objections are technically correct—apart from the two-way business, Hancock would not have been allowed to transmit on the emergency frequency that the boat would have been using—and in any case, no one of Hancock's evident incompetence would have been able to get a licence to transmit in the first place (operators have to pass a fairly stiff examination in the technical side of radio). But this is, of course, a comedy programme; the importance of these departures from technical reality depends on the individual viewer.

'The Bedsitter', 'The Lift', and 'The Radio Ham' have all been published in script collections, either in the André Deutsch book in 1961 or in the 1974 Woburn Press book with the frame enlargements. 'The Radio Ham' and 'The Lift' are also available on gramophone records ('The Radio Ham' in a re-enactment) and so are very well known. What is surprising is that the fourth show as recorded, 'The Bowmans' has never been as popular, even though the script has been published (again in the Woburn Press book). It is Alan Simpson's favourite from the series, and shows Hancock at the absolute peak of his profession. It is also his last really great performance, for reasons which will emerge later.

'The Bowmans' is a daily radio serial, and is of course a parody of *The Archers*. At the time of writing, sixteen years after 'The Bowmans', *The Archers* is still running, and Walter Gabriel ('me old pal, me old beauty') continues to provide rustic comic relief as he has done for over twenty-

BBC Publicity

'The Bowmans' (broadcast 2.6.61) : the dog (Peter Glaze), Old Joshua Merryweather, and Mr and Mrs Bowman (Brian Oulton and Constance Chapman)

five years, so that Hancock's barbed impression of him is just as relevant now as it was in 1961.

The show opens with a close-up of an illuminated 'On The Air' sign (never used in BBC radio studios in actual fact) as we hear a clever inversion of 'Barwick Green', the signature tune for *The Archers*. 'Dan Bowman', 'George' and 'Gladys Bowman' are discussing the carryings-on of Dan and Gladys's daughter, when 'Old Joshua Merryweather' approaches. This is Hancock's part, and he is determined to make the most of the characterization. He is wearing what he obviously considers to be a rural hat, carrying a rural walking stick, and begins by singing a rural nonsense song about having 'mangel wurzels in my garden', which, from the puzzled reactions of the rest of the cast, is plainly not in the script. The actor playing his trusty dog (Peter Glaze) yaps at him in an effort to keep him to the script, and an altercation develops between them, only stopped by the producer (Patrick Cargill) waving frantically from the control cubicle. The scene continues, with 'Old Joshua' ad-libbing and the dog snarling in an effort to keep him to the text, until the end of the episode, which has the usual

'Archers' technique of repeating the cliff-hanging line over and over again until it is drowned out by the signature tune.

As soon as the programme is off the air a row develops between Hancock and the other actors. Hancock is convinced that he is the mainstay of the programme, which does nothing to endear him to the others. Then the producer storms in, complaining about Hancock's unwarranted additions to the script. He hands out the scripts for Monday's episode. Hancock is horrified to discover that Old Joshua falls into the threshing machine and is taken to hospital, where he dies on Tuesday night. Hancock protests.

HANCOCK: Well I'm not standing for it, I shall go straight to the top.

PRODUCER: My instructions have come from the top.

HANCOCK: Oh. Well, it's the scriptwriters—they don't know what they're doing. They're making me far too unsympathetic. Last week I kicked the dog three times.

PRODUCER: Well that was *not* in the script.

HANCOCK: Well no, but he asked for it, shoving in yelps . . .

PRODUCER: I'm sorry—there's nothing more to be said.

HANCOCK: Look—I've been in this programme for five years—I've acted my heart out for you.

PRODUCER: Oh yes, that's another thing—your acting.

HANCOCK: And what about my acting?

PRODUCER: Well it's erratic. We never know from show to show what performance to expect next. And what is more, people are beginning to notice your accent.

HANCOCK: My accent is perfect. I spent six months on a cider farm in Devon getting it right.

PRODUCER: It is never the same two performances running. Sometimes it's Somerset, sometimes it's Suffolk, then a bit of Welsh, Birmingham—last week I could swear we had a bit of Robert Newton in there. It's just not good enough. And these ridiculous clothes that you're wearing—this is a radio show.

HANCOCK: I wear these clothes to get the feeling of the part. Of course, if you're completely ignorant of the Stanislavsky school of acting, I'm obviously wasting my time with this load of tat here.

PRODUCER: We don't want method actors in here.

HANCOCK: I'm not a method actor. I don't just rush around the studio scratching myself. What do you know about it anyway— you come in here—an ex-sound-mixer for *Sports Report*, and talk to me about acting?

122

Radio Times
'The Bowmans'—Hancock with 'the producer' (Patrick Cargill).

On the Monday Hancock has his death scene. Determined to make the most of it, he takes four times as long as he is supposed to and nearly wrecks the programme. In the end he has to be forcibly restrained by the producer and the rest of the cast, and the closing announcement is made with a battle royal raging in the studio.

We then see Hancock pursuing his career. He auditions for a part in *Hamlet*, unsuccessfully, and is eventually reduced to making TV commercials for Grimsby Pilchards. ('You're never alone with a pilchard.') The sales of Grimsby Pilchards plummet, and Hancock is fired. Back in his bedsitter, he is musing on the injustice of it. 'They can't blame me for what's inside the tin. I told them it was the tomato sauce that's turning people off. They should have taken the heads off. Very unnerving to open a tin and see six heads staring up at you. No, they have to have a scapegoat, go on, blame it on the artist.'

The postman arrives with a great sack of letters expressing sympathy for the death of Old Joshua Merryweather. Hancock is bewildered until he remembers that the programmes are recorded in advance. (The plot creaks a bit here, because all the arguing in the studio in the earlier sequences is really only applicable if the programmes were live, whereas if the programmes were pre-recorded, as it now suddenly appears they are, Hancock's ad-libbing could have been cut out. This however is really only carping, as few viewers are likely to be worried by the inconsistency.) The letters are followed by a large wreath from the local florist, and a reporter, who tells him that the stunned listeners have been jamming the BBC switchboards.

The BBC approaches Hancock to come back into the serial, as Joshua's twin brother.

HANCOCK: How very ingenious.

BBC OFFICIAL: You like it?
HANCOCK: Yes, I think it's a very, very, good idea. There's only one snag.
OFFICIAL: What?
HANCOCK: I'm not doing it . . . unless . . .
OFFICIAL: Yes?
HANCOCK: Unless you agree to my terms. Ten thousand a year, five year contract, I get top billing, I write all me own scripts, and a free radio licence.
OFFICIAL: Write all your own scripts?
HANCOCK: Yes, we're not having any more of this falling into the threshing machine.

Reluctantly, the BBC agrees, and we see Hancock in the first episode of: 'The Merryweathers, an everyday story of Old Ben Merryweather'.

ACTOR: Good Morning, Ben—how are you today?
HANCOCK: Oh, arr, me old pal, me old beauty.
ACTOR: What's the weather goin' to be like today, then, Ben?
HANCOCK: Well, I seen a crow on the wing this morning—he went round in three circles and flew off to the north, arr, it'll be raining by lunchtime.
ACTOR: Oh look, coming across the fields—there be Dan Bowman, Mrs Bowman, their daughter Diane, and George and Fred his farmhands, the Squire and his wife, old Jim who owns the tobacconists, the Vicar, and the Manager of the Turk's Head. Half the village be coming across.
HANCOCK: Dang me, they shouldn't be walking across that field.
ACTOR: Why not?

(*The rest of the cast cry out in unison. This is followed by silence.*)

HANCOCK (*flat*):   Oh dear, what a shame—they've all fallen down that disused mineshaft.

124

With half the village dead, Hancock plans to stock it up with Old Ben's relatives, and we leave him as he lapses into broad Robert Newton: 'Ahhaarrr, harr harrr . . .'

The script for the next show, 'The Blood Donor', arrived on the last day of rehearsals for 'The Bowmans'. Hancock and Wood looked at it and thought it first class, and Wood suggested that Patrick Cargill, who was excellent as the radio producer in 'The Bowmans', would be an ideal choice for the doctor in 'The Blood Donor'. Hancock agreed, and so Cargill was asked to do that part before he had even finished in 'The Bowmans'.

As has been said, 'The Bowmans', recorded on May 26th 1961, shows Hancock in brilliant form. The years of hard work he had put into learning his craft and overcoming his nerves, and the good luck which had brought him into contact with the writers and producers who were ideally suited to his style, had taken him to the very top of his profession.

On the way home after the recording his luck ran out. Cicely was driving, and the car ran into some roadworks. Hancock went through the windscreen; he was not badly hurt, but within twenty-four hours he had two massive black eyes that made him look like a panda. He felt unable to embark on learning 'The Blood Donor', as his normal difficulties in learning his lines were made far worse by the accident. Duncan Wood was on the point of cancelling the recording session, but Hancock was very anxious to go ahead, and asked whether he couldn't be made up to cover the black eyes—which was simple enough—and whether something could be done about his inability to learn the lines. Wood got round this problem by re-working the camera script to allow for the use of teleprompters—television monitors placed in strategic positions, which carry the script on a rolling caption. This is the modern equivalent of the older technique—still occasionally used—of writing the lines on large cards, or 'idiot boards' as they are unkindly known in the trade. Hancock had to learn one section of the script—where he wanders round the waiting room reading the posters—but otherwise he performed the entire show from the teleprompters.

'The Blood Donor' is the most famous of all Hancock's performances. It is the most often quoted as an example of his skill, and even within the BBC seems to be regarded as his best work. Certainly at the time few viewers seem to have noticed the fact that Hancock was reading his lines, and possibly even today's more observant audience would not have noticed when the show was repeated in 1976 if *Radio Times* had not drawn attention to the whole teleprompt business. Looked at with a knowledge of the circumstances, however, the show becomes extremely irritating. Not only is Hancock quite obviously reading his lines, but he is not even acting properly—he is behaving very much as if he was on a run-through, and giving a rather muted performance, whereas everybody else is acting normally. He also does not give some of the lines the correct delivery, which is unusual for him. The gramophone record of 'The Blood Donor' is a studio re-make, recorded shortly after the transmission, with Hancock reading his lines from a script; it is a much better performance than the original.

Wood now says that he wishes that he had insisted on postponing the recording until Hancock was well enough. Not only did 'The Blood Donor' suffer as a result of the conditions under which it was made, but, more significantly, Hancock developed the idea that teleprompters were the permanent answer to his learning problems, and that no-one could tell that he was using them.

In fact he never developed the knack of using teleprompters undetectably, and his delivery suffered when he used them. It is not true that he never learnt a line again, as has been claimed, but whenever he found himself in difficulties, which was to be increasingly often, his first reaction was to fall back on teleprompters to save him the strain of learning his lines.

This was the immediate, and most generally known, effect of the car accident. It also may have had a more serious and longer-term effect on him, and this will be examined in the next chapter.

There was one more recording to be made in the series—'The Succession—Son and Heir'. Hancock made some effort to learn his lines for this, but he insisted on having teleprompters on the set. As it happens it is not as obvious as it might have been because the show begins with a long monologue to the camera, so that with a teleprompter on the camera there is no problem about Hancock looking in odd directions; and he plays another section of the show in horn-rimmed spectacles, which effectively mask the tell-tale side-to-side eye movements of someone who is reading his part.

Neither Duncan Wood nor Simpson and Galton have a particularly high opinion of this show, either as a script or as a performance, but there are some good moments in it. Hancock is suffering from the realization that he will never amount to anything of importance. He decides that he must leave a son behind him as his contribution to civilization. Unfortunately this means marriage. He examines his address book, and, after a long process of elimination, is left with three candidates.

The first is Olive Hobbs, an ordinary, unpretentious ex-girl friend (Myrtle Read). He offers her a complete defrozen four course meal, but makes the mistake of taking the tin foil off it in her presence. She doesn't want tin poisoning and declines the meal. He offers her wine. Unfortunately, she happens to know about wine because her boss takes her out to dinner, and is unimpressed by his 1959 Chateau Bottled Albanian Burgundy. He asks her whether she has ever thought of

Radio Times

Hancock and fiancées—Gwenda Ewan, June Whitfield and Myrtle Reed—in 'The Succession—Son and Heir' (broadcast 30.6.61)

getting married-and-settled-down. She would like to have a son, she says, so that she can call him Elvis. This is more than enough for Hancock, who hurries her out of the room.

The next candidate is Veronica Stillwell, an intellectual beatnik dressed in jeans, a woolly sweater several sizes too large, and heavy horn-rimmed glasses (June Whitfield). Hancock is also wearing horn-rimmed glasses, and keeping up a flow of bogus intellectual chat. He tries to offer her the same defrozen dinner, but she is a vegetarian and a health food fanatic, and politely declines. They discuss a play Hancock is supposed to be writing. Hancock is having trouble with the main character: 'All the way through he was saying "What's the point of this" and "What's the point of that"—and in the end I agreed with him and turned it in'. He is now thinking of doing a musical about the Spanish Inquisition. Hancock tackles her on the subject of children. She agrees that the race must be continued, but when she realizes that he is proposing to her she explains that she regards marriage as a barbaric primitive hangover from superstitious cave dwellers, and that she would only be prepared to enter into a 'free and voluntary contract'. Hancock is shocked, and shows her out, muttering that he never thought he'd hear a vicar's daughter talk like that.

His final choice is Pamela Ffortescue-Ffrench, a débutante (Gwenda Ewan). She seems much more promising—she eats the frozen dinner

127

without complaint, and readily falls in with his proposal of marriage. However, her engagement book is full for the next three years—and her enthusiasm evaporates when she realizes that the object of the exercise is to have children—her pet dachshund Boo-Boo would be too upset. Hancock says it is all off, whereupon she threatens to sue him for breach of promise.

Then Olive bursts in—she has reconsidered, and is prepared to improve herself to meet Hancock's standards. She is closely followed by Veronica, announcing that she has decided that the furtherance of the race is more important than principles, and that she will even have the word 'obey' in the marriage service. The three women start shouting at each other.

HANCOCK: Will you kindly sit down and work this out quietly, please!
OLIVE: You keep out of this.

(Hancock reacts and goes to the wardrobe and starts slinging things in a suitcase).

VERONICA: He's mine—we're going to produce a race of geniuses.
OLIVE: They won't be very good looking, will they. I mean, you can get brains at school, but you can't get good looks, though, can you?
PAMELA: You can't acquire breeding either. My family is the second oldest in England.
OLIVE: I'm not surprised, looking at you!

(They start shouting all at once. Hancock creeps out of the room and closes the door behind him.)

HANCOCK: So exits the last of the Hancocks . . . Good luck!

And as he walks disgustedly away, the last of his BBC shows comes to an end. He had made sixty-three shows in the seven series for BBC Television; now he was about to change his approach to his work in an attempt to widen his audience.

9. 1962–63

Up to the last BBC Television series Hancock had not been difficult to work with, and not once in any of these BBC telerecordings is there the slightest trace of even the after-effects of drink. He had been reasonably co-operative with those around him, although of course he was always determined to have things done in what he saw as the best way for his style of comedy; but he remained open to suggestions and on the whole made few problems for his colleagues. Some of the people less closely connected with him were a little surprised to find that he was rather morose and uncommunicative when he was working; part of this would be his concentration on the job in hand, and a good deal of it would be nerves. Ray Galton says: 'It was never a good idea to go and see him in his dressing-room before transmission. During rehearsals, he would be fine; and then there would be an hour's break, and it would be best to keep away because he would be in his dressing-room alone. He'd be very, very nervous; he'd be so tense that your presence would be unwelcome.'

Now things started to go wrong. Hancock wanted to give television a rest and make another film, still hoping for international recognition. Galton and Simpson discussed a theme with Hancock, and went away to write a screenplay. Half-way through it, Hancock rang up to say that he had changed his mind and didn't like the idea. They discussed another approach, and went away to write that one. Again Hancock rang up while they were still working on it to say that he didn't think it would be what he wanted. They got him to agree that he would wait while they wrote a third screenplay, and not comment on it until it was complete and he had read through it. They took a further three months to complete the screenplay, by which time they had been working for six months without earning any money. They sent it to Hancock, and a week or so later he rang them up, sounding very embarrassed, and said that he didn't like the script. Galton and Simpson pointed out that they had to earn some money, and it was agreed that they should go back to writing for television while Hancock had a further think about his film.

Then Hancock called a meeting with Galton, Simpson and Beryl Vertue, who had been his agent for some years, and in effect terminated their relationship. He was rather brusque about it, and Beryl Vertue was extremely upset. However, Simpson and Galton were approached by the BBC to write a series of separate plays under the title *Comedy Playhouse*; the fourth was 'The Offer', which became the first *Steptoe and Son*.

Meanwhile Hancock was setting up his new film. From now on his general behaviour was far more difficult than it had been in the past. His writers and directors found him difficult to deal with, and over the next few years the drinking began to interfere with his performances for the first time. Why should a man who had been comparatively easy to work with, and who had been able to keep his drinking under control, suddenly become difficult? Obviously, his increasingly nervous state, arising out of the sheer fear of performing, and the process of self-examination which his friends saw as having been intensified by *Face to Face*, were contributory causes; but the car accident on the way home after 'The Bowmans' had a considerable effect on him. Through not badly hurt—he was not knocked unconscious, and later the same evening was on his feet and talking perfectly coherently, so that there appears to have been no serious concussion—he was badly shaken, and the fact that Cicely was hurt and had to have stitches, may also have affected him. People involved in this sort of accident are liable to be very upset for some time, because the narrow escape reminds them that they *can* be killed—a fact which most people do not really believe until they are forcibly reminded of it. William Cleverly, a long-standing friend of the Hancocks and also their doctor for many years, confirms that before the accident, and despite his increasingly troubled mind, Hancock was confining his drinking to after working hours, drinking heavily but not excessively. Cleverly noticed a marked change in Hancock's drinking habits after the accident—he was now drinking during the day, and increasingly using alcohol as a 'prop'. It was about two years before it became obvious that Hancock had gone over the tenuous line that marks the beginning of alcoholism, and was becoming physically dependent on alcohol.

(There is still a tendency to regard alcoholism as something which the sufferer could stop 'if he really wanted to', but it is not as simple as that. The point at which alcohol ceases to be an external influence and becomes a necessity—the point at which the habit becomes an addiction—passes before it is noticed. Once addicted, an alcoholic can only be stopped from drinking by medical intervention. He is no longer drinking because he wants to, but because the withdrawal symptoms are too unpleasant to be contemplated.)

It was in this intensified state of nervousness that Hancock made the first preparations for his new film. He approached Philip Oakes, a poet, film critic and novelist who is probably best known for his novel *The God Botherers*, and asked him to collaborate on the screenplay. Oakes has described his experiences in his book *Tony Hancock*, in the series *The Entertainers*. They started to discuss the plot, which was to be about a Punch and Judy man in a tired seaside resort, and then in October 1961 broke off for a short time while Hancock went to New York for the American première of *The Rebel*. Unfortunately, there was at that time

Popperfoto

The Punch and Judy Man—*Hancock poses with Punch*

an American TV series called *The Rebel*, dealing with the Civil War, and
the distributors re-titled the film *Call Me Genius*. This title appears to
have incensed the New York film critics. They tore it to shreds, and
Hancock was so upset that he could not face coming back to London.
Instead he went to Paris, where Oakes joined him, and continued to
work on *The Punch and Judy Man*, punctuated by large amounts of
alcohol. Oakes rebelled after a few days of this and they returned to

131

Lingfield, where the writing was further affected by the increasing atmosphere of strain between Hancock and Cicely.

Gradually the screenplay emerged, not without considerable effort being expended by Oakes to keep Hancock on the job in hand. The plot (see page 255 for a synopsis) looked promising, and arrangements were made to start shooting. One of the difficulties was that Hancock seems to have wanted to emulate Chaplin—not the Chaplin character (Hancock despised pathos) but Chaplin's overall control of his films—Hancock would have liked to write, act, direct, get the tea, operate the camera and write the music. As he had no musical ability, the score was safe, but he gave everybody concerned with the film a few bad moments by threatening to direct. In the end, it became necessary to find a director at fairly short notice because the contractual negotiations had taken so long, and the production company hired Jeremy Summers, a young, technically extremely competent, director trained in television. What Hancock really needed was a tough director of the old Hollywood type, who could have kept him in order, but he would have seen such a director as a threat. Another way in which he seemed to be emulating Chaplin was in his perfectionism. Chaplin's scenes were shot over and over and over again until they were perfect; hours and hours of rehearsal would go into getting the timing perfect to the split second before shooting even started. Chaplin and his actors raised their performances to an incredible pitch of perfection by this technique. Hancock always gave his best performance on the first try, and subsequent repetition only resulted in it deteriorating. This made him ideal for television; but in the film studio the result was that the takes which he finally accepted were usually nowhere near as good as the first takes. Hancock was not Chaplin. Writing in 1969, J. B. Priestley said 'Hancock lacked Chaplin's steely ego, his hard well-tried will, which kept the sentimental tramp on the screen, not in the studio'.

Even so, Hancock contributed some good ideas to the film, and parts of his performance are excellent. He plays the Punch and Judy Man, Wally Pinner, who lives over a souvenir shop run by his wife Delia (Sylvia Syms). In the opening sequence, played with very little dialogue, they give a penetrating demonstration of breakfast in the house of a couple whose marriage is breaking up. After some altercations, Wally makes his way out through the souvenir shop. In a moment of malice, he picks up a spotted china pig and a bunch of flowers. Originally the flowers were meant to go into its snout, but 'It's not strong enough' said Hancock, 'they have to go up its arse'. So a china pig was constructed with a suitable orifice, and in the film Wally rams the flowers up it with every appearance of malicious satisfaction.

The interesting thing about *The Punch and Judy Man* is that it works rather better on television than it does in the cinema, perhaps because

The Punch and Judy Man—*Wally Pinner (Hancock) expresses dissatisfaction*

Hancock's performance is underplayed in cinema terms. It has been broadcast several times on BBC Television, and stands up much better than critical reaction at the time of its release would lead one to expect. There are flawed moments, but much of it is good, with an overall effect of fairly gentle and well observed comedy. In one scene Wally finds himself trapped by a rainstorm in the company of a small boy (Nicholas Webb) who has been hanging round the Punch and Judy show. They go into an ice-cream parlour, and Wally treats the boy to an expensive ice-cream concoction with a cherry on top. Not to be out-done, Wally has one too, and a long mime sequence follows with Wally, unsure of the etiquette of eating such exotic food, watching the boy carefully before imitating every move. In the end, with an expression of triumph, he throws the cherry in the air and neatly catches it in his mouth. Seen on television, it is an excellent and relaxed piece of 'business', and not a moment too long.

At the end of the film, Wally reluctantly agrees to give a performance at a reception to mark the official switching-on of the illuminations by

Lady Jane Caterham (Barbara Murray). On the balcony outside the town hall, the mayor makes a speech of welcome, and Hancock's friend from his pre-war days, George Fairweather, can be seen briefly as a heckler at the front of the crowd. At the gala dinner, the Punch and Judy show is at first ignored by the diners (shades of the Election Night Ball at Claridges twelve years earlier) until a drunk starts to heckle Punch. A bun-fight develops. This is one scene where a more experienced director would have been a great advantage; the bun-fight builds up far too fast—the scene should have been several minutes longer so that the gala dinner could deteriorate more slowly. Overall, however, the film is very enjoyable, and as Sylvia Syms recalled in a later radio interview, it is only a pity that Hancock could not have been persuaded to let well alone instead of running good ideas into the ground by trying too hard to perfect them.

Filming finished in a rather bitter atmosphere. Cicely and Hancock were by now falling out spectacularly. Tired of standing around at Lingfield while Hancock and his colleagues drank heavily, she started drinking herself. Hancock, ironically, could not bear to see a woman drunk. Rows and recriminations were followed by physical violence. Hancock usually came off worse in these encounters because Cicely had some ability at judo and was very strong. She would visit him on the set of *The Punch and Judy Man* and her presence would upset him and disrupt the work.

Hancock started to lay plans for his next TV series. He approached Galton and Simpson, but they were now committed to writing the second series of *Steptoe and Son*, and could not find time. It is doubtful whether they would have wanted to go back to writing for him in any case. They could not help but be upset at the way Hancock had refused even to read some of their final work for him; and, in *Steptoe and Son* they had discovered the joy of writing for actors rather than comedians. Actors don't argue—they don't reject scripts as unsuitable—they just get on and read the lines. Writing for a comedian is in some ways irritating for a writer. John Muir, co-writer of Hancock's 1966/7 television material, says: 'If you write a good script, and it is performed well, people just say "What a funny man he is".' Frank Muir and Denis Norden have described the writer's position as 'comedian's labourer'; and most writers have found that there is a social barrier between them and the performer who depends on their work—caused often by the performer's slight resentment at his own dependence on other people's skills. Of all comedy writers, only Galton and Simpson, Muir and Norden, and Johnny Speight have become identified by the general public (Muir and Norden more particularly since they became personalities—'My Word' and so on—rather than a writing team, and Speight because of the publicity surrounding Alf Garnett's bad language); and only Galton and Simpson have managed to get their names billed above the title of the programme.

Hancock retained Philip Oakes as script adviser on the new series, but Oakes did not like the scripts which Hancock then commissioned from other people, and they split up. Hancock approached ventriloquist Ray Alan, who writes under the name 'Ray Whyberd', and a first draft of the script which later became 'The Assistant' emerged. It was not entirely satisfactory as it stood, and Hancock brought in another writer, Terry Nation, who a year later was to achieve a kind of fame as the creator of the Daleks in *Doctor Who*. With Nation as script adviser and chaperone, Hancock went on a short theatrical tour, opening at Southsea on October 8th 1962, and following with a week at Liverpool and a week at Brighton. This time he did a continuous act, running for about thirty-five minutes and including much of the familiar material, in the second half of the show, and the first half was filled by singer Matt Munro.

The TV series began recording in November, for ATV. The BBC had made attempts to get Hancock back, without success. He was offered the lead in a play by N. F. Simpson, *The Form*, and attempts were made to reunite him with Sidney James, but Hancock was not interested; and later, when an internal suggestion was made for a television version of *The Yeomen of the Guard* with Hancock as Jack Point, the BBC did not think it worth approaching him.

If Hancock's break with Galton and Simpson was disastrous for him, his decision not to work with the BBC in future was equally so. He was his own producer on the ATV series, which enabled him to keep a closer control over casting and production than he could have had with the BBC. However, he was not really cut out to be a producer, and would have done far better to leave all the worry associated with that side of the business to people trained to deal with it, even though he had considerable help from his brother Roger, who had been representing him at Associated London Scripts since the break-up with Beryl Vertue, and who later continued to do so in an independent capacity.

The BBC has many faults, but one of its great virtues is that it is very good when dealing with people—permanent staff or contract artists—who are in difficulties. Staff suffering from sudden illness, bereavement, or personal difficulties, have often found the Corporation extremely generous and helpful; and the classic case of help to outside artists was that of Morecambe and Wise. When Eric Morecambe had a heart attack, and was told that he must reduce the strain of his work, the BBC took the unprecedented step of allowing them to double the time it took to do each programme—two weeks rehearsal and two days in the studio doing the recording. It paid off in the form of some superb comedy shows. ITV, on the other hand, has a financial responsibility to its shareholders and advertisers, and cannot afford such luxuries—in fact many ITV

comedy programmes look under-rehearsed. If Hancock had stayed with
the BBC they might well have found ways to reduce the pressure on
him; but the conditions under which the ATV series was made would
have been a strain on many a more hardened performer.

Hancock did a deal with Bernard Delfont, who then presented the
series as a package to Lew Grade at ATV. Alan Tarrant, who was an
executive producer of Light Entertainment for ATV, was brought in as
director. Since ITV had been trying to persuade Hancock away from the
BBC for many years, this was ATV's big chance to produce a high
prestige comedy series; but the rushed manner in which the recordings
were done contrasted oddly with the care taken and the money spent on
casting. Once again, Hancock was surrounded by straight actors rather
than comics; and the cast lists for the series are most impressive,
featuring many actors who were at that time already well-established on
television or in the West End. They include Martita Hunt, Kenneth
Griffith, Patrick Cargill, Peter Vaughan, Allan Cuthbertson, Denholm
Elliott, Dennis Price, James Villiers, Geoffrey Keen, Edward Chapman,
Derek Nimmo, John Le Mesurier, John Junkin and Francis Matthews.
Several programmes are also enlivened by the appearance of Wilfrid
Lawson as a paper-seller, and his bleary and alcoholically aggressive
confrontations with Hancock provide some of the funniest moments in

ATV
*Hancock confronted by the paper man (played by an hilariously bleary
Wilfrid Lawson) in 'The Man on the Corner' (broadcast 31.1.63)*

the series.

Alan Tarrant met Hancock shortly after *The Punch and Judy Man* had finished shooting. They got on well, and Tarrant was delighted to have a chance to work with Hancock. They discussed the show in general terms. The first few scripts were written by Godfrey Harrison, who had written the 'Fools Rush In' sketches in *Kaleidoscope* in 1951, and who is best remembered for his excellent scripts for *A Life of Bliss*. Harrison's scripts were always most professional, but his methods of writing were alarming in the extreme. In his book *Laughter in the Air* Barry Took quotes a typical *Life of Bliss* session, with Harrison still writing as the recording started, and delivering the remaining pages in fits and starts, with the result that the recording also progressed in fits and starts. Harrison's peculiar methods were to be one of the major difficulties of the ATV series.

Hancock and Harrison went to America to see the ECAM system in action on the Lucille Ball show. This is an arrangement whereby cameras using standard 35mm cine film are fitted with miniature TV cameras as viewfinders, and have special interlocking arrangements so that they can be operated as if they were TV cameras for continuous working in front of an audience; but produce a result on film which is more compatible for foreign TV companies operating on different technical standards. They were both interested in the possibility of using it, but in fact the ATV series was done in the usual way because of objections from the film and television unions, and it was not until 1968, in Australia, that Hancock came face-to-face with the ECAM system.

It had been intended that there should be a month for preparation before studio work began but in the end Tarrant went to see Hancock during the theatrical tour, and it was only ten days before shooting that they really got down to organizing details. The shows were fairly ambitious, perhaps too much so in view of the short time for preparation. Most of the programmes began with Hancock standing on a street corner, and getting involved in various happenings. The sets were large, representing a good part of the street, and the designer even got in real paving stones to get the right sound as people walked by. There was no audience, the shows being recorded, edited as necessary, and then played back to an audience so that their reaction could be dubbed on. This was almost the same system that Hancock had tried to persuade the BBC to use in 1959. As Duncan Wood had predicted, Hancock really needed an audience to get his best performance, and in fact it is noticeable in some of the shows that actors occasionally speak their lines across a laugh, whereas had they been able to hear the audience they would have waited until the laugh had died down.

The first programme was recorded on November 4th 1962. Transmissions did not begin until January, and Alan Tarrant altered the order of the shows to balance the series a bit better, so that the first as recorded, *The Eye-Witness*, went out second, and the first as transmitted was actually the seventh to be recorded. Godfrey Harrison had delivered the first two or three scripts by the time the first show went on the studio floor, but although good they were far too long. Hancock and Tarrant ran the first script through and found that it was half-an-hour over length—more than twice as long as it should have been. They made some cuts, but time was now catching up with them, and they went into the studio with it still too long. Hancock had learnt the script properly—contrary to general belief, he did the first half of the series without teleprompters, and it was only when things started to go wrong that he reverted to their use, with all too obvious results. Once on tape, the programme still over-ran by about twenty minutes, and had to be shortened by editing—by now a perfectly feasible technical process, but of course the script suffered from being hacked about in this way. It would have made a very funny hour, but Harrison seemed unable to work to the required length.

The recordings continued. Harrison was getting more and more behind with his writing, and after a few weeks was handing in the last pages of script on the morning of the recording. Harrison's scripts are well written, and take into account the requirements of the Hancock character; their main trouble is that they tend to have over-complicated plots, and of course they inevitably suffer if one compares them with the Galton and Simpson scripts. No-one else could write with their depth, and they had gradually dispensed with complicated plots and 'business' in favour of slower pace and character development. Harrison's second script, 'The Shooting Star', which has Hancock involved with the making of a film, is very funny, and has a brilliantly written scene in which he tries to act a part for the film camera and gets his lines and his business hopelessly muddled up. It is well done, and the only criticism is that it would probably be equally funny in the hands of any experienced comedian—it relies too much on 'business' and gags, and not enough on Hancock.

The third show, as recorded, 'The Girl', is more effective as a vehicle for Hancock.

Hancock is discovered standing on a street corner, pointedly ignoring a flower seller (Nancy Nevinson). 'It's no good you ignoring me,' she says. 'I've been ignored by all the crowned heads of Europe.' A young and attractive nurse (Judith Stott) walks by, and, breaking the heel of her shoe, falls into Hancock. He gallantly tries to help her mend the shoe, but makes a mess of it. She is grateful to him for trying, and hurries off to catch a bus, leaving Hancock with a starry expression on his face.

The flower seller says 'You know what you ought to do if you want to see her again? Buy some of my lucky heather.' Hancock: 'Oh, shut up.'

ATV
*Hancock and an unsympathetic doctor (Dennis Price) in 'The Girl'
(broadcast 24.1.63)*

At home, Hancock is trying to forget her, but the radio insists on playing love songs and there is a hospital drama on the television. He is annoyed with himself. 'I don't know what's got into me. Is she any different to any other girl? Yes, she's different altogether. Hair the colour of corn, soft brown eyes . . . there's definitely something wrong with me. I'm sick.' The only thing he knows about her is that she is a nurse, so he decides to try the local hospital.

He approaches a doctor (Dennis Price). 'Good evening—I'm looking for a nurse.'—'Don't you think we should find out what's wrong with you first?'—'I just want to speak to her for a moment.'—'This is a hospital, not a social club.'—'I said "speak", not the next dance.' Hancock claims the nurse is a friend of his, but when asked for her name is only able to say 'fair hair, brown eyes'. The doctor is unimpressed. 'There are more than a hundred nurses here, at least twenty-five per cent of whom have fair hair, either by accident or design. Would you like me to arrange for them to parade past you in single file?'—'No, just an informal group' says Hancock. They glower at each other, and after further altercations the doctor orders Hancock out.

Nothing daunted, Hancock creeps back when the doctor has gone, but runs into further trouble with a nursing sister. Hiding from her, and having put on a doctor's white coat that is lying around, he runs into a hypochondriac outpatient (Norman Chappell), and is forced to make an impromptu examination of him to preserve his incognito. He goes through all the routines of tapping the stomach, taking the pulse, and poking the ribs: 'Does that hurt?'—'Yes, a bit.'—'Just as I thought.'— 'What?'—'I'm pressing too hard.' The patient demands to have his temperature taken, because the hospital does so every time he comes. Hancock: 'How long have you been coming here?'—'Three years.'— 'Well, they're bound to know it by now.' Finally escaping from the patient, Hancock runs into the doctor again and is thrown out.

Wandering past a restaurant, Hancock sees the nurse alone at a table. He joins her, and strikes up a shy conversation; she remembers his kindness over her shoe. They are just beginning to get more friendly when the waitress shows a middle-aged husband and wife (Robin Wentworth and Patsy Smart) to their table, much to Hancock's annoyance. His attempts to continue his conversation are continually interrupted because neither of the couple has brought their spectacles, and Hancock unwillingly finds himself having to read the menu to them. They argue between themselves about what to order, and Hancock is unable to get any further with his attempts to explain his feelings to the nurse. Then the waitress dumps his pot of tea in front of him, and the nurse gets up to go—she has to meet some friends. He asks when they

ATV
'The Girl'—Hancock with Judith Stott (as Nurse Rawlings) and Dany Clare (the waitress); Patsy Smart and Robin Wentworth (standing) as the intrusive couple

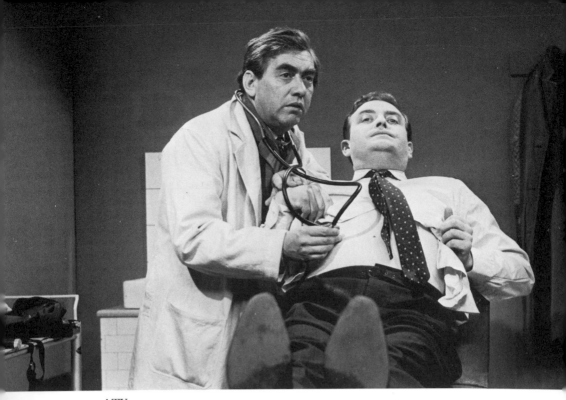

ATV
'The Girl'—Hancock and hypochondriac (Norman Chappell)

can meet again, and she agrees to give him a ring at six-thirty. As she leaves, the middle-aged couple want to know whether there are any cakes on the menu. With mounting annoyance, Hancock looks at the menu and reads 'cakes, assorted'. 'That's not much help.'—'You're right, it's not,' he agrees, and, going over to the cake trolley, he ironically gives them a brief description of the available range. 'Anything else you want to know, don't hesitate to give me a ring', and he slams down the money for his order and storms out. The wife looks after him: 'There's something funny about him.'—'What?'—'He didn't drink his tea.'

Hancock waits with mounting anxiety for the 'phone call, and at a quarter past eight decides to go back to the hospital. As soon as he has gone out, the 'phone rings. At the hospital, Hancock has a further heated argument with the doctor until the nurse comes by and promises to see that Hancock leaves the hospital quietly. She and Hancock go outside, and the doctor turns to the commissionaire: 'You must admit he's got taste. He's certainly livened things up—I can't remember anything like this since my last students' rag.'

Outside the hospital, the nurse explains that she couldn't get to a telephone before eight o'clock. Hancock is relieved. 'Well, that's all right, then.' 'Well, no, it's not all right, because you see, I'm engaged.' Hancock manfully hides his feelings. 'Oh! Congratulations.' 'Well, I know how you felt . . . but you've just been so marvellous . . . I'll think of you every time I put my shoes on' she says as she goes. 'Thank you very much indeed', says Hancock more to himself than to her. He looks up at a large sign saying 'Casualty'. 'That's me all right.'

We next see him on the street corner, boasting to the flower seller that he will be seeing the girl again, in his own good time. A girl passing by breaks the heel of her shoe and falls against Hancock. He rapidly buttonholes a young man and passes the girl and the shoe into his care. 'We usually sit on the steps there while you fix it.' The man and the girl start to become friendly as they look at the damaged shoe. Hancock points at the flower seller. 'If I were you I should buy some of her lucky heather . . . you're probably going to need it.'

The sixth show in the series was 'The Politician', which Tarrant didn't like. He tried to persuade Hancock to throw it out, but Hancock said 'I'll make it funny'. Tarrant was not happy with the result (though in point of fact the show is quite effective, partly because the plot is reasonably simple). Harrison got cross with his material being cut about and withdrew; he was in any case none too popular because the overruns were resulting in increased pressure of work for Tarrant and Hancock— they would be editing until midnight after the recording, and then would be back again the following morning to read through the next script, only to find that it was over length as well. Harrison's increasingly late delivery didn't help matters, and Hancock was having to knuckle down and do a lot of extra work, which he did not really want to do, as the producer of the series. The net result was that both Hancock and Tarrant were not getting enough sleep and were under increasing tension.

New writers had to be found to replace Harrison. Terry Nation's script 'The Assistant' was recorded, and Tarrant thought the show so successful that he placed it first in order of transmission.

Hancock, watching a tailor's dummy being dressed in the window of a department store, feels embarrassed when the shop assistant removes the coat it was wearing to reveal its underwear. Not realizing that there is no glass in the window, he holds his coat over the dummy, falls into the window, and, as the shop girl retreats hurriedly and pulls down the blind, finds himself struggling in the street with a near-naked female tailor's dummy. He takes it into the shop, and tries to hand it over to a shop assistant. She calls him a dirty old devil, and a row develops, only quelled by the arrival of the manager (Patrick Cargill). Hancock complains about the deterioration of the store; the manager complains about the deterioration of Hancock's account. He points out that some customers are enough to make anyone lose their temper. Hancock replies that a gentleman never loses his temper. 'It's a question of breeding, and you cannot whack good breeding. Now, you take my lot

143

ATV
Hancock as a reluctant 'Uncle Bunny' and Patrick Cargill as the manager in 'The Assistant' (broadcast 3.1.63)

for a start. I can go back to "Hancock the Red".' The manager wants to know who this was. 'Well, he was my father actually. The pater was a dear friend of Lenin. Dear old Lenin—I saw him the other day.' The manager points out that Lenin is dead. 'Yes, I though he was a bit quiet—but I digress.' The manager: 'Yes, I noticed that you digressed when I mentioned your account'. In an attempt to make Hancock see his point of view, the manager suggests a deal whereby, if Hancock can work in the store for a week without being rude to a single customer, the manager will pay off the outstanding account. Hancock accepts.

He begins in the packing department, assisting Owen Bowen (Kenneth Griffith) who instructs Hancock in the art of throwing valuable merchandise about, and treats him to a recital of how the Welsh villagers stood out against the English Army during the depression. Hancock, of course, gets very wrapped up in this, and imagines himself in the front line, defying the wicked English. Hancock's final effort in the packing department is to try to wrap an inflatable rubber dinghy. As he inadvertently operates the self-inflating device, he has a certain amount of difficulty getting it into a small cardboard box—a problem he solves by stabbing it with a pair of scissors.

He is then promoted to working in the children's part of the store— taking over from Mario Fabrizi as 'Uncle Bunny', dressed up as a rabbit, complete with one ear bent over and a large spotted bow-tie. Hancock: 'Look, this is ridiculous—I look like Nanook of the North'. The manager: 'You will *act* like Uncle Bunny the children's friend'. A small girl brings him a doll to wrap. (She is played by a very young Adrienne Poster, now known as Adrienne Posta.) Hancock is brusque with her. She is upset. 'You're not Uncle Bunny!'—'Yes I am.'—'You're not! Uncle Bunny is good and kind and gentle.'—'And I am good and kind and gentle, and if you don't give me the doll I shall fetch you one round the ear.' The girl's mother appears and Hancock rapidly assures her that he was only joking. He takes the doll, which goes 'Mama'. Hancock: 'You can belt up as well.'

He is rescued by the manager who details him to the games department. He demonstrates a football game to Mrs Hart (Martita Hunt), who promises to buy several for her grandchildren. They enjoy several games, with Mrs Hart thoroughly enjoying herself, with the result that she ends up too tired to bother about buying anything. The manager sends him back to being Uncle Bunny and Hancock exits, bitterly muttering friendly Uncle-Bunny-type phrases. We never find out whether he succeeds in keeping his temper for a week.

The series was by now in difficulties, and under pressure because of the rapidly approaching transmission dates. After 'The Assistant' there was a fortnight's break over Christmas, and by the time the next show was recorded the transmissions had already started. Two more writers were brought in, Richard Harris and Dennis Spooner. They found themselves having to write scripts under extreme pressure for an artist they were not directly familiar with, and it is hardly surprising that, in the circumstances, their scripts are pretty bad. In their first, 'The Craftsman', Hancock rashly claims to be a master carpenter, and finds himself involved in helping an acquaintance to erect a fitted wardrobe. The standard of the show is down to that of a very average situation comedy, and worse was to come. About this time, Hancock started really hitting the bottle, and from the next show onwards clear signs can be seen of it. He is not drunk in the studio, but his voice deepens in pitch, his delivery slows, and obvious bags appear under his eyes. As the series progresses his facial reactions become more wooden, and he can clearly be seen to be using 'idiot boards'. For some reason he had his hair cut— shorn is really more the word—around the time of 'The Early Call', the show which followed 'The Craftsman' in order of recording. He turned up on the set with this haircut, which was so short that it was almost a crew cut; with his heavy face and thick eyebrows the effect was most macabre—it made him look like a convict. Alan Tarrant stared at him in horror. 'What have you done!' he said. 'I asked for a short back and sides,' muttered Hancock.

'The Early Call' is a disaster. Harris and Spooner unwisely attempted to emulate 'The Bedsitter' and wrote a solo performance in which Hancock is concerned because he has to get up early the next morning and, his alarm clock being unreliable, books an alarm call from the telephone operator. Their script, being written in a hurry, fails to make some of the reasoning clear, and Hancock is obviously in no condition to be attempting a long solo performance. They also seemed to think that Hancock ought to have a strong fantasy life, and in most of their scripts he goes off into imaginary sword-fights and the like. It just doesn't work, partly because they have misjudged it, and partly because Hancock was now out of his depth. The pressures of trying to produce and act, and the pressure of trying to do a thirteen week series in as many weeks, was all too much for him, and he drank more and more and slept less and less. On one occasion Tarrant went into Hancock's dressing room to find him hitting himself against the wall in an effort to make himself relax.

The first shows started being transmitted in January, at the time when the Harris and Spooner shows were being recorded. By a quirk of fate, the BBC started the second series of *Steptoe and Son* earlier on the same evening as the first of Hancock's series. Hancock's name was enough to ensure good viewing figures for the first show. It got mixed reviews; *The Times* reviewer said that Hancock had shown that if Simpson and Galton did not need him, he did not need them; but in general, critical opinion was not enthusiastic. Neither was the public. By the end of January the show was out of the Top Twenty in the viewing figures.

Hancock blamed the difficulties with the public electricity supply, which was causing voltage reductions. He told the *Daily Express:* 'All the viewers could see on their sets was a postage-stamp-sized Hancock, and so they switched off. There is nothing, absolutely nothing, wrong with my new series.' More probably the public simply did not like the changes, however slight, which had been made in the Hancock image. Whatever the reason, Hancock was having to record the remainder of the series with the knowledge that even the better shows at the start of it were not being as successful as he had hoped.

There were four more shows to record. Nation wrote three of them, Harris and Spooner wrote the other one. The scripts are, on the whole, mediocre without being actually bad; but Hancock was by now in no fit state to improve the material through his performance. Tarrant remonstrated with Hancock about the use of teleprompters, but Hancock insisted that no-one would be able to tell. By the end of the series Tarrant had more teleprompt machines on the studio floor than cameras. Everyone was thankful when the last show was finished.

It is a little alarming to watch the whole series. The early shows, if not in the Simpson and Galton class, are still well performed and highly enjoyable. The second half of the series, once the strain had begun to have its effect, is startlingly different—so much so that it is almost difficult to believe that it *is* the same series. One wonders how things would have gone if more time had been allowed for recording the series, and if the original script difficulties could have been overcome.

10. 1963–65

The next three years were a succession of disappointments and abortive projects, although there were some successful moments. Hancock was booked by Bernard Delfont to appear at the Talk of the Town, the theatre-restaurant in Charing Cross Road; but as the date drew near Hancock's nerve went and he withdrew. Nevertheless in August when Arthur Haynes, who was appearing at the Palladium, became ill, Hancock volunteered to go on in his place. He did nearly eight weeks, from August 6th 1963; and, although audience reactions were mixed at first, he was a reasonable success. He used the same material that had been in his stage act for years, but in the circumstances no-one could expect him to provide a new act.

He appeared in some newspaper advertisements for British Railways, which were intended to sugar the pill of Dr Beeching's cuts. The texts of the adverts were written by a young copywriter, David Gillies, who listened to some of Hancock's records and wrote some pastiche Galton-and-Simpson. The *Daily Mail* asked Galton and Simpson to comment: they stuck their tongues firmly in their cheeks and announced 'We have hereby been done out of a job . . .'. The advertisements caused a certain amount of trouble, however. An official enquiry into cuts in the Cardiff area was told by a representative of the local City Council that an advertisement showing Hancock making a mock attack on the Beeching cuts was an attempt to undermine the enquiry by trying to persuade people not to object.

Various high-flown plans were made. Hancock conceived the idea of playing the Fool in *King Lear*—with Wilfrid Lawson as Lear. As a fantasy, it was great fun—but there was never the slightest chance of it happening. Lawson's drinking put Hancock's in the shade, and no-one in their right minds would have backed such a venture. There was a suggestion that he should play the lead in a film of *Harvey*, the play about a man who has an invisible six-foot rabbit for a constant companion, which had starred Sid Field on stage and had been filmed in 1950 with James Stewart; but nothing came of it.

He was given a small part in *Those Magnificent Men in Their Flying Machines*, an overblown comedy blockbuster about a London to Paris air race in 1910. The cast was crammed with star names, but most of them were over-shadowed by the flying machines themselves, and some impressive stunt work. Hancock had very little to do, and had his foot in plaster at the time with what he proudly described as a 'Potts fracture'; he attacked his part with little apparent enthusiasm.

He was asked to appear in a film of *Rhinoceros*, from the stage play by Ionesco; he was to play Bérenger, who refuses to join the rest of humanity who are quietly turning into rhinos. Clive Exton wrote the screenplay, and the director was to be Alexander McKendrick; the producing company was Woodfall, then at the height of its fame. Hancock's brother Roger and McKendrick went to New York to persuade Zero Mostel to join the cast. All looked to be going well, but as the time when Hancock would be definitely committed to it drew nearer, he began to have second thoughts. Roger Hancock says that his brother was very keen to get international recognition, and thought that *Rhinoceros* might have achieved this; and that he was seeking some kind of intellectual satisfaction which the film would certainly have provided. However, in the cold light of dawn, Hancock's commercial instinct (sharpened perhaps by one of his periodic drying-out sessions in hospital) told him that it would be the wrong thing for him to do. In fact,

148

since Roger had set out to protect him by making sure that the producer, director, scriptwriter and cast were of the highest calibre, it is unlikely that the film could have been a total critical or commercial failure, whatever happened; but Hancock's sense of what was right for him held him back when the plans started to become a reality.

As a result of the abandonment of *Rhinoceros*, the brothers agreed to terminate their agent-performer relationship; Roger went on to run his own agency, and Hancock transferred to Billy Marsh at London Management, who acted as his agent for the rest of Hancock's life.

Marsh was older than Hancock, and his many years experience in the business had led him to see the agent's rôle as a detached island of stability for artists who are often nervous about their performances. 'Your job is to get them bookings when they're unknown,' he says, 'and look after their affairs when they get to the top. You can't go on for them.' He did not get caught up in Hancock's nervous and alcoholic problems, and consequently Hancock found Marsh's office one place where the pressures stopped. Marsh says that, whatever difficulties Hancock may have made on the studio floor, in his business affairs he was always impeccable. Most of his bookings were made on a word and a handshake; and Hancock never once let Marsh down.

On November 15th 1964 Hancock appeared in ITV's Premier variety programme, *Sunday Night at the London Palladium*, in top placing. Something, says Marsh, seemed to worry Hancock about seeing his name in lights at the top of the bill; the responsibility of such a position, which would act as a stimulant to many performers, strained Hancock's nerves. His performance was reasonably good, but not one of his best.

All through this period his home life had been getting more and more difficult. The marriage with Cicely was breaking up, and his friendships with Freda (Freddie) Ross, who had been his publicist and general helper since 1954, had developed into something between a love affair and a patient-nurse relationship. Freddie put tremendous efforts into trying to keep Hancock sober, but her emotional involvement with him made this almost impossible, and there were many violent scenes.

On Christmas Day 1964, Hancock appeared in a forty-minute programme on radio, recorded four days earlier. Called *'Ancock's Anthology*, it was produced by Richard Dingley and consisted of Hancock introducing records, reading excerpts from Stephen Leacock and others, and interviewing Stirling Moss. The programme is well thought out and written, but Hancock was not at his best reading for radio and since he was not playing a part but being himself, his voice is not the familiar slightly aggressive one, but much quieter and more diffident. In short, he sounds what he was—shy. The programme makes pleasant enough listening, but is unremarkable. Dingley was not entirely satisfied with it, but his superior, Con Mahoney, thought that the idea would be worth pursuing, and plans were laid for a series of six thirty-five minute programmes on the same pattern. Philip Oakes was brought in by the BBC as writer; Dingley had a meeting with Hancock and Oakes, after which he reported that he could visualize himself having the same problems that he had on the original programme, in that Hancock seemed reluctant to get down to work. Disagreements arose between Hancock and Oakes, and Dingley came in one morning to find that Hancock had 'fired' Oakes—something he had no right to do, since Oakes had been hired by the BBC. If Dingley was none too pleased, Oakes was furious. Hancock refused to work with Oakes, and the BBC refused to let the programme go ahead without Oakes; so a deadlock was reached and the whole project abandoned.

In 1965 the Walt Disney studio asked Hancock to appear in a film called *Bullwhip Griffin*. Hancock was to be an itinerant Shakespearian actor in the Wild West. Hancock went to Hollywood, and began to prepare for the part. He was lonely, he found the heat unbearable, and his behaviour became strained. Freddie flew out to look after him. On May 27th Hancock collapsed in the studio, probably from the heat. In view of his past record, the Disney officials suspected drink, although in fact it seems that he had kept sober over this period. Disney's, however, were not going to risk any chance of their studio's hermetically pure image being upset. Hancock left for Paris and the film went on without him.

He got his nerve up and this time went ahead with a six-week engagement at the Talk of the Town, appearing every night at 11.30 p.m. He did all the old stage routines again, plus one or two new bits thrown in; he was moderately successful. He was not, however, happy. Dennis Main Wilson was telephoned one night and asked to go down to try to see whether he could help—Hancock was in a state. He went down; Hancock refused to see him.

On July 6th Cicely got a divorce from Hancock, citing Freddie.

In October BBC Television began a long repeat series in which they screened the entire last three series of *Hancock's Half-Hour*—his best period.

In November he went to Australia for a three week appearance at the Chevron Hilton Hotel in Sidney; he was a smash hit. The Australians had seen his best BBC work as a result of the Television Enterprises sales, and they welcomed the man himself warmly.

Another project which came to nothing was a musical version of André Obey's play *Noah*, adapted by Simpson and Galton, with music by Leslie Bricusse. Bernard Delfont and the designer, Sean Kenny, suggested Hancock to Simpson and Galton for the title-rôle. They were not very happy with the idea, but went along with it. Hancock himself was very taken with the possibilities, but gradually the other people

150

involved backed out, and despite Hancock's optimism the project was abandoned.

During this time Hancock made his last feature film appearance, in *The Wrong Box*, Bryan Forbes' film based on the novel by Robert Louis Stevenson and Lloyd Osbourne. The novel is a hilarious romp detailing the complications arising between the families of the last two survivors of a Tontine (a form of lottery in which the total investment eventually goes to the last surviving subscriber). The film is packed with stars and comic invention—in fact too much so, and becomes rather undisciplined—with some very funny performances, particularly from Ralph Richardson and John Mills as the two survivors and a magnificently pickled Wilfrid Lawson as the butler to one of them. Hancock plays the detective who appears in a few short scenes in the last twenty minutes of the film, and who finds himself trying to unravel the complications at the end of a chase involving three hearses, a brewers' dray, a corpse, the proceeds of the Tontine in banknotes and all the main characters. He makes the most of the little he is given to do, but his expressive and exasperated reactions are rather sabotaged by over-quick editing; one is left wanting to see more every time a new bewilderment heaps itself on him.

He finished this period of his career on a bright note by appearing in a set of very funny television commercials for the Egg Marketing Board with Patricia Hayes once more appearing as his charlady, Mrs Cravatte.

His personal life was also looking up. On December 12th 1965 he married Freddie; the marriage was happy for a time; and in May plans were laid for a new television series.

11. 1966–67

This time the producing company was ABC Television. The director was Mark Stuart, who asked two young writers, John Muir and Eric Geen, to write the shows. Muir and Geen had started out as a comedy act but hadn't lasted long, and they had turned their hands to writing for other comics: they had just done a series for Mark Stuart with Tommy Cooper.

John Muir remembers that they first met Hancock on Hancock's birthday, May 12th 1966. He was then forty-two. They had lunch, and afterwards went back to Hancock's flat in Belgravia. Freddie told them that Hancock had been 'dry' for some time, but certainly on this occasion he was drinking fairly heavily. There was some talk of Jimmy Grafton and Jeremy Lloyd also working on the scripts, and they were at this meeting, but Hancock and Lloyd fell out; Grafton tried to smooth over the argument, but in the end Grafton and Lloyd left and so Muir and Geen were left as the sole writers for the series.

There was no more drinking, and up to the start of the series Hancock behaved quite normally. The show was an hour-long variety programme with Hancock as compère and doing his sketches, and was recorded in the ABC Theatre Blackpool earlier on the same evening as each broadcast. The plan was that there should be three guests, giving Hancock about twenty minutes for his material, but in the end there were four guest artists in each show.

Before the series proper started a 'pilot' programme was performed and recorded, but not transmitted. The guest artists were little-known names, and the session gave everyone an opportunity to get the feel of the programme. The following week, on the first transmitted show, the same script was used, with amendments for the new guest artists, who were top-flight performers. Hancock was supported by John Junkin as a regular foil, together with Peter Gordeno and his dancers, and the ABC Television showband.

The 'pilot' was performed on Sunday June 12th 1966. John Muir says: 'It was really fantastically successful. It was a big theatre, but he really paralysed them; he was quite as funny as he had ever been.' With the identical script a week later, Hancock's nerves were strained, and it was nowhere near as successful a performance. 'We got away with it,' says Muir, 'it was all right, but it wasn't anything like it had been the week before.'

After a dance number, the show begins with a girl entering carrying a board: 'Tony Hancock Jr.'. She exits, and the band plays a noisy introduction as Hancock enters.

HANCOCK: Have you gone raving mad? Who were you expecting? Sammy Davis? Well you've got me, Hancock, and like it. We don't want any of that cheap American stuff here . . . in future my music will be . . . (*mimics 'Hancock's Half-Hour' theme*) . . . Right? Ladies and gentlemen, may I apologize for that fiasco, and may I say I am privileged and honoured to be called upon to address the nation via television. It has been some years since I graced the small screen . . . and since then one or two things have happened. First there was the war . . . then the general strike . . . but I am pleased to note that the legend of Hancock lives on, perpetuated by

152

BBC repeats and Jack Jackson's record show. And if I hear 'The Blood Donor' again I'll smash the set. And while I'm on the subject I would just like to scotch a rumour and put you at your ease. *The Best of Hancock* will not be shown for the eighth time this year. I am pleased to say that the films have finally fallen to pieces . . . and what's left of them is in the Victoria and Albert Museum.

He goes on to complain about the methods of modern television producers, and then calls for a stool.

HANCOCK: Where's me stool? That's nice, isn't it. All this money and no stool. If I was Sinatra they'd be falling over themselves to bring on a stool. You'd think they were a bunch of landladies back there.

(John Junkin walks out very slowly carrying a stool.)

HANCOCK: Oh come along! 'Course it's my head that's going to roll. Not his. The critics are waiting for stuff like this. Oh, shift your carcass, you great white-faced baboon. Put it down here! . . . (*simmering down*) . . . I'm sorry about that—what's your name?

JUNKIN: Evelyn.

HANCOCK: (*Raises his eyes—'Heaven help us'.*) I'm sorry about that, Evelyn. I didn't mean to say those things . . . (*to audience*) Got a lot to do, these stagehands. I shouldn't knock 'em. (*Puts his arm round Junkin.*) But I want you to know you're doing a great job, Evelyn. I know you don't get much money—you don't have to tell me that. You don't have much glamour, much recognition, or thanks . . . but without you the show wouldn't go on. 'All the World's a Stage . . .' we each have our part to play . . . (*truculently*) and your part is to bring on the stool, so put it down and get off. And don't take a bow either. And next time don't wear make-up.

Muir and Geen also wrote for this show an up-dated version of Hancock's old 'Crooner' routine.

HANCOCK: Today you have to be versatile—if you're not versatile you've had it. Take Sammy Davis he sings, dances, mimes—does impressions—not my cup of tea, but it's what they want. That's the secret—versatile, but casual. Of

153

course this won't be my first stab at the Top Twenty as the more mature pop-pickers amongst you know . . . I got to 83 with 'Lullaby of the Leaves' . . . pensioners don't buy many records. Then I recorded 'These Boots Are Made for Walking'. It didn't sell, but I got some very funny fan mail . . . but you don't want to be put off . . . if the Singing Nun can do it, we all can. First of all you have to have the hip movement . . . (*starts swaying hips*) . . . Then the Bob Hope jaw movement . . . the fingers . . . (*starts snapping his fingers*) . . . it's more important to be a good snapper than a singer. Finally you need a fag. That's in the contract. (*Takes out a packet of cigarettes; taps the packet for one*) . . . See, it's all done dead casual— and it helps to be Jewish or Italian—but I can't do anything about that. (*Taps the packet—nothing happens*) I bet Dino never had this trouble. Of course I'm really too tall to be a singer . . . I tried walking on my knees but I had a nasty experience with a dalmation. To get the breaks you've got to be four foot two and wearing a wig. But I'm more the chocolate box Steeve Reeves type. Still, there's always room for a great new talent . . . Look at Streisand, with my nose she could do quite well. (*Angrily tapping the packet*) How do they do this? (*Gives one God-Almighty thump at the packet; the cigarettes spray all over the floor . . . he kicks them away.*) Marvellous, isn't it? (*Reaches into his pocket, pulls out a used butt—straightens it—stuffs it into his mouth—pats his pockets for a light—can't find one, shrugs, throws the butt away.*) And now, Ladies and Gentleman, with one eye cocked at the hit parade and the other eye watching my coat . . . I should like to wander over to the old joanna, and render for you—'Button Up Your Overcoat'. Thank you. (*Walks over to piano; sits, runs his fingers up and down the keys.*) Here's a song I know you'll know . . . (*chord*) I brought it back from Miami on a recent visit (*chord*) It was a big hit in Miami and more recently in the Barnsley Miners' Welfare Club . . . (*chord . . .*)

(*Junkin walks out, and plonks a pint of beer on to the piano.*)

HANCOCK: Just a moment . . . what's this?

JUNKIN: Mild and bitter.

HANCOCK: (*Leaps up from his stool*) Mild and bitter! You are uncouth! This is my Sinatra kick, not the Dawlish Darby and Joan Club.

JUNKIN: But you said in the pub last night . . .

HANCOCK: Don't tell me what I said in the pub last night—kindly remember your place—you artistic savage. Do you think

154

Frank would sing 'One for the Road' swigging mild and bitter out of a bucket? I told you to bring out a bourbon on the rocks . . . whatever that is . . . and while I'm at it—I really wanted a glass top on here with a candelabra.

JUNKIN: Well Sinatra does two hours out there with just a hat.

HANCOCK: Well get off and get me a hat. Sinatra—who's he?

He then goes on to sing 'Brother can you spare a dime'.

To the viewers, who had not seen the much more effective pilot show, the programme was quite successful, even though Hancock forgot the name of one of the artists he was introducing and had to fudge his lines. The show went straight to the top of the audience ratings. The television critic of *The Observer* complained that the show was 'slow and dim', and that 'some phantom saboteur had produced an ingenious method of lighting that made performers often indistinguishable from their surroundings', but described parts of Hancock's performance as 'titanic' and said that the 'Brother can you spare a dime' routine was 'near perfect'.

The series continued, tolerably successfully even though Hancock was finding it something of a nervous strain. One of the difficulties was that the format of the show made him almost a stand-up comic—always his weakest point. Muir and Geen gave him situations to react to as far as was possible. John Muir says: 'You couldn't really do much monologue with him—he did harangues within the course of a situation very well, but when he came to harangue the audience, it didn't seem to work, because what was funny was that he was haranguing imbeciles, within the context of his story line. If he did the same thing to the audience, it didn't really work.'

Battles began between Hancock and the ABC-TV executives about various aspects of the show. The executives couldn't find the nerve to tackle Hancock direct, so they used Muir and Geen as a buffer, passing them one set of instructions while Hancock was giving them another.

During this time Hancock was living in London during the week, travelling to Liverpool on the Saturday, staying in a hotel there, and travelling to Blackpool for the rehearsals and the recording. On the morning of the fourth show his marriage to Freddie, which had been increasingly punctuated with rows, violence and drinking from him and threats of suicide from her, came to its lowest point. Freddie did not have Cicely's physical strength to fight back, and admits, in her book* co-written with David Nathan, that her suicide attempts did not act as a deterrent to Hancock's drinking and very probably in fact made it worse. On the morning of the day before the fourth programme,

* *Hancock*, by Freddie Hancock & David Nathan, William Kimber & Company, 1969.

Hancock, substantially drunk, was getting ready to go north. Freddie took an overdose of tablets—her fifth suicide attempt. On previous occasions she had always had friends around to walk her up and down and make her vomit. Hancock ignored her and went on to Liverpool. But Freddie had misjudged it this time; she was found unconscious by the daily help, and taken, in a critical condition, to the Middlesex Hospital. Hancock arrived at the hotel in Liverpool to find the foyer stiff with reporters. He told them he thought the tablets were Ex-Lax.

They were both furious about the incident, Freddie because she felt that she had been callously abandoned by him, and Hancock because he felt that the incident was an attack on his career. Freddie had intended no such thing, of course, but Hancock, who had seen her do this before, may have thought that this time would be like the previous occasions, an annoyance which he could well do without in the middle of a series. Whatever his reasoning, he was angry in the extreme. He gave interviews to the press in which he said a number of things which they very charitably did not print. He went on with the show, rehearsing and performing like a zombie.

He returned to London and visited Freddie in hospital. There was another row, and the marriage was over bar the formalities. It had lasted seven months.

The incident was the kiss of death to the television show. Hancock became totally reliant on 'idiot boards', which, as these severely limited his movement on stage, restricted Muir and Geen's writing. Two weeks later, on July 24th, Hancock turned up for rehearsals feeling unwell. Mark Stuart sent for a doctor, who insisted that Hancock should go to bed immediately. Dave Allen, who had a seven-minute spot in the show, took over the job of compère, and John Junkin apologised to the viewers for Hancock's absence.

Hancock did only one more week, and the last programme of the series was taken over by Bruce Forsyth.

Despite the strain behind the scenes, the series had done well in the ratings, and Hancock's performances had come over quite acceptably. The ABC-TV executives were pleased with it, and were complimentary, but Muir and Geen were not very keen on the idea of writing any more for Hancock. The experience had been something of a nightmare for them, although they did not feel antipathy towards him. John Muir says: 'I've had horrible experiences with other performers, but they've been differently horrible; you got awfully sick of Hancock, but you never actually became hostile like you do with some of them.' There was always in Hancock a helplessness that made people, even those who had been through difficult situations like the Blackpool series, feel that they could not abandon him. A little reluctantly, they agreed to provide a new act for Hancock, who was now laying plans for a solo performance at the Royal Festival Hall. John Muir: 'He said he wanted a completely new act; well, of course, he wasn't capable of learning it, this was the great problem. We did write a new act; he got it, and he read it, and he was delighted with it. He literally did not put that script down for three weeks—he always had it clenched, rolled up, in his hand; and he never got past the first page. We went down to Bournemouth with him to try it out in a week of variety, but he virtually didn't touch the new stuff. He tried to, but then he'd forget it.'

The appearance at the Royal Festival Hall took place on September 22nd 1966. In the first half of the evening singer Marian Montgomery was effectively sabotaged by trouble with the public address system, and got a rather hostile reception from the audience. In the second half, Hancock was on-stage for nearly an hour. The act was recorded by the BBC for their new second television channel, but no transmission date was scheduled so that it could be scrapped if the performance was not good enough—and in fact Hancock was given the right of veto. A telerecording still exists, and even though one can detect the tremendous sympathy of the audience, who seemed to be willing Hancock to succeed, the cold eye of the television camera shows the performance as empty, lacking the power and warmth of the real Hancock. In the hall itself, the atmosphere of the audience made the performance seem rather more successful than it really was—sufficiently so to persuade David Attenborough, the Controller of BBC-2, and Hancock himself that it was worth broadcasting. Of the BBC executives present only Tom Sloan had reservations; he was over-ruled and the recording was transmitted on October 15th.

Hancock comes on-stage to a huge round of applause, as the band plays 'Mr. Wonderful'. Muir and Geen's opening material had been written on the assumption that the evening would not go exactly smoothly.

HANCOCK: Good evening. I don't think I've ever seen such an ornate garage. And good evening to you in the Big Dipper. (*applause*) I was told this place was 'acoustically perfect'. (*Huge round of applause—someone in the audience shouts 'We didn't hear you, can you say that again?'*) If you can't hear, shout out! Any case, I expected a battery of microphones round here—this show is going out to all nations, and by 'Early Bird' to my mother in Bournemouth. (*Turns to look at the choir seats.*) Always bothers me a bit when the audience is behind you. Seems to bring in a strange sort of person. Any case, I don't like these places where there's no smoking and coffee and Tchaikovsky in the interval.

He is obviously very nervous, and consequently sounds uncertain of himself, fluffing occasionally over his lines. He said later, in an interview with *The Observer :* 'I decided that if I'd got fifteen minutes in and hadn't got anywhere I'd make this terrible speech—no, I can't possibly repeat it, it was *terrible*—and that would be the finish of a career.'

He announces that he is going to go through the card—and he does. He does a composite version of Galton and Simpson's 'The Crooner' and Muir and Geen's updated version of it from *The Blackpool Show*. He does Robert Newton, Laughton in *Mutiny on the Bounty*, George Arliss ('What do you mean, never heard of him—he's only been dead forty years') and the Hunchback of Notre Dame; but the once mobile face muscles have gone stiff, and the eyes no longer bulge out as they once did. Even so, it all goes down very well with the audience. He does a long skit on *Richard III*, and a parody of closing 'thank you' speeches with the musical director, Tony Hatch, and his supporting actor Joe Ritchie. The sheer size of the Festival Hall seems to bother him; his nerves, and the need to project to such a huge audience (even though he has a microphone, he has to put the material over in a very 'large' way), result in the whole performance never quite coming off; at any rate when seen in cold blood on the recording.

The broadcast did not include the excerpts from 'The Blood Donor' that Hancock had decided to do to fill out the length. He had not been able to learn any of it, and Muir and Geen wrote out his lines on large pieces of card which they held up in the wings. Unfortunately they did not think to write the last line on each card again on the *back*, so that they found that they had no idea when they were supposed to change cards. Hancock did the whole sequence peering into the wings.

On November 13th 1966 Hancock appeared on ITV as a guest in *Secombe and Friends*. For the last time he wore his famous budgerigar disguise; and Jimmy Grafton, with the permission of Galton and Simpson, adapted the original sketch. The old lady who owns the budgie announces to the Vicar that she has a new mate for him.

HANCOCK: Oh, no, not again—as soon as you start looking moody they think you need a mate! Well I can only hope they've had a good look this time . . . I had a lot of trouble with the last fellow.

OLD LADY: Perhaps you'd open the door, Vicar—I can introduce his new friend.

HANCOCK: Oh, charming, that's typical, isn't it—they might have given me a chance to tidy up. Look at me—what *do* I look like? A second-hand flue-brush!

OLD LADY: There now, say hello to your new little friend.

Hancock as Richard III, at the Royal Festival Hall (22.9.66)

(Secombe enters the cage dressed as a budgerigar.)

HANCOCK: *Little* friend? You must be joking!

SECOMBE: *(Whistles; budgie business.)* Good afternoon madam.

HANCOCK: Madam? Don't you know that the male bird is the bright-feathered attractive one? The female is dull and plain.

SECOMBE: Exactly, darling! Shall we dance?

HANCOCK: Oh blimey, they've done it again! Will you get off me! I'm a fellow, like you!

SECOMBE: Oh no! Blimey, I was expecting a mate!

HANCOCK: So was I. We'll just have to put up with it, that's all.

SECOMBE: Hello—just a minute ... *(laughs)* I'm your replacement, mate!

HANCOCK: What do you mean?

SECOMBE: Well look at you—haven't got long to go, have you! Loose feathers, chalky feet,—I wouldn't be surprised if you'd got

HANCOCK: *(with him :)*   a touch of the red-mite!

HANCOCK: Yes. We've had all that. Now don't you worry, mate.

SECOMBE: Careful.

HANCOCK: All right, then, 'old man'. I've a good few years left in me! And I'm senior bird here, and don't you forget it.

SECOMBE: All right, then. My name's Joey—what's yours?

HANCOCK: I'm not telling you.

SECOMBE: Come on, they must call you something—what is it? Bill? Eric? ... Fluffy? ... I know—Chalky!

HANCOCK: Oh, very funny!

SECOMBE: Come on, tell me.

HANCOCK: Well, promise you won't laugh.

SECOMBE: Promise.

HANCOCK: It's 'Cheeky'.

SECOMBE: *(Giggles)* Hallo Cheeky!

HANCOCK: Oh blimey, we've had enough of that. Look, if we've got to stick here together I'd better show you the ropes. Now let's look at the general geography here—you've got your cuttlefish up there for sharpening the beak—if you want to keep fit, swing up there—mirror there ... bath, bottom left.

SECOMBE: What about the ... ahem!

HANCOCK: The usual offices.

SECOMBE: What's the grub like?

HANCOCK: Oh, not bad, you know—you get a pretty fair supply—birdseed, groundsel, chickweed, lettuce, the odd spray of millet you know. Yes, so if you run out or feel a bit peckish just give the bell a bang with your beak.

SECOMBE: Oh—like that? (*Bangs the bell.*)

HANCOCK: No, no—not now, you stupid great oaf!

SECOMBE: Who are you calling a big oaf? I'm just about the size for you, mate.

HANCOCK: Oh, you are? Well have a go, then . . . just watch it, mate, I'm warning you . . . (*etc. etc.—they scuffle.*)

OLD LADY: They're playing together—isn't it sweet!

VICAR: Do you suppose this is some kind of love-making?

SECOMBE (*shocked*): Love-making?

HANCOCK: That's nice, isn't it—these vicars are all the same!

The sketch was the highlight of the programme, with Hancock in good form.

The ABC-TV executives were sufficiently pleased with *The Blackpool Show* to want to embark on another series, but after the difficulties behind the scenes they were beginning to feel cautious; so they devised a supposedly 'sure-fire' formula in which Hancock would be the manager of a night-club and would alternate his own sketches with introducing various acts. The theory was that if things deteriorated there could be less Hancock and more variety. This 'safety-net' approach doomed the show before it even got started.

Hancock agreed to the proposals, although inevitably they would again cast him in the rôle of a stand-up comic for part of the time. He never seemed to realize that it was his weakest point. Muir and Geen discussed the show with him, and though Hancock obviously had a very clear idea in his mind of what he wanted, they could not latch on to it until, quite suddenly, Muir realized that what Hancock was talking about was a succession of sketches very much in the style of the old music-hall—not in the sense of being corny, but using set-pieces. Shortly after this, Muir happened to see on television a screening of Sid Field's film *London Town*, which contains several of Field's most famous sketches. Muir realized how much Hancock's style was based on Field's, and they wrote all the material as if for Field. Hancock variously took the parts of the wine waiter, a gypsy fiddler, a croupier, the hat-check man . . . all written in the style of a music-hall routine.

It was probably the best possible approach to the situation. The series began tolerably well, except that there was the usual battle over the use of 'idiot boards', which Hancock won; this resulted in him reading his lines off a roller and consequently being rooted to the spot for a fair amount of the time. The regular supporting team was Joe Ritchie and June Whitfield, with Nat Temple and his Orchestra. Joe Ritchie had appeared in the Festival Hall performance, but he was not really suitable for this series, which left June Whitfield as the main foil. As in the past,

Hancock was not at his best with a woman as his partner.

In the second show to be recorded, Hancock firstly has an altercation with June Whitfield because she is selling cigarettes, cigars, kewpie dolls ... and then does a routine with guest singer Dick Haymes. After the commercial break, we see the band playing while some 'extras', as patrons of the night-club, dance.

(Hancock and Ritchie approach the band simultaneously, Ritchie carrying a large tray loaded up with pints of beer—they meet in front of the band.)

HANCOCK: Just a minute, Toulouse, where are you going with that lot? We haven't got the rugby crowd in, have we?

RITCHIE: No, it's for the band.

HANCOCK: The band? It's not your job to serve the band—anyway, who's paying for it?

RITCHIE: You are, I suppose.

HANCOCK: There must be a very grave mistake on somebody's part—I'm not playing Dr Schweitzer to this load of layabouts. Take the beer away.

(The band stops playing in mid-tune. They grind to a halt and put down their instruments. Ritchie takes a step away and 'hovers' during the next bit ... at one point he sips one of the pints ... he is well aware that ultimately the band will get the drinks.)

HANCOCK: Hey—just a moment—what's happened to the music?

NAT TEMPLE: Mr Hancock, without the beer my orchestra will not provide music.

HANCOCK: Orchestra?

TEMPLE: Their contract is for seven-and-six a night and all the beer they can drink.

HANCOCK: All the beer they can drink? This could put me out of business.

TEMPLE: You told me to get the cheapest musicians, and this is the best I can do.

HANCOCK: A bunch of drunken Geraldo rejects—and I'm paying for it.

RITCHIE: Do you want the beer or not?

HANCOCK: Keep out of this, Toulouse.

(Ritchie shrugs and steps away ... goes back to the occasional sip.)

HANCOCK: It's not as if they know what they're doing. I mean, look at this layabout. I shouldn't be at all surprised if he's not a proper musician. (*The pianist plays an exquisite arpeggio.*) Don't get clever with me—just shut your mouth and sit up straight. (*To Temple*) And have him

162

	buff those keys up . . . I don't want them looking like his teeth.
BAND:	Oi, Oi! (*They stand up.*)
HANCOCK:	Oh sit down!
TEMPLE:	We don't have to listen to your personal remarks, Mr Hancock. We're here to provide music, not to be the butt of your personal remarks.
HANCOCK:	Stone me, Sir Laurence! The last bandleader to adopt that tone of voice with me felt the benefit of my boot up his rostrum.
RITCHIE:	What about the beer?
HANCOCK:	Oh shut up. Now—are you going to extract some music from this crew, or do I fetch in Henry Hall?
TEMPLE:	(*Firmly*) Not until they get the beer!
HANCOCK:	Here we go—the voice of the union.
TEMPLE:	No beer, no music.
HANCOCK:	Well, it's extortion, but I suppose I've no choice . . . as a country we are but slaves to the unions, and this is merely another episode in a sorry story. Fifty-four—serve the beer. I'll speak to you two later.

Popperfoto
The Gypsy Fiddler sketch from Hancock's—*Hancock with Damaris Hayman and Frank Crawshaw (broadcast 30.6.67)*

The show continues with a song from Dick Haymes, and ends with Hancock's appearance as a gypsy violinist. He is dressed in a full gypsy rig-out, much to the amusement of June Whitfield.

JUNE: Isn't there something I could do to help? Perhaps I could go round the tables and announce you (*breaking into a giggle*) or warn them, or something, of your approach . . .

HANCOCK: Young lady, I've noticed that trait in your character before and I am not at all sure I care for it.

JUNE: Well, I'm sorry, but you must admit you do look rather foolish dressed like that—a man of your build.

HANCOCK: I am not a man of my build.

And he goes on to make himself a nuisance to the customers.

The series, under the title *Hancock's*, began recording at the beginning of April 1967, for transmissions weekly from June 16th. By the third week Hancock was feeling the strain, and tried to make a week's break by objecting to the script—something he had never done before with Muir and Geen. They stayed up three nights running and produced a re-written script in time for the recording.

The TV executives were still trying to use Muir and Geen as buffers rather than deal with Hancock direct, and the writers, who were then in their early twenties, found themselves in the impossible position of being in the cross-fire between high-powered executives and a high-powered star in one of his most difficult moods. Hancock's complaints about the series were not all unjustified. ABC-TV tried to impose a plot where 'Hancock's' was visited by an American film company, with Hancock just being pushed round and most of the lines being given to the other actors. Hancock, of course, refused to co-operate. Then ABC

Popperfoto
The Croupier sketch from Hancock's, *(broadcast 4.7.67)*

decided that the last show, which had not yet been written, should end with the night-club being raided and closed down by the police. Hancock, who fully intended to do another series on the same lines, realized that there would be no second series if this idea was allowed to go through, and refused to permit Muir and Geen to write such a script. ABC were furious that their instructions had been disobeyed, and Muir and Geen were by now so sick of being in the middle that they told the ABC executives to talk directly to Hancock.

After all the trouble on the third show, they came to rehearse the next programme, for which Muir and Geen had written a sketch with Hancock as a croupier. Hancock was absolutely sober on the read-through, and at the end he said 'This is as good a script as has ever been written for me'. He felt that he had no excuses this time, and that it was up to him to give a good performance. He complained to the director, Mark Stuart, that he was not getting enough close-ups and quoted the old BBC Television shows where much of the work had been done in close-up. Stuart was well aware of this, but had felt unable to use close shots because Hancock's face had now badly deteriorated due to the years of drink; the muscles were stiff, and there were great bags under the eyes. Stuart asked Muir and Geen whether he should do the close-ups as Hancock asked, and they said: if that was what Hancock wanted, let him have it. It was a bad miscalculation. There was a play-back of the show, and after it a long awkward silence. Then Hancock said: 'I look just like a fucking frog'. After that he went completely to pieces; his nerve failed and he went back to drinking extremely heavily, turning up at the studio in a bad condition.

Whether the series might have worked if Hancock had been more tactfully handled, particularly by the ABC-TV people, is impossible to say. He had not lost all his old skills and at the beginning approached the work in a responsible manner, but faced with the strain of week-by-week working and the tense atmosphere, it was inevitable that he would crack. 'All the way along', says Muir, 'you got your best performance from him at the first read-through; after that it was just a steady decline. On the first read-through it would be funny—and you'd wonder how it could be, as it was the first time he'd ever seen it. I think he could have gone on working, in radio, if you rehearsed the rest of the cast, and then suddenly stuck him in front of the microphone with a script. He probably could have gone on for ever, and really that's what he should have done.' But to Hancock, that would have been a going back. He still felt he had to go on, to try and gain the international acclaim he had wanted for so long. *Hancock's* was badly received by the critics, and was not popular with the viewers. It was Hancock's last series on British television.

In July 1967 he and Hughie Green went to Aden for a week to entertain the troops. The hotel they stayed in was under fire, and they had to have armed guards between there and their various engagements.

The failure of *Hancock's* must have been a blow to him, but he was determined not to be beaten and, in a final effort to re-establish himself, he returned to Australia, where he had made such a hit in cabaret in 1965; but his bad luck went with him.

12. 1967–68

Hancock went out to Australia at the beginning of October 1967 to appear in stage engagements arranged by John Collins, an entrepreneur associated with Willard King Productions. The principal appearance was for three weeks at the Dendy Cinema in Melbourne, where Hancock opened on October 4th. At this time he had been 'dry' for some time and the performances went quite well until Tuesday, October 10th. A party was thrown for Hancock around this time, at which he was drinking tomato juice. Apparently one of the guests—a man who knew Hancock's condition—laced his tomato juice with vodka. The result was inevitable—to an alcoholic one drink is enough to cause a total return to dependence on alcohol. On October 10th Hancock was allowed to go on-stage—apparently at his own insistence—in a completely incapable condition. He fell over several times, and at one point made a false exit and crawled back up the stairs onto the stage. The audience booed and cat-called and Hancock ordered a spotlight to be shone on a heckler. The theatre staff made the mistake of complying with this order, and uproar broke out. Hancock was helped off-stage. He was back on form the next night, beginning 'As I was saying when I fell off the stage . . .'. He went through the act with no difficulty, and received a tremendous ovation. On the following Sunday he gave a free performance for those who had been in the audience on the Tuesday.

Apart from this incident the three weeks at the Dendy Cinema were successful. The Australian audiences responded warmly to him, and if he was not up to the standard of his best years he still gave an excellent performance. The act was still the same as it had always been, of course, with a few interjections suitable to the occasion.

HANCOCK: Anyway, tonight you are getting the lot—I shall not be hanging around—I shall not be rushing on here shouting

John Fairfax & Sons Ltd
Hancock in the opening sequence of the Australian TV film

'stone me' and 'he's gone bonkers' and 'fetch him a punch up the bracket'—there will be no mention of an armful of blood. Tonight you are getting the lot—you'll be getting Terpischore . . . dancing . . . sword-swallowing . . . (painful, but lucrative) . . . impressions, Shakespeare—I shall be going through the card, because you are looking at Mr Show Business himself.

He did his impressions, and introduced 'The Crooner' by saying: 'Ah, the times Dame Nellie Melba and I had together . . . singing, you know . . . of course, they named a pudding after her . . .'

The last performance at the Dendy Cinema was on October 22nd. Thank-you speeches were made by Robert Ward, the manager of the Dendy, and the local mayor, who made favourable comparisons between Hancock's act and the *Hancock's Half-Hour* TV shows and records. If this rankled with Hancock, who was trying to forget those days, he did not show it.

Despite Hancock's relative success on-stage, his condition was deteriorating. Collins felt that he should keep him occupied and set up a television series with ATN7 in Sydney. Hugh Stuckey, who had been the first writer for television when it opened in Australia in 1956, was then under contract to Collins, and began to write the series. Hancock signed a contract with Collins, doing so without reference to Billy Marsh.

At this time the BBC Television recordings of *Hancock's Half-Hour* were very familiar in Australia, and of course the later and less satisfactory ITV programmes had never been exported. Consequently the management of ATN7 thought that they were getting the Hancock of 1961. Hancock was in Melbourne; ATN7 is in Sydney—a distance of six hundred miles. This is not considered an excessive distance in Australia and is only an hour by plane, but it was far enough to keep Hancock's condition away from the notice of the television management. Hancock was being shunted around from one hotel to another; he frequently rang his mother in Bournemouth and worried hotel managers would present bills of over $1,000 for a week's telephoning. Hancock always paid them without a murmur.

He went on to Hobart, Tasmania, to appear in cabaret at the main hotel there. A worried 'phone call from Collins sent Stuckey out to look after Hancock, who was getting into a bad state again. The technique Stuckey developed was to keep Hancock fully occupied. 'He was a very unsophisticated man, he loved simple things', says Stuckey. 'I took him to an agricultural fair in Hobart—he bought a cap and a scarf and dark glasses and wandered around—he thought he was in disguise—everybody said "Hello Tony"—he loved that, it kept him dry for about three days.' An interesting sidelight on Hancock's attitude to his own

168

fame emerged when Stuckey offered to introduce him to two famous Australian Test cricketers who were friends of Stuckey's—Len Maddox and Norman O'Neill. Hancock could hardly believe that they would come to see him. They went to one of Hancock's performances, and after the show Stuckey took them round to Hancock's dressing room. 'He sat with O'Neill on one side and Maddox on the other', recalls Stuckey, 'and he was absolutely starry-eyed. They talked for an hour or two'— Hancock was a great cricket fan—'afterwards I walked them down to their car and when I came back Tony was sitting there saying "They'll never believe me, that I had Len Maddox and Norman O'Neill all to myself for an hour".'

Hancock went back to England in December, in the company of a seven-foot-tall yellow teddy bear he had bought. He and the bear gave interviews to the press about his forthcoming television series. 'My best is yet to come' he announced in the *Sunday Express* on December 17th. But his colleagues in England were less optimistic. As Hancock had signed the contract for the series on his own authority, Billy Marsh felt unable to take any part in the matter; Hancock asked Muir and Geen to come to Australia to help with the writing, and Duncan Wood to help with the production, but they were not willing to do so.

ATN7 approached Eddie Joffe, who had experience of television direction in Britain, to direct their series, and Michael Wale, a young writer, went out with Hancock to assist Hugh Stuckey with the scripts. Hancock returned to Australia in March 1968, and work began. He stayed with Stuckey and became very friendly with him and his wife. When the time came for Hancock to move on to Sydney, where the series was to be made, he ran back at the last moment from the aircraft and broke down, saying 'Don't let them take me'. The Stuckeys persuaded him onto the plane.

Collins was by now a very worried man. He introduced Hancock to a psychiatrist specializing in alcoholism, and Collins and Stuckey went to see the television management, excusing Hancock's absence by saying that he was busy on the scripts. Hancock was installed in a motel; Stuckey stayed in the next room, only going home to Melbourne at weekends. Stuckey says: 'Hancock only had the capacity to trust one person at a time—at this time I just happened to be that person'. He found himself staying up half the night talking to Hancock, and searching the room for hidden bottles. They became very friendly. 'Whatever that magic quality is that gets to audiences, was in the man,' says Stuckey; 'he was so vulnerable, you just had to do something.'

Michael Wale and Stuckey re-wrote the scripts, and the time arrived when Hancock had to make a 'pilot' episode. By now the management had realized Hancock's condition, and everyone was getting rather nervous. Wale and Stuckey chose a script that they thought would give

Hancock the best chance, and not ask too much of him. The pilot was a disaster; Hancock was in no fit state to be in the studio and the resultant film was so bad that ATN7 ordered it destroyed. Jim Oswin, the managing director, laid the law down in no uncertain manner to Hancock. He also did so to Collins, who was bought out of his contract, and the show then became an ATN7 production.

On the orders of the station Hancock was put in the charge of a psychiatrist, and alternated between living in a nursing home and with the psychiatrist. Hancock really made an effort and eventually was sober and ready to start work. He knew that this was his last chance and put everything he had into the painful process of sobering up. He was, of course, not the old Hancock. The effect of the years of alcohol ensured that he could never again be that.

Work started at the end of May. Hancock learnt his lines, managing without 'idiot boards', and as usual, gave his best performance on the first try every time. But other factors intervened to make things more difficult for him. The system in use for making the episodes was not the usual electronic television system, but a development of the ECAM film system that Hancock had seen in operation in America in 1962. At that time, the system simply consisted of three ciné cameras running in synchronization, and operated in much the same way as television cameras, complete with electronic viewfinders (small television cameras fixed to the ciné cameras) that relayed the picture from each camera position to a control cubicle. The result was three rolls of film which could be intercut to produce the final programme. The main trouble with this system was that it was wasteful of film, and by 1968 the technique had been developed so that, watching the monitors that showed the outputs from the electronic viewfinders, the director could 'cut' from one camera to another just as in a TV studio. Only one camera at a time would run, and on cutting from one camera to another the second camera would start and, when it had run up to speed, the first one would stop. The system was in common use in America, because the international sale of electronically recorded television programmes is hampered by the fact that line and colour standards differ in different countries, whereas film standards are universal. ATN7 had chosen to use it because it enabled them to film in colour—at that time there was no colour television in Australia—and they used the 35mm version of it, which is about four times as expensive in film as the 16mm version, in the hope of world-wide sales of a top-quality product which would not be outdated by any advances in television technology.

Unfortunately for Hancock no-one in Australia was used to the equipment. It was extremely new, and they had at that time done one outside sports session with it (a quite different set of problems) and one studio session in black-and-white. Filming in colour brought a number of problems because of the very high lighting level required. The company hired Eddie Joffe because they wanted a director with television rather than film experience, but Joffe had never worked with the ECAM system before. It had been tried in Britain, but the film union had objected to the use of film cameras in a television manner because a TV crew is much smaller than the minimum number laid down for a film crew. Joffe had gone into the system in some detail with the ECAM agents in Britain, but theoretical knowledge of technical equipment is quite another thing from actual practical experience of it, and it would have been unfair to expect Joffe to handle it with the confidence he could have brought to ordinary television equipment.

In order to help him assess his work, Joffe asked for a small video tape recorder to be attached to the output of the cutting desk, so that the results of the cutting between cameras could be studied immediately instead of days later when the film had been developed and edited; ATN7 refused on grounds of cost.

With almost any other performer these problems might have been incidental, but Hancock was only able to give one good performance of any scene. The first time he would be, if not his old self, at least funny enough to fill the studio staff with optimism; but the technical problems necessitated re-takes, sometimes many re-takes, by which time Hancock's performance had deteriorated beyond recognition.

Only three episodes of the projected thirteen were completed, and eventually they were strung together to make *The Tony Hancock Special*, filling a ninety-minute commercial TV slot; this was broadcast on January 25th 1972 on HSV7 Melbourne.

The story begins on board the ship on which Hancock is emigrating to Australia. He has with him an Australian valet, Mervyn (Don Crosby), whom he met in England. Crosby's performance is very odd throughout the film; he seems to be sleepwalking, and reads his lines in a monotone—perhaps he was trying to emulate Bill Kerr at his most slow-witted. After arriving in Australia, Hancock is told by the Customs Officer (Don Reid) that a stuffed owl in his baggage must be put into quarantine for six months. Following some shots, filmed later, of a 'double' arriving at the Hotel Dumont, Hancock is seen in the hotel foyer. He has an altercation with a bored hotel clerk (Max Phipps), and goes to his room. In flashback we see his last night in England—he goes to a pub where he is obviously well known as a bore, but when he announces that he is leaving for Australia he immediately has to buy a round of drinks. Back in the hotel room, the maid (Doreen Warburton) advises him that the hotel overcharges migrants and recommends him to a flat owned by a Mrs Gilroy.

Mrs Gilroy (Gloria Dawn) proves only too willing to have Hancock as a tenant—she becomes rather over-amorous and Hancock has some

171

difficulty persuading her to leave.

All through these sequences Hancock is obviously trying hard, but apart from occasional flashes of the old Hancock he gives a very muted performance, his voice sounding almost as if it had been slowed down. He is not reading his lines, but can be seen making the effort to remember them most of the time with the result that his reactions to other people tend to be spoilt. There was, of course, no audience at the time of filming; after the film was assembled it was shown to an audience and their reactions added to the soundtrack. This was the system which Hancock always approved of, but the result demonstrates only too clearly the accuracy of Duncan Wood's comments—in the absence of an audience, Hancock's timing has disappeared completely and he is failing to leave pauses for laughter. As a consequence, lines which deserve, and in fact get, a good laugh are followed immediately by another line, so that the sound mixer has had to hold the laughter down. The technical side also tends to sabotage Hancock; he is obviously never too sure where to look, partly because he cannot know which camera is on him as he would in television, and he does at least one important monologue sideways on. The soundtrack has been put through a compressor (a rapid-acting automatic volume control) which has the effect of making the background noises sound far too loud—and in fact in one sequence they almost smother the dialogue.

The show comes rather more to life with the next sequence. Hancock, now alone in his new flat, investigates the automated kitchen, which has rows of control knobs on the walls. The first makes the telephone slide about; the second causes the broom-cupboard door to open, whereupon a broom falls out. He gets radio programmes out of the rings on the electric cooker; one of the programmes is muffled until he takes the kettle off the ring which the music is coming from. Yet another knob opens the door of a cupboard high up behind him and a plate falls out; the cupboard door shuts immediately. Some toast pops out of the electric toaster, which he drops into a foot-operated pedal-bin; he then takes to dropping unbreakable cups onto the bin, sending them flying with the lid. Hancock's reactions in this sequence are much better than in the earlier parts of the film, and though the sequence never really takes off, it works quite well.

Mervyn arrives, and the standard of the show drops again, with Hancock all too obviously concentrating on his dialogue and Crosby giving his strange somnambulistic performance. They discuss the rôle of Australia. Hancock: 'This country has broken away from Mother England and is now standing on its own four feet.' Later, Hancock is seen preparing his breakfast. He investigates the cereal packet and finds a plastic toy in it: 'Oh no, I've got the giraffe again, I've got three of these, why can't I get the packet with the hippopotamus?' The whole sequence, although it contains some good lines, fails to work as it should because Hancock is not leaving pauses between his lines; and he is not helped by some irritating and unnecessary background music.

The milkman (Lex Mitchell) arrives, and immediately takes it upon himself to improve Hancock's physical fitness. He invites Hancock to join him at the local sporting club, but it turns out that the only exercise that the lads there get is lifting glasses of beer. Later, when everybody is well-oiled, a fight almost develops between Hancock and a cocky Australian, which is only stopped by the barmaid pointing out that nobody has paid her for the drinks. At this point, which would have been the end of the third episode, the film ends.

Everyone concerned with the shooting seems to have been over-optimistic about the quality of the series, partly because Hancock was showing up fairly well in comparison with the supporting cast, who were professionals but not in his class. Stuckey was commissioned to write another series, and Hancock himself watched the rushes and felt that he was getting back on form. Rehearsals went ahead for the fourth episode, and there were definite signs of improvement.

Then, on the morning of June 25th, Hancock was found dead. He had taken a large overdose of barbiturate tablets and a bottle of vodka. In his suicide note he said 'Things seemed to go wrong too many times'.

Everyone concerned has their own theory as to just why Hancock committed suicide. Perhaps he suddenly saw the decline in his career clearly; or it may have been more personal. Freddie obtained her *decree nisi* a few days before his death (which meant that they would have been completely divorced after a short period had elapsed and the decree had been made absolute). Apparently Hancock rang Cicely and asked if she would have him back, and she refused. She was in any case now very ill, her own alcoholism having reached a severe level.

Whatever the reason, most people feel that suicide was inevitable, sooner or later. Hancock had become bent on self-destruction; and in any case he could only have continued to decline. For him, the quick way out would have been infinitely preferable to a long and pathetic slide into obscurity.

13. The Lad Himself

Anthony Aloysius St John Hancock II, of 23 Railway Cuttings, East Cheam; dressed in a Homburg hat and a heavy overcoat with an astrakhan collar of uncertain age; a failed Shakespearean actor with pretensions to a knighthood and no bookings; age—late 30s but claims to be younger; success with women—nil; financial success—nil; a pretentious, gullible, bombastic, occasionally kindly, superstitious, avaricious, petulant, over-imaginative, semi-educated, gourmandising, incompetent, cunning, obstinate, self-opiniated, impolite, pompous, lecherous, lonely and likeable fall-guy.

This character, who held millions enthralled in front of their television sets, was not of course the real Tony Hancock; but there was more of the real Hancock in the imaginary lad from East Cheam than Hancock ever realized. His own personality—exaggerated, distorted, sometimes with particular characteristics inverted, but always essentially himself—was what held together the most complex comic characterization ever created for television. He was so much a part of the East Cheam character that his attempts to break away from it were doomed to failure; but he felt that he had wrung every last drop of comedy out of it, and had to find another persona to act as a vehicle for what he wanted to say. Perhaps the nearest to what Hancock was looking for is the film *The Punch and Judy Man*—a 'serious comedy' in which the characters are real people and the situations for the most part true to life. Though flawed, the film has many good points and looks better with the passing of time; and Hancock never realized that the character he played in it was himself.

His great ambition was international recognition—a chimera he pursued relentlessly for the latter years of his life. He has often been criticized for doing so, with the implication that national fame should have been enough for him; but Hancock was a man who was never satisfied to stand still—had he been so, he might well never have risen beyond the level of being Archie Andrews' tutor—and the constant desire to improve, to expand, to widen his abilities is surely to be admired rather than condemned. Unfortunately, it is a hard fact of life, which Hancock could never accept, that international fame is simply not possible for television stars—unless they are American. The cinema has spread the American way of life—its slang, its attitudes, its surroundings—throughout the world ever since the nineteen-thirties; but, to the majority of Americans, Britain is an attractive foreign country whose social order and outlook is in many ways as incomprehensible as that of Nepal is to the British. Hancock thought that if he cut out the slang and spoke clearly he would be acceptable—but it was not his words the Americans could not understand—it was him.

Few artists can ever have been so bitterly and publicly criticized as Hancock was in the few years following his death. Those close to him for the most part either spoke truthfully and sympathetically of his problems or held their peace, but the writings of many other commentators have vilified him for 'shutting the door' on all his friends, usually ascribing this to professional or personal jealousy. The most resented of all his breaks was of course the one with Sidney James. James, however, though upset about not continuing with a man who was—and remained—a very close friend, understood Hancock's feeling that all the possible variations had been wrung out of the East Cheam situation; and in fact James later said that he felt that there could only have been one more such series anyway.

Hancock's death also acted as the trigger for column upon column of newsprint examining his alcoholism in distressing and often un-necessary detail. Now that some years have gone by, the drinking can perhaps be put into perspective; it clouded the last third of a twenty-year career, and can be seen to be rooted in a fear of performing and a difficulty in learning his lines; an ill-advised process of self-examination begun in an attempt to understand himself and intensified by his appearance on *Face to Face*; and the nervous strains brought about by working on television week in, week out. These factors caused him worries and depressions, and what are glibly called 'personality problems'—a desperate searching for his own identity; but it is just possible that he might have survived them, at least for a while longer, if his stability had not been shattered by the car crash in 1961, which shook his already troubled nerves and was probably the turning-point beyond which the drinking habits changed to the long descent into alcoholism.

On the credit side, he had a tremendously warm and likeable personality; and indeed had he not had the ability to inspire affection his friends would hardly have stayed by him, as they did when his problems over-powered him. He had a deep and joyous sense of humour, and often laughed so much that he had to sit on the floor, holding his sides. He could be extraordinarily kind and thoughtful—but stories of his thoughtfulness have tended to be over-balanced by the more spectacular occasions when alcohol caused him to behave unpleasantly. His generosity was considerable, although it was oddly contrasted by his irritating habit of never carrying cash and forgetting to pay back what he borrowed.

His contribution to comedy is incalculable. He inspired Galton and Simpson to write scripts of a depth and intensity unparalleled in broadcasting history. His insistence on the increasingly natural style of situation comedy led firstly to Galton and Simpson's re-working of the

175

Hancock-James relationship in the junk-yard of Albert and Steptoe, and from there by descent to the large number of situation comedies on television that owe a huge debt to the pioneering work of *Hancock's Half-Hour*.

His best epitaph must be the thirty-seven telerecordings of *Hancock's Half-Hour* carefully stored in the vaults of the BBC Film Library. These include some of the earlier shows, but, most importantly, the complete fifth, sixth and seventh series—twenty-six programmes, of which every one is excellent. Even when seen, several in succession, in an uncomfortable viewing room on a noisy and flickering viewing machine of indeterminate antiquity, they stand out as masterpieces of comedy. 'Genius' is a word whch has been devalued by being over-worked; but used in its true sense it is not too strong a description of the man who could give the richly comic performances preserved on these films. Neither the television nor the more readily available radio programmes stale with repetition—perhaps the most severe test of the quality of comedy—for in laughing at Hancock's pretensions and uncertainties we are laughing at ourselves. Although his world is firmly the Britain of the nineteen-fifties, he himself is timeless; and his defiance of the trying situations which beset him will remain as the core of the deepest, most complex, and humanly funny characterization we are ever likely to see.

176

Research Sources

The principal sources of the information in this book were: the existing telerecordings and sound recordings; BBC files on Hancock and *Hancock's Half-Hour* and the documentary information on the broadcasts which forms the basis of Part Two of this book; and interviews kindly granted to me by the following: Dr W. G. Cleverly (25-2-77), Ray Galton and Alan Simpson (10-1-77), Eddie Joffe (31-1-77), Glyn Jones (1-3-77), Billy Marsh (25-2-77), John Muir (2-2-77), Hugh Stuckey (26-1-77), Alan Tarrant (18-1-77), Johnny Vyvyan (2-3-77), Dennis Main Wilson (25-1-77) and Duncan Wood (18-1-77) (the interviews with Cleverly, Joffe and Vyvyan being done over the telephone). I also 'phoned George Fairweather, who filled in details of Hancock's early career, and Peter Eton; and was given considerable help and information by Roger Hancock.

The listing below details sources (other than BBC files, etc.) which are not clearly identified in the text.

page	CHAPTER 2
14	George Fairweather, and a biographical story in the *Sunday Times*, 22-7-62.
16	Quote from an article by Hancock in *TV Times*, 2-12-62.
16	Quote from Philip Oakes's book 'The Entertainers—Tony Hancock' details on page 261.
17	Dennis Main Wilson.
20	Theatre programme for 'London Laughs'.
22	Quote from Peter Brough in a tribute programme, broadcast from station 3LO Melbourne, Australia, on 14-1-69
22	Dennis Main Wilson interview.
25	Dennis Main Wilson interview.

	CHAPTER 3
29	The story of Hancock's 1949 broadcast was given in Freddie Hancock and David Nathan's book *Hancock*, and came principally from Phyllis Rounce.
30	Dennis Main Wilson.
31-2	Dennis Main Wilson.
34	Dennis Main Wilson.
35-6	Peter Eton.
36	Dennis Main Wilson.
37	The story of the audience experiments with ITMA was told by Barry Took in his book 'Laughter in the Air' (see page 261).
37	Dennis Main Wilson.
40	Dennis Main Wilson.

CHAPTER 12

166   Hugh Stuckey; the *Sun* 11-10-67; the *Evening Standard* 11-10-67; the *Sun* 12-10-67.
168   Hugh Stuckey interview.
169-71 Hugh Stuckey; Eddie Joffe; Michael Wale writing in *The Times*, 1-2-69.
173   Hugh Stuckey.

Photograph by Harry Secombe

PART TWO

The Career of Tony Hancock

HANCOCK'S STAGE APPEARANCES

All Hancock's public performances that have been traced are listed; performances made to clubs in the early years and the last few years of his career have been ignored, as have his performances while in the RAF.

On tour with Ralph Reader's 'WINGS'

28- 4-47 for one week	Opera House, Blackpool
5- 5-47 for one week	Theatre Royal, Nottingham
12- 5-47 for one week	New Theatre, Hull
19- 5-47 for one week	Empire Theatre, Sheffield
26- 5-47 for one week	Theatre Royal, Birmingham
2- 6-47 for one week	Hippodrome, Coventry
9- 6-47 for one week	Empire Theatre, Newcastle
16- 6-47 for one week	Empire Theatre, Edinburgh
23- 6-47 for one week	Empire Theatre, Liverpool
30- 6-47 for two weeks	Palace Theatre, Manchester
14- 7-47 for one week	Hippodrome, Brighton
21- 7-47 for two weeks	King's Theatre, Southsea
11- 8-47 for one week	Palace Theatre, Plymouth
18- 8-47 for one week	New Theatre, Oxford
25- 8-47 for one week	Hippodrome, Dudley
1- 9-47 for one week	Winter Gardens, Morecambe

Children's matinée 25-12-47;
26-12-47 to 24- 1-48 } 'CINDERELLA' (as an Ugly Sister) at the Playhouse Theatre, Oxford.

26- 4-48 to 1- 5-48 — 'PEACE IN OUR TIME' (three small parts) at the Playhouse Theatre, Oxford.

12- 7-48 to 21- 8-48 — With Derek Scott in 'REVUDEVILLE No 214' at the Windmill Theatre, London.

13- 6-49 until the end of September — 'FLOTSAM'S FOLLIES' (in four sketches) at the Esplanade Concert Hall, Bognor Regis.

19-11-49 Saturday only — Victoria Hotel, Sidmouth

Winter 1949/50 — 'CINDERELLA' (as Buttons) at the Royal Artillery Theatre, Woolwich.

23- 2-50 — Election night ball at Claridges.

17- 6-50 to 16- 9-50 — 'OCEAN REVUE' at the Pier, and then the Ocean Theatre, Clacton.

Variety appearances:

2-10-50 for one week	Hippodrome, Birmingham
9-10-50 for one week	Empire Theatre, Liverpool
16-10-50 for one week	Empire Theatre, Newcastle
30-10-50 for one week	Empire Theatre, Glasgow

184

23-12-50 to 10- 3-51	'LITTLE RED RIDING HOOD' (as Jolly Jenkins) at the Theatre Royal, Nottingham

Variety appearances:

21- 5-51 for one week	Empire, Shepherd's Bush
4- 6-51 for one week	County Theatre, Reading
6- 7-51 midnight matinée	Ritz Cinema, Nuneaton
9- 7-51 for one week	Palace Theatre, Chelsea
16- 7-51 for one week	Palace Theatre, East Ham
23- 7-51 for one week	Empire Theatre, Finsbury Park
1- 8-51 midnight matinée	Century Cinema, Clacton
20- 8-51 for one week	Empire Theatre, Sunderland
26- 8-51 for one day (Sunday)	Spa Theatre, Scarborough
17- 9-51 for three days	Winter Gardens, Bournemouth
20- 9-51 for three days	Winter Gardens, Eastbourne
24- 9-51 for one week	Ritz Cinema, Weymouth
1-10-51 for one week	Empire Theatre, Nottingham
8-10-51 for one day	Empire Theatre, Edinburgh
12-10-51 for one day	Odeon Theatre, Southampton
14-10-51 for one day	Charity performance at the Palace, Walthamstow
15-10-51 for one week	Palace Theatre, Blackpool
22-10-51 for one week	Opera House, Belfast
3-11-51 for one day	Dome Theatre, Brighton
12-11-51 for one week	Gaumont, Southampton
19-11-51 for one week	Embassy Theatre, Peterborough
3-12-51 for one week	Hippodrome Theatre, Dudley
21-12-51 to 19- 1-52	Prince of Wales Theatre, London, in 'ARCHIE ANDREWS' CHRISTMAS PARTY' (matinées) & 'PEEP SHOW' (evenings)

Variety appearances:

6- 1-52 Sunday only	Trocadero, Elephant and Castle
13- 1-52 Sunday only	Gaumont, Lewisham
20- 1-52 Sunday only	Odeon, Barking
4- 2-52 for one week	Empire Theatre, Sunderland
11- 2-52 for one week	Empire, Shepherd's Bush
17- 2-52 Sunday only	Charity performance for News Vendors' Benevolent Fund at the Alexandra Theatre, Birmingham
18- 2-52 for one week	Empire Theatre, Hackney
25- 2-52 for one week	Palace Theatre, Leicester
3 -3-52 for one week	Empire Theatre, Leeds
10- 3-52 for one week	Granada, Rugby
17- 3-52 for one week	Hippodrome, Birmingham
24- 3-52 for one week	Empire Theatre, Glasgow
31- 3-52 for one week	Empire Theatre, Liverpool
12- 4-52	'LONDON LAUGHS' at the Adelphi Theatre, London with Jimmy Edwards and Vera Lynn.
28- 7-52 – 2- 8-52	Theatre closed
15-12-52 – 22-12-52	Theatre closed
26- 1-53 – 21- 2-53	Hancock not billed
30- 3-53 – 3- 4-53	Theatre closed

185

10- 8-53– 8- 9-53	Hancock not billed
7-12-53	Hancock replaced by Tommy Cooper until the show finished on 6-2-54.

Variety appearances:

1- 6-52 Sunday only	Villa Marina, Douglas, Isle of Man
22- 6-52 Sunday only	Pavilion, Sandown, *and* The Theatre, Shanklin, Isle of Wight
31- 8-52 Sunday only	Butlins, Filey
3-11-52	ROYAL VARIETY PERFORMANCE at the London Palladium
30- 8-53 Sunday only	Pavilion, Sandown, *and* The Theatre, Shanklin, Isle of Wight.
23-12-53 to 27- 2-54	'CINDERELLA' (as Buttons) at the Theatre Royal, Nottingham

Variety appearance with Jimmy Edwards:

17- 5-54 for one week	Hippodrome, Brighton

'THE TALK OF THE TOWN', with Jimmy Edwards and Joan Turner.

5- 6-54 to 9-10-54	Opera House, Blackpool
8-11-54 to 13-11-54	New Theatre, Oxford
17-11-54	Adelphi Theatre, London
April–25- 6-55	Hancock replaced first by Bonar Colleano, then Dave King.
22- 8-55–25- 8-55	Hancock replaced by Maria Pavolou.
31-10-55	Hancock replaced by Dave King until the show finished on 10-12-55.

Variety appearances:

19- 8-57 for one week	Palace Theatre, Manchester
26- 8-57 for one week	Hippodrome, Bristol
2- 9-57 for one week	Hippodrome, Birmingham
9- 9-57 for one week	Empire Theatre, Finsbury Park
24- 3-58 to 15- 4-58	Mediterranean tour—Malta, Tripoli and Cyprus, entertaining the troops; returning on Sundays 30-3-58 and 6-4-58 for radio recordings.
4- 8-58 for one week	Empire Theatre, Liverpool
27-10-58 for one week	Empire Theatre, Hanley
3-11-58	ROYAL VARIETY PERFORMANCE at the London Coliseum. Hancock appeared in the budgerigar sketch with Hattie Jacques.

On tour in his own show, with Johnny Vyvyan, Audrey Jeans, Albert and Les Ward, Alec Bregonzi, Neil and Pat Delrina, The Three Ghezzis, and The Skylons.

6- 3-61 for one week	Granada, Shrewsbury
13- 3-61 for one week	Empire Theatre, Newcastle
20- 3-61 for one week	Gaumont, Southampton
27- 3-61 for one week	Hippodrome, Brighton
3- 4-61 for one week	Hippodrome, Bristol
10- 4-61 for one week	New Theatre, Oxford

On tour in his own show, appearing in a continuous act in the second half; Matt Munro filled the first half.

8-10-62 for one week	King's Theatre, Southsea
15-10-62 for one week	Empire Theatre, Liverpool
22-10-62 for one week	Hippodrome, Brighton
15- 7-63 for one week	Theatre Royal, Nottingham
23- 7-63 for one week	Palace Theatre, Manchester
6- 8-63 to 28- 9-63	substituting for Arthur Haynes at the London Palladium
28- 6-65 to 7- 8-65	Appeared at 2330 in cabaret, overall title 'Fatal Fascination' at the Talk of the Town theatre-restaurant, London.
2-11-65 for three weeks	Cabaret at the Chevron Hilton Hotel, Sydney, Australia.
5- 9-66 for one week	Winter Gardens, Bournemouth
22- 9-66 one performance	Royal Festival Hall, London (also televised)
2- 7-67 Sunday only	Villa Marina, Douglas, Isle of Man
17- 7-67 for five days	Entertaining the troops in Aden
4-10-67 to 22-10-67	Dendy Cinema, Brighton, Melbourne, Australia

Followed by cabaret at a hotel in Hobart, Tasmania.

INTRODUCTION TO LISTING OF HANCOCK'S BROADCASTS

This section lists all Hancock's known broadcasts, both on radio and television. For the sake of clarity, they have not been listed in strict chronological order since this would result in his single broadcasts being mixed up with his radio and TV series, which also alternate.

Firstly, there is a list of Hancock's single broadcasts. Some of the shows in this list are from a series, such as 'Variety Bandbox', but Hancock did not appear regularly in them. Following this are the details of other people's series in which he appeared regularly—'Happy-Go-Lucky', the second series of 'Educating Archie', and the various 'Forces' and 'Star Bill' programmes.

Then the six series of 'Hancock's Half-Hour' on radio are listed in detail, with titles and brief plot synopses. The television series began after the third radio series, but for clarity the TV and radio series have been kept quite separate. The listing of radio series is followed by details of subsequent repeats, a list of the shows held by BBC Sound Archives, and a list of shows issued by the BBC Transcription Services.

The seven BBC Television series of 'Hancock's Half-Hour' (the last series under the title 'Hancock') are then listed in similar detail to the radio series; as the cast lists for these shows are fairly large, they are listed together after the series lists rather than actually with the shows. The cast lists are followed by details of subsequent TV repeats, and a list of shows held in the BBC Film Library.

The various Independent Television shows are then listed, beginning with the two Jack Hylton series, the first of which actually preceded the first BBC-TV series. The remaining ITV series were all broadcast after the BBC series ended; they are 'Hancock' (1963), 'The Blackpool Show' (1966) and 'Hancock's' (1967). The final series to be listed is the incomplete one made for Australian TV.

The following abbreviations are used for networks throughout this section:

HS =	BBC Home Service (now replaced by BBC Radio 4)
LP =	BBC Light Programme (now replaced by BBC Radio 2)

187

R1 =	BBC Radio One
R2 =	BBC Radio 2
R4 =	BBC Radio 4
GOS =	BBC General Overseas Service (now the BBC World Service)
ATV =	Associated Television (one of the Independent TV companies)
AR-TV =	Associated-Rediffusion (one of the Independent TV companies)
BBC-2 =	second BBC-TV channel
ABC =	Associated British Cinemas (Television) Ltd (an ITV company)

The recording numbers quoted for BBC sound recordings contain prefixes which indicate the type of recording and the location of the recording room (which is not necessarily the same as the studio).

SLO =	33⅓ rpm coarse groove 17¼″ disk recorded at Broadcasting House.
SAL =	ditto recorded at Aldenham House.
SOX =	ditto recorded at 200 Oxford Street.
SBS =	ditto recorded at Broadcasting House, Bristol.
DLO =	78 rpm disk(s) recorded at Broadcasting House.
DBS =	ditto recorded at Broadcasting House, Bristol.
TLO =	15 ips tape recorded at Broadcasting House.
TBU =	ditto recorded at Bush House.
TOX =	ditto recorded at 200 Oxford Street.
TBM =	ditto recorded at Broadcasting House, Birmingham.
TBS =	ditto recorded at Broadcasting House, Bristol.
TMR =	ditto recorded at Broadcasting House, Manchester.
TTU =	ditto recorded by Transcription Services.
MLO =	15 ips tape recorded by the mobile van based in London.
MBM =	ditto recorded by the mobile van based in Birmingham.
YCTLO =	copy, at 7½ ips, of a TLO.

BBC-TV recordings fall into two types; the earlier system involves photographing a television screen onto ciné film (using special equipment to ensure a steady picture); the video tape system in common use today, which provides a picture indistinguishable from a live transmission, was introduced in 1958. The recording numbers include prefixes which indicate the system in use, and the purpose for which the recording was made; a recording made on one system and subsequently transferred to another retains its number but changes its prefix.

35/T =	telerecording on 35mm film, made for subsequent transmission or repeat.
35/INT =	ditto, but made for internal use; e.g. as a check on the success of a live transmission.
16/ =	16mm telerecordings, with letter codes as above.
VT/T =	video tape made for subsequent transmission or repeat.
T/M =	early number applied to video tapes, soon replaced by VT.

The fact that a recording number is quoted, for either radio or television, does not necessarily mean that it still exists—in fact in many cases recordings were destroyed after use. Lists of 'Hancock's Half-Hour', radio and TV, which still exist, together with the handful of other programmes which have survived, will be found in the sections dealing with BBC Sound Archives (page 220) and BBC Film Library (page 245).

In the case of the series listings, the dates on which the programmes were pre-recorded are shown in brackets underneath the tape numbers, except where the shows were all recorded a fixed time before transmission. It was normal practice to record Variety programmes on the Sunday before transmission, so that the artists would be free for theatrical engagements during the week; occasionally two programmes would be recorded on the same day to allow a week's break. Sometimes several programmes (in the case of the sixth radio series, all but one) were recorded in advance, and then the order was altered before transmission to make a better balanced series. In these cases I have always listed, and numbered, the shows in order of *transmission* (although the scripts may be numbered in order of recording).

SINGLE BROADCASTS, RADIO AND TELEVISION

This list includes all known out-of-series broadcasts, with the series listed by starting date and indexed to the appropriate page. The abbreviation *HHH* is used throughout this list for *Hancock's Half-Hour*. For reasons of space, other artists taking part in Variety programmes, but with whom Hancock did not actually work, are not listed. Producers are not listed in the case of programmes such as *Workers' Playtime* where Hancock contributed his own solo routine and the producer's contribution to the proceedings would have been minimal. All transmissions were live unless otherwise stated.

6- 6-41   'A La Carte—a mixed menu of light fare'; from Bristol. Produced by Leslie Bridgmont. BBC Forces Programme 1100-1130.

1-11-48   'New to You'; Hancock appeared with Derek Scott. Produced by Richard Afton. BBC-TV 1500-1530.

9- 1-49   'Variety Bandbox'; from the Cambridge Theatre, London. LP & GOS, 2100-2200.

27- 3-49   'Variety Bandbox'; from the Kilburn Empire. LP & GOS, 2100-2200. Repeated 2-4-49, HS, 1310-1350 (shortened) on SLO 48515.

25- 9-49   'Variety Bandbox'; from the Camberwell Palace. LP & GOS, 2100-2200. Hancock omitted from shortened repeat on 1-10-49.

10-10-49   'Stars of Tomorrow'; HS 1820-1845. Repeated 12-10-49, HS, 1230-1255 on SLO 59744.

8-12-49   'First House—Look Who's Here'; HS 1820-1845. Repeated 12-12-49, HS, 1230-1255 on SLO 62927.

1- 1-50   'Variety Bandbox'; from the Camberwell Palace. LP & GOS, 2100-2200. Repeated 7-1-50, HS (not Scotland) 1215-1255 (shortened) on SLO 63946.

27- 1-50   'Workers' Playtime'; from Messrs Sterling Metals Ltd, Coventry. HS, 1230-1255.

20- 2-50   'Flotsam's Follies'; produced by Walton Anderson. Hancock appeared with Reg Purdell, Barbara James, Dilys Laye and Patricia Riley in sketch 'The Conjuror' (6' 10"). BBC-TV, 2130-2210.

19- 3-50   'Variety Bandbox'; LP & GOS, 2100–2200. Repeated 25-3-50, HS, 1215-1255 (shortened) on SLO 68115.

15- 4-50   'BBC Ballroom'; dance music, including two cabaret turns, one of which was Hancock. LP 2215-2356.

2- 5-50   'First House—Look Who's Here'; HS 1820-1845.

28- 5-50   'Variety Bandbox'; from the Camberwell Palace. LP 2100-2200. Repeated 3-6-50, HS, 1215-1253 (shortened) on SLO 71331.

25- 8-50   'Summer Showtime'; from Clacton—Hancock appearing in 'Ocean Revue'. LP, 2045-2130; recorded 20-8-50 on SLO 75913.

27- 8-50   'Variety Bandbox'; LP 2100-2200. Hancock omitted from shortened repeat on 2-9-50.

12-11-50   'Variety Bandbox'; LP, 2100-2200. Repeated 18-11-50, HS, 1310-1350

	(shortened) on SAL 27818.
30-12-50	'Radio Parade'; introduced by Bebe Daniels and Ben Lyon. Hancock was one of eleven acts. Produced by Tom Ronald and Michael North. HS 1945–2100; recorded 3-12-50 on SLO 81248. Repeated 2-1-51, HS, 1310-1410 (shortened).
7- 1-51	'Variety Bandbox'; LP 2100-2200. Repeated 13-1-51, HS, 1310-1346 (shortened) on SAL 28699.
21- 1-51	'Variety Bandbox'; LP 2100-2200. Repeated 27-1-51, HS, 1310-1350 (shortened) on SAL 28894.
11- 2-51	'Variety Bandbox'; LP 2100-2200. Repeated 17-2-51, HS, 1310-1350 (shortened) on SAL 29180.
11- 3-51	'Variety Bandbox'; LP 2100-2200. Repeated 17-3-51, HS, 1310-1350 (shortened) on SAL 29812.
24- 3-51	'Variety Ahoy'; from on board HMS Woolwich, off Harwich. HS 1225-1255, recorded 19-3-51 on MLO 9884. Repeated 29-4-51, LP, 1030-1100.
1- 4-51	'Variety Bandbox'; LP 2100-2200. Repeated 7-4-51, HS, 1310-1350 (shortened) on SAL 30176.
29- 4-51	'Variety Bandbox'; LP 2100-2200. Repeated 5-5-51, HS, 1310-1350 (shortened) on SAL 30579.
4- 5-51	'Kaleidoscope'; including 'Fools Rush In', a comedy series by Godfrey Harrison, starring Hancock as 'George', & Robert Perceval (as 'Bill Braun'), June Sylvaine (as 'Fay'), and J. Webster-Brough (as 'Mrs Hutton-Hythe'). Produced by Graeme Muir. BBC-TV 2045-2145.
14- 5-51	'Variety Ahoy'; from on board HMS Indefatigable, off Portland. Produced by Duncan Wood. HS 1945-2015, recorded 6-5-51 on DBS 3033.
18- 5-51	'Kaleidoscope'; including 'Fools Rush In' with Hancock & Anthony Shaw (as 'Col B. Smyth'), Sheila Gunn (as 'Dulcie'), Dodd Mehan (as 'Mr Steel'), Andrew Massey (as 'Foreign Gent'), and Brian Roper (as 'Page Boy'). BBC-TV 2015-2115.
1- 6-51	'Kaleidoscope'; including 'Fools Rush In' with Hancock & Charles Farrell (as 'Harry'), Virginia Winter (as 'Lucy'), and Olga Dickie (as 'Waitress'). BBC-TV 2031-2130.
6- 6-51	'Western Music Hall'; produced by Duncan Wood. West of England Home Service only, 2000-2100; recorded 27-5-51.
15- 6-51	'Kaleidoscope'; including 'Fools Rush In', with Hancock & Eleanor Summerfield (as 'Fiona'), Tommy Duggan (as 'Cornie'), and Harry Lane (as 'The Burglar'). BBC-TV, 2049-2151.
19- 6-51	'Workers' Playtime'; from Gracey Brothers Canneries, Hillhall, County Antrim. HS 1230-1255.
21- 6-51	'Workers' Playtime'; from Heller Confectionery Ltd, Bangor, County Down. HS 1230-1255.
22- 6-51	'Workers' Playtime'; from Messrs. Teady McErlear Ltd, Clady, Portglenone. HS 1230-1255, recorded 20-6-51 on SLO 90930.
29- 6-51	'Kaleidoscope'; including 'Fools Rush In' with Hancock & Joan Seton (as 'Esme'), Norman Mitchell (as 'Andy'), and Jean Hardwicke (as 'Lillian'). BBC-TV 2016-2117.
21- 7-51	'Festival Parade'; the last of six fortnightly galas celebrating the Festival of Britain. Introduced by Bebe Daniels and Ben Lyon. Produced by Tom Ronald and Michael North. Hancock was first of ten acts. HS 1945-2100, recorded 15-7-51 on SLO 91937. Repeated 24-7-51, HS, 1310-1423.
1- 8-51	'The Lighter Side—a humorous slant on current affairs—No. 1—'Food'.

Script edited and compiled by Godfrey Harrison. With Patricia Hartley, Patricia Hastings, Ivan Staff, Christopher Hewett, Sidney Vivian, Barry McGregor, Oliver Burt, Jean Webster-Brough, Tony Hancock (as 'The Civil Servant'). Betty Blackler, Ysanne Churchman, Roy Grant, Marguerite Young, and Michael Green. Commentator Lionel Gamlin. Orchestra directed by Eric Robinson. Produced by Gilchrist Calder. BBC-TV 2035-2105.

2- 8-51 *'Happy-Go-Lucky' begins : runs to 10-12-51 (see p. 197).*

3- 8-51 *'Educating Archie' (2nd series) begins : runs to 25-1-52 (see p. 198).*

5- 8-51 *'Calling All Forces' (for details see p. 200).*

8- 8-51 'Variety Ahoy'; from the Royal Naval Hospital, Haslar, Gosport. Produced by Duncan Wood. HS & LP, 1225-1255; recorded 8-7-51 on DBS 3502.

9- 8-51 'Western Music Hall'; from the Victoria Rooms, Bristol. Produced by Duncan Wood. West of England Home Service only, 2130-2230; recorded 22-7-51 on SBS 2627.

26-12-51 *'Archie Andrews' Party' (for details see p. 199).*

31-12-51 'Bumblethorpe'; Robert Moreton, Avril Angers, Valentine Dyall, Kenneth Connor, Graham Stark, Spike Milligan, and Tony Hancock as 'this week's Bumblethorpe'. Script by Spike Milligan, Larry Stephens, and Peter Ling. Produced by Peter Eton. HS 1945-2015; recorded 31-12-51 on SLO 496.

25- 2-52 *'Calling All Forces' (for details see p. 200).*

2- 3-52 'National Radio Awards of 1951' from the London Coliseum. From 'Educating Archie', Brough, Hancock, and Hattie Jacques appeared for about 5 minutes. LP, 2100-2200.

3- 4-52 'Workers' Playtime'; from Messrs. Maurice Lee-Unger Ltd, Boothstown, Manchester. Hancock appeared with Peter Brough and Archie Andrews. HS 1230-1255.

14- 4-52 *'Calling All Forces' begins : runs to 28-7-52 (see p. 200).*

29- 6-52 'Hullo There—a weekly radio magazine for younger listeners'. Edited and produced by Lionel Gamlin. LP, 0930-1000. Programme recorded 26-6-52 on DLO 10224; insert 'Let's Hear the Other Side' (a musical quiz) with Marcel Stellman and Tony Hancock pre-recorded 17-6-52 on DLO 11091. Repeated 5-7-52, LP, 1000-1030.

13- 8-52 'Henry Hall's Guest Night—Highlights of the Show World'; presented by Henry Hall. Produced by Alistair Scott-Johnston. HS, 1845–1930; recorded earlier same day, on SLO 12765. Repeated 17-8-52, LP, 1330–1415.

15- 9-52 *'Forces All Star Bill' (for details see p. 201).*

27- 9-52 Recording for Radio Luxembourg, from the London Palladium. Transmission date untraced.

1-10-52 'Henry Hall's Guest Night'. HS, 1900-1945; recorded earlier same day on SLO 15433. Repeated 5-10-52, LP, 1445-1530.

5-11-52 'The Guy Fawkes Show'—a musical-comedy travesty of history, written by Jimmy Grafton.

Hancock, the butler, and his ancestor
Guy Hancock-Fawkes.................... Tony Hancock
Lady Fitz-Badely/Miss Winter .... Joy Nichols
Thomas Winter .... Max Bygraves
Robert Catesby .... Wilbur Evans
Thomas Percy/Sir Francis Tresham Graham Stark

with the George Mitchell Singers, The Augmented Dance Orchestra conducted by Stanley Black; and Jimmy Edwards. Produced by Dennis Main Wilson. LP, 2000-2045; recorded 30-10-52 on SLO 17989.

3-12-52   'Henry Hall's Guest Night'; HS 1830-1915; recorded earlier same day on SLO 18824. Repeated 7-12-52, LP, 1445-1530.

13-12-52   Recording for Radio Luxembourg—'Showtime' from the London Palladium. Transmission date untraced.

6- 1-53   *'Forces All Star Bill' begins: runs to 26-6-53 (see p. 201).*

6- 5-53   'Henry Hall's Guest Night'; HS 2135-2215; recorded earlier same day on SLO 28142. Repeated 10-5-53, LP, 1415-1455.

30- 5-53   'Variety Cavalcade'; introduced by Benny Hill; Hancock was one of nine acts. Produced by Duncan Wood. West of England Home Service only, 2000-2100; recorded 19-5-53 on SBS 8550.

7- 6-53   *'Star Bill' begins: runs to 25-10-53 (see p. 202).*

1-11-53   'Top of the Town'; Terry-Thomas with Joan Sims and Leslie Mitchell. 'On top of his town this week—Tony Hancock, and his home town, Birmingham'. Script edited by James Grafton. Produced by Dennis Main Wilson. LP 2100-2200.

23-11-53   'The Frankie Howerd Show'; Frankie Howerd introducing personalities of show business, including Hancock. Script by Ray Galton and Alan Simpson, with Eric Sykes. Produced by Alistair Scott-Johnston. LP 2115-2200; recorded 22-11-53 on SLO 39241.

29- 1-54   'What Goes On'; Hancock interviewed by Philip Garston-Jones. Programme introduced by Paul Martin, produced by David Frankham. Midland Home Service only, 1830-1900. Hancock's interview pre-recorded 27-1-54, in Nottingham, on MBM 3742.

28- 2-54   *'Star Bill'—second series—begins: runs to 2-5-54. (see p. 203).*

15- 5-54   'Gala Performance—A Welcome to Her Majesty the Queen' introduced by Jack Buchanan and Margaret Lockwood; Hancock was one of 19 acts in first section, HS and LP 1930-2100, recorded 9-5-54 on TLO 54779. (After the News at 2100 the special programme continued with 'Out and About' and a concert.)

24- 6-54   'Variety Fanfare'; from the Hulme Hippodrome, Manchester. LP, 2130-2200; recorded 20-6-54 on TMR 2976.

2-11-54   *'HHH' 1st series (radio) begins: runs to 15-2-55 (see p. 204).*

19- 4-55   *'HHH' 2nd series (radio) begins: runs to 5-7-55 (see p. 206).*

19-10-55   *'HHH' 3rd series (radio) begins: runs to 29-2-56 (see p. 207).*

27- 4-55   *'The Tony Hancock Show' 1st series (AR-TV/Hylton) begins: runs to 1-6-56 (see p. 247).*

6- 2-56   'Jack Hylton Presents'; variety introduced by Arthur Helliwell. Included the Lighthouse Keeper sketch from 'The Talk of the Town', filmed at the Adelphi Theatre (but without an audience) on 14-9-55, with Hancock and Reg O'List (Jimmy Edwards's understudy). Duration of sketch 7' 06". Programme broadcast on AR-TV, 2130-2200. *The sketch still exists on 35mm film.*

1- 7-56   'House Magazine'; included Hancock with Ray Galton, Alan Simpson and Duncan Wood in a trailer for the forthcoming BBC-TV Series. BBC-TV, 1430-1500.

6- 7-56   *'HHH' 1st series (BBC-TV) begins: runs to 14-9-56 (see p. 224).*

20- 7-56   'The Laughtermakers—No. 3: Tony Hancock'. Script by Gale Pedrick, Produced by Tom Ronald. With Tony Hancock, Graham Stark, Ray

Galton, Alan Simpson, Leslie Bridgmont, Clifford Davies, Derek Scott and Philip Slessor. HS 1310-1340; recorded 15-7-56 on TLO 7875.

14-10-56   *'HHH' 4th series (radio) begins : runs to 24-2-57 (see p. 204).*

16-11-56   *'The Tony Hancock Show' 2nd series (AR-TV/Hylton) begins : runs to 25-1-57 (see p. 247).*

31-12-56   'The Man Who Could Work Miracles' by H. G. Wells, adapted by Dennis Main Wilson from H. G. Wells' screenplay.

        George McWhirter Fotheringay .... Tony Hancock
        Toddy Beamish .... Warren Mitchell
        Miss Maybridge............................Hattie Jacques
        Mr Cox.. Fred Yule
        Old Man with a dog....................... Deryck Guyler
        Bill Stoker....................................... Harry Fowler
        Ada Price .... Miriam Karlin
        Maggie Hooper............................. Marcia Ashton
        Effie Hickman................................. Maria Charles
        Housekeeper .... Hattie Jacques
        Major Grigsby .... Charles Lloyd Pack
        P. C. Winch...................................... Alfie Bass
        Mr Bampfylde .... Hugh Morton
        The Rev Silas Maydig .... Kenneth Williams
        Moody...Fred Yule
        Colonel Winstanley...... Howard Marion Crawford
        Superintendent Smithells .... Deryck Guyler
            with Roger Snowdon and Sidney Keith
    The Prologue & Epilogue (pre-recorded 13-12-56 on TLO 19090/B)
        The Observer .... André Morell
        Indifference...................................... Dennis Price
        The Player .... Robert Eddison
        Music (pre-recorded 21-12-56 on TLO 19090/A)
        by Wally Stott (using the themes from 'Hancock's
        Half-Hour') and played by the BBC Augmented
        Revue Orchestra conducted by Harry Rabinowitz.
            Produced by Dennis Main Wilson.
    HS, 2115-2245; recorded 20-12-56 on TLO 19090.

18- 1-57   'A–Z' (the ABC of Show Business). Included the first appearance of the famous 'budgerigar' sketch, with Hancock as the Budgerigar, Irene Handl as his owner, and John Deverill as the Vicar. Written by Simpson and Galton. BBC-TV, 1940-2030.

1- 4-57   *'HHH' 2nd series (BBC-TV) begins : runs to 10-6-57 (see p. 224).*

5- 8-57   'Desert Island Discs' introduced by Roy Plomley, produced by Monica Chapman.
    Records Chosen:
        Overture: The Thieving Magpie (*Rossini*) (NBC
        Symphony Orchestra)
        Symphonic Variations (*César Franck*) (Walter
        Gieseking, piano, and the London Philharmonic
        Orchestra)
        The Man that Got Away (*Arlen, Gershwin*) (Judy
        Garland)
        The Swan of Tuonela (*Sibelius*) (The Danish State
        Radio Symphony Orchestra)
        Migraine Melody (*Rose, Dickinson*) (David Rose

and his Orchestra, vocal by Hal Dickinson)
Gloomy Sunday (*Javor, Seross, Lewis*) (Artie Shaw and his Orchestra, with vocal refrain)
Soleares (flamenco) (*traditional*) (Pepe de Almeria, guitar)
Un Jour tu Verras (*van Parys, Mouloudji*) (Mouloudji with Michel Legrand and his Orchestra) (obviously only excerpts were played, except the Garland, the David Rose, and the Mouloudji)
HS, 1310-1340; speech recorded 23-7-57 on TLO 34699.

28- 9-57 'These Are The Shows'—Hancock and James appeared on behalf of 'Hancock's Half-Hour'. The programme produced by Francis Essex. BBC-TV 2000-2045.

30- 9-57 *'HHH' 3rd series (BBC-TV) begins : runs to 23-12-57 (see p. 225).*

7-12-57 'In Town Tonight'—Hancock interviewed by John Ellison. (3' 25") HS 1930-2000.

25-12-57 'Pantomania—Babes in the Wood'

Merry Man	Eamonn Andrews
A Robber	Derek Bond
Baron Eville	Sam Costa
School Inspector/Lawyer	Kenneth Connor
Sheriff	Charlie Drake
A Robber	Peter Haigh
Minstrel	Benny Hill
Minstrel's Minstrels	Peter Crawford Trio
Aladdin/Robin Hood	Tony Hancock
Forrester and Lion	Terry Hall with Lenny the Lion
The Genie/Friar Tuck	Sidney James
Merry Man	Derek Hart
Merry Man	Cliff Michelmore
The Babes	Bill Maynard Ted Ray
Widow Higgins	Jack Payne
Platinum Back-scratcher	Pauline Tooth
Merry Man	Huw Wheldon
Merry Man/Sherwood Commentator	Peter Dimmock
1st Villager/Woodcutter	Alex Macintosh
Maid Marion	Sylvia Peters
Floor Manager	Len Mitchell
Fairy Queen	Jean Metcalfe

Eric Robinson Orchestra and the George Mitchell Singers conducted by George Clouston.
Produced by Graeme Muir.
BBC-TV, 1930-2030; telerecorded 17-12-57 on 35/T/3846

18- 1-58 'Saturday Night on the Light'; Hancock and Tom Ronald interviewed by Charles Richardson (2' 42"). LP 1930-2230; Hancock interview prerecorded 17-1-58 on TLO 46572.

21- 1-58 *'HHH' 5th series (radio) begins : runs to 3-6-58 (see p. 211).*

9- 2-58 'The Government Inspector' by Nicolai Gogol; English version by D. J. Campbell; adapted for television by Barry Thomas.

194

Hlestakov....................................... Tony Hancock
Yosif..Reginald Barratt
The Mayor .... John Phillips
Anna..Helen Christie
Marya.. Susan Maryott
School superintendent .... Peter Copley
Health Commissioner .... Philip Leaver
The Judge.. Noel Howlett
The Postmaster...........................Wilfrid Brambell
Bobchinsky ....Michael Segal
Dobchinsky ....John Gill
Abdulin ....Harold Kasket
2nd Merchant................................ Denis Homes
3rd Merchant................................ Hamilton Dyce
Police Superintendent................. Reginald Hearne
Innkeeper .... Frank Sieman
Mishka...Gertan Klauber
Gendarme................................ Alexis Bobrinskoy
1st Constable ....Douglas Blackwell
2nd Constable...................................Derris Ward
Soldiers.. Roy Dotrice
Daniel Moynihan

Townspeople:
Alice Greenwood, Betty Woolfe, John Herrington,
John Tucker, Bernard Callaghan, Bert Simms,
David Grahame and Jose Tregoningo.
Produced by Alan Bromley
BBC-TV, 2030-2115. A telerecording is in BBC Film Library on 35/TU/3972.

3- 8-58 'Welcome to London—a gala performance from the London Coliseum in honour of athletes who are being entertained in London after taking part in the Commonwealth Games'. Hancock, Sid James and Bill Kerr appeared in a five minute sketch by Simpson and Galton. The programme produced by Tom Ronald. LP, 2100-2230.

28- 9-58 'Educating Archie'—with Peter Brough and Archie Andrews, Bernard Bresslaw, Gladys Morgan, Dick Emery, and special guests Max Bygraves, Tony Hancock, Harry Secombe (all three pre-recorded) and Warren Mitchell. Script by Ronald Wolfe, Ronald Chesney and Marty Feldman. Produced by Jacques Brown. LP 1345-1415; recorded 7-9-58 on TLO 65937 (Hancock's contribution pre-recorded 26-8-58 on DLO 66486). Repeated 1-10-58, LP, 1930-2000.

9-11-58 'The Royal Variety Performance'—highlights introduced by Brian Johnston. Hancock performed a modified version of the budgerigar sketch with Hattie Jacques. LP, 2100–2200; recorded 3-11-58 on TLO 70311.

20-11-58 Recording made for 'This is Britain', a programme sent overseas by the BBC Transcription Services for use by foreign broadcasting stations: Hancock was interviewed.

25-12-58 'HHH' Christmas Special (see p. 213).

25-12-58 'Christmas Night with the Stars'; Hancock appeared in a repeat performance of the budgerigar sketch, with Tottie Truman Taylor and Alec Bregonzi, and whistling by Percy Edwards (off-screen). Script by Simpson and Galton. Complete programme produced by Graeme Muir. BBC-TV, 1830-1940; telerecorded 5-12-58 (links only, the programme is mostly

195

assembled from pre-telerecorded items) on overall number 35/T/5232. Hancock's sketch pre-recorded 2-12-58. *The complete programme is in BBC Film Library.*

26-12-58   *'HHH' 4th series (BBC-TV) begins : runs to 27-3-59 (see p. 227).*

4- 1-59   *'HHH' (radio) — Transcription series remakes : runs to 25-1-59 (see p. 214).*

4- 1-59   'What's My Line?'; Hancock appeared as guest celebrity. The panel were Gilbert Harding, Lady Isobel Barnet, Pippa Stanley and Cyril Fletcher. Master of ceremonies Eamonn Andrews. Produced by John Warrington & Kenneth Milne-Buckley. BBC-TV, 2000-2030.

25- 9-59   *'HHH' 5th series (BBC-TV) begins : runs to 27-11-59 (see p. 228).*

29- 9-59   *'HHH' 6th series (radio) begins : runs to 20-12-59 (see p. 214).*

7- 2-60   'Face to Face'; Hancock interviewed by John Freeman. BBC-TV 2130-2200; video taped 28-1-60 on VT/T/7160.

4- 3-60   *'HHH' 6th series (BBC-TV) begins : runs to 6-5-60 (see p. 230).*

9- 7-60   'In Town Tonight'; Hancock interviewed by Tony Bilbow (3' 30") HS 1930-2000; Hancock's interview pre-recorded 8-7-60 on TLO 23654.

4- 3-61   'In Town Today'; Hancock interviewed about 'The Rebel' by Tony Bilbow (2' 58"). HS 1310-1340; recorded 2/3-3-61 on TLO 44861; Hancock's interview pre-recorded 2-3-61 on TLO 44515.

4- 3-61   'London Mirror'; Hancock interviewed by Wilfrid Thomas (2' 00"). GOS 1830-1915; recorded 2-3-61 on TLO 44173; repeated 11-3-61, GOS, 0030-0115.

7- 3-61   'Picture Parade'; Hancock interviewed by Robert Robinson (7' 10") BBC-TV 2226-2305; Hancock's interview pre-recorded 22-2-61 on T/1090.

23- 5-61   'Today' introduced by Jack De Manio.
First edition HS 0715-0735; Hancock interviewed by Richard Innison, (3' 02") pre-recorded 18-5-61 on YCTLO 53208.
Second edition HS 0815-0835; same interview used in version shortened to 2' 49".

26- 5-61   *'Hancock' (7th BBC-TV series) begins : runs to 30-6-61 (see p. 231).*

5- 5-62   'In Town Today'; Hancock interviewed by McDonald Hobley about 'The Punch and Judy Man' (3' 10"). HS 1230-1255; recorded 3/4-5-62 on TLO 81995.

3- 1-63   *'Hancock' (ATV series) begins : runs to 28-3-63 (see p. 248).*

22- 7-63   'Scene at 6.30'; interview pre-recorded the same day. Granada TV, 1830–1900.

12- 8-63   'Today' (first edition only); Hancock interviewed by Tim Matthews (1' 55"). HS 0715-0735; interview pre-recorded 9-8-63.

17- 8-63   'In Town Today'; Hancock interviewed by Nan Winton at the London Palladium (3' 33"). HS 1230–1255; recorded 15/16-8-63, on TLO 17564.

19-10-63   'That Reminds Me'; Midland Home Service 0930-1000; Hancock prerecorded in Nottingham on T/NOT 83, 18-7-63; complete programme recorded 16-10-63 on TBM 32956.

15-11-64   'Sunday Night at the London Palladium'. ATV London 2025-2125.

5-12-64   'Open House' compèred by Gay Byrne and Peter Haigh. Hancock was interviewed 'live'. BBC-2, 1600-1715.

25-12-64   ''Ancock's Anthology'. Hancock talked, read from Stephen Leacock and A. A. Milne, introduced records, and interviewed Stirling Moss. Produced by Richard Dingley. HS, 1200-1240; recorded 21-12-64 on TLO 54573.

26- 6-65   'Late Night Saturday'; Hancock interviewed 'live' by Pete Murray. LP, 2300-0200 on 27-6-65.

5-10-65   'Late Night Line-up'; Hancock interviewed by Michael Dean (18' 55")

196

BBC-2, 2310-2335. Hancock's interview pre-recorded 2-10-65 on VT/6T/13/0538.

19- 6-66   *'The Blackpool Show' (ABC-TV) begins : runs to 7-8-66 (see p. 252).*

31- 7-66   'The Entertainers'; complete programme consisted of an interview with Hancock by Colin Hamilton. (8' 24").
BBC World Service, 1035–1045 (GMT); recorded 20-5-66 on TBU 443006. Repeated 1-8-66, North American Service, 1645-1655 (GMT) and 5-8-66, World Service, 1845-1855 (GMT).

16- 9-66   'Late Night Line-Up'; Hancock interviewed 'live' about his RFH show by Joan Bakewell. (13' 40"). BBC-2, 2308-2348.

15-10-66   'Hancock at the Royal Festival Hall'; with Joe Ritchie, Tony Hatch (musical director), and June Whitfield (out of vision). Produced for television by Derek Burrell-Davis. BBC-2, 2106-2154; video taped 22-9-66 on VT/6T/35166.

13-11-66   'Secombe and Friends'; Harry Secombe with Michael Bentine, Tony Hancock, Danny Lá Rue, Adele Leigh, Jeremy Lloyd, Nora Nicholson, and Jack Parnell and his orchestra. Script by Jimmy Grafton, who (with the permission of Simpson and Galton) adapted the budgerigar sketch to provide Hancock with a 'mate'—Secombe. Producer Jon Scoffield. ATV Network production; 2025-2125. (It is not known whether this programme was pre-recorded.)

19- 1-67   'The Frost Programme' AR-TV 2302-2342.

20- 1-67   'The Frost Programme' AR-TV 2235-2310.
In the first programme, Hancock mentioned a sentimental ballad that his father used to sing professionally, but which he could no longer remember. Frost invited anyone who had a copy to send it in. Someone did (very promptly!) and Hancock was invited back the following evening to give a rendition of it.

16- 6-67   *'Hancock's' (ABC-TV series) begins : runs to 18-7-67 (see p. 252).*

14- 1-68   'The Eamonn Andrews Show'; ABC-TV, 2315 to closedown.

21- 1-68   'The David Jacobs Show': Hancock interviewed 'live' (5') R1 and 2, 2200-0000.

12- 6-68   'Something Special—Nancye': Hancock appeared in a 10 minute guest spot in this show hosted by Nancye Hayes. Channel HSV7, Melbourne, Australia, 1930-2030. Recorded the previous October.

25- 1-72   *'The Tony Hancock Special'—the three completed episodes of the Australian TV series were strung together and shown on Channel HSV7, Melbourne, 2030-2200 (see p. 253).*

'HAPPY-GO-LUCKY'

Derek Roy, Doreen Harris, Peggy Cochrane, Jack and Daphne Barker (except where stated), Harry Noble and Frances King, The Sam Browne Singers and the Augmented BBC Dance Orchestra conducted by Stanley Black (except no. 8). Tony Hancock, Peter Butterworth, Graham Stark, and (in first four only) Bill Kerr appeared in self-contained 'Eager Beavers' sketch (except last two programmes).

Some shows also had guests (detailed below, but with whom Hancock did not work), and a married couple from the audience celebrating their wedding anniversary, who were interviewed by Roy and acted in a short sketch with him: these latter are not listed.

Nos 1-11 produced by Roy Speer; nos 12-14 produced by Dennis Main Wilson.

Scriptwriters detailed below: RP = Ralp Peterson, JL — John Law, BC — Bill Craig, LW = Laurie Wyman, JV = John Vyvyan, RR = Rona Ricardo, EKS = E. K. Smith, AS = Alan Simpson, RG — Ray Galton.

2100-2200 LP, except no 9, 2105-2200. No repeats.

Thursdays
1   2- -8-51   SLO 92598   with Suzette Tarri, Benny Hill and John Hanson. (Script
            (28-7-51)   RP, JL and BC, LW and JV)

2   9- 8-51   Live   with Charlie Chester, Harry Locke and Edmundo Ros;
            without J and D Barker. (Script as no 1 + RR)
3   16- 8-51   SLO 93549   with Beryl Reid and Dick Emery (Script RP and RR,
            (11-8-51)   LW and JV)
4   23- 8-51   SLO 93945   with Avrill Angers, Ken Platt and Jimmy Young. (Script
            (18-8-51)   RP, JL and BC; LW, RR and JV)
5   30- 8-51   Live   From the National Radio Show. With Terry-Thomas
            and Freddie Sales; Bill Kerr leaves. (Script RP, LW, RR
            and JV)
6   6- 9-51   SLO 94332   with Maudie Edwards and Eddie Malloy; without J. and
            (1-9-51)   D. Barker. (Script RP, LW, RR and JV)
7   13- 9-51   Hancock absent
8   20- 9-51   SLO 94930   with Janet Brown and Bernard Speer: The BBC
            (15-9-51)   Augmented Revue Orchestra conducted by Robert
            Busby. (Script as no 6)

Mondays, fortnightly ('Variety Bandbox' on alternate weeks); LP 2100-2200.
9   1-10-51   SLO 96282   without J. and D. Barker. (Script RP, RR, LW and
            (30-9-51)   EKS)
10   15-10-51   SLO 96397   without J. and D. Barker. (Script RP, EKS, RR, with
            (14-10-51)   additional material by AS and RG)
11   29-10-51   Hancock absent
12   12-11-51   SLO 97978   without J. and D. Barker. Benny Hill replaced But-
            (11-11-51)   terworth. (Script AS and RG, EKS and RP, RR)
13   26-11-51   Hancock rehearsed but did not contribute to recording.
14   10-12-51   SLO 99800   without J. and D. Barker; without Butterworth; with
End of series.   (9-12-51)   Dick Emery. (Script AS and RG, RP) and RR)

'EDUCATING ARCHIE'—2nd SERIES
Peter Brough and Archie Andrews with Hattie Jacques, Tony Hancock, Peter Madden,
The Tanner Sisters (except 'Archie Andrews' Party'), The Hedley Ward Trio (except
'Archie Andrews' Party'); Anton and his Orchestra (nos 1-12), The BBC Revue
Orchestra conducted by Robert Busby (13 onwards, except 25); and additional cast as
noted below. Scripts by Eric Sykes and Sid Colin with additional material (lyrics to
signature tune) by Walter Ridley. Produced by Roy Speer.

Fridays, 2045-2115 LP (except no. 9, see below); all except no. 8 repeated Sundays 1800
LP; 21-26 also repeated Mondays 1225 HS.

1   3- 8-51   SLO 93152   with Max Bygraves and Julie Andrews.
            (29-7-51)
2   10- 8-51   SLO 93158   with Max Bygraves and Julie Andrews.
            (5-8-51)
3   17- 8-51   SLO 93384   with Max Bygraves and Julie Andrews.
            (12-8-51)
4   24- 8-51   SLO 93969   with Max Bygraves and Julie Andrews.
            (19- 8-51)

198

5	31- 8-51	SLO 93970	with Max Bygraves and Julie Andrews.
	(19-8-51)		
6	7- 9-51	SLO 94385	with Max Bygraves and Julie Andrews.
	(2-9-51)		
7	14- 9-51	SLO 94386	with Max Bygraves and Julie Andrews.
	(2-9-51)		
8	21- 9-51	SLO 94599	with Max Bygraves and Ronald Chesney.
	(16-9-51)		

Number 8 was not repeated; number 9 was first transmitted in the advertised repeat placing for number 8, then repeated in its advertised first placing, and further repeated in its advertised repeat placing.

9	23- 9-51	SLO 95044	with Max Bygraves and Ronald Chesney.
	at 1800 LP (16-9-51)		
(repeated 28-9-51)			
10	5-10-51	SLO 96035	with Max Bygraves and Julie Andrews.
	(30-9-51)		
11	12-10-51	SLO 95381	with Alfred Marks and Julie Andrews.
	(7-10-51)		
12	19-10-51	SLO 95382	with Alfred Marks and Julie Andrews.
	(7-10-51)		
13	26-10-51	SLO 97093	with Gilbert Harding and Julie Andrews.
	(21-10-51)		
14	2-11-51	SLO 97094	with Gilbert Harding and Julie Andrews.
	(21-10-51)		
15	9-11-51	SLO 98020	with John Sharp and Julie Andrews.
	(4-11-51)		
16	16-11-51	SLO 98021	with John Sharp and Julie Andrews.
	(4-11-51)		
17	23-11-51	SLO 98294	with John Sharp and Julie Andrews.
	(18-11-51)		
18	30-11-51	SLO 98295	with John Sharp and Julie Andrews.
	(18-11-51)		
19	7-12-51	SLO 700	with Robert Moreton and Julie Andrews.
	(9-12-51)		
20	14-12-51	SLO 701	with John Sharp, Max Bygraves and Julie Andrews.
	(9-12-51)		
21	21-12-51	SLO 626	with Gilbert Harding and Ronald Chesney.
	(20-12-51)		

SP	26-12-51	SLO 623	ARCHIE ANDREWS' PARTY at the NAAFI Club,
Boxing (Wed)	(16-12-51)		Colchester. Without the Tanner Sisters or The Hedley
LP 1930-2000			Ward Trio; with the Ilford Girls' Choir.

22	28-12-51	SLO 627	with Jack Train and Ronald Chesney.
	(27-12-51)		
23	4- 1-52	SLO 628	with Albert Modley.
	(27-12-51)		
24	11- 1-52	SLO 1713	with Bernard Miles and Ronald Chesney.
	(6-1-52)		
25	18- 1-52	SLO 1714	with Gilbert Harding and Ronald Chesney; the BBC
	(13-1-52)		Revue Orchestra conducted by Charles Shadwell.

199

26   25- 1-52   SLO 1765   with Max Bygraves and Ronald Chesney.
Last of series   (20-1-52)

Number 12 of this series is in BBC Sound Archives, on MT 17237.

APPEARANCES BY HANCOCK IN THE *FORCES*/*STAR BILL* PROGRAMMES
'CALLING ALL FORCES'

Hancock appeared in the edition of Sunday 5-8-51, LP 2100-2200 (repeated Friday 11-8-51, HS 1310), working with Googie Withers, Geraldo and compère Ted Ray, as well as working solo. Script (not the solo spot) by Bob Monkhouse and Denis Goodwin; produced by Leslie Bridgmont and Frank Hooper. Recorded 4-8-51 on SLO 93226.

On 31-12-51 'Calling All Forces' moved to Mondays at 2100-2200 LP, the slot vacated two weeks earlier by 'Happy-Go-Lucky'; Ted Ray remained the compère.

Hancock appeared in the edition of 25-2-52 (repeated Saturday 1-3-52, 1310 HS), doing his own act solo, then working with Ted Ray, Pauline Stroud, Geraldo, Denis Goodwin, Alan Skempton and Leslie Welch. Script and production as above. Recorded 23-2-52 on SLO 3430.

On Easter Monday Ted Ray was replaced as compère by Charlie Chester and Hancock. Since Hancock, as co-compère, usually worked (albeit briefly) with the musical guest (the 'Music Master') and also did a sketch with the main guest, the full bill for each show has been quoted below. Apart from working with the guests, Hancock usually did a sketch with Chester and a supporting actress.

Regular artists: Charlie Chester and Tony Hancock (compères), Leslie Welch, Carole Carr, and (except where stated) the Mitchellaires and The BBC Augmented Dance Orchestra conducted by Stanley Black. Produced by Jacques Brown and John Hooper. Scripts for the first ten by Bob Monkhouse and Denis Goodwin.
All programmes 2100-2200 LP (Mondays); repeated the following Saturday at 1310 HS; recorded the previous Saturday.

14-4-52   SLO 5898   with Arthur Askey, Eddie Calvert; Edna Fryer (in sketch with Hancock); and the George Mitchell Singers instead of the Mitchellaires.
21-4-52   SLO 6508   with Jack Warner, Ken Mackintosh; Joan Heal, Bob Monkhouse; and the George Mitchell Singers.
28-4-52   SLO 7188   with Peter Cavanagh, Monia Liter; Hattie Jacques; and the George Mitchell Singers.
5-5-52   SLO 7231   with Terry-Thomas, Nat Temple; and Josephine Crombie.
12-5-52   SLO 8946   with Cardew Robinson, Jack Simpson; Miriam Karlin and Denis Goodwin.
19-5-52   SLO 7850   with Robb Wilton, Kenny Baker; and Patricia Gilbert.
26-5-52   SLO 8354   with Robert Moreton, Steve Race and Malcolm Lockyer; Diana Decker and Denis Goodwin.
2-6-52   SLO 8934   with Cyril Fletcher, Tollefsen; Joan Heal; and the Augmen-
(Whit Monday)   ted Variety Orchestra conducted by Paul Fenoulhet.
9-6-52   SLO 9071   with Bill Kerr, Ronnie Aldrich; Pat Cutts; and the Augmen-ted Variety Orchestra conducted by Paul Fenoulhet.
16-6-52   SLO 9828   with Harry Secombe, Johnny Dankworth; and Lisbeth Kearnes.

Ray Galton and Alan Simpson took over as scriptwriters.
23-6-52   SLO 10117   with Richard Murdoch, Wally Rockett; and Edna Fryer.
30-6-52   SLO 10454   with Derek Roy, Winifred Atwell; and Jennifer Ramage.
 7-7-52   SLO 10396   with Jimmy Edwards, Freddie Randall; and Billie Whitelaw.

Charlie Chester joined Simpson and Galton as scriptwriter.
14-7-52   SLO 11116   with Bernard Braden, Tommy Reilly; and Primrose Milligan.
21-7-52   SLO 11354   with Peter Sellers, Stanley Black (solo piano); and Miriam
                      Karlin.
28-7-52   SLO 11893   with Eric Barker, Humphrey Lyttleton and Wally Fawkes;
Last of series.   and Edna Fryer.

'FORCES ALL-STAR BILL'

*Took over immediately from 'Calling All Forces', in the same slot—Mondays at 2100-2200,
LP, but with no repeats. The compère changed weekly.*

Hancock appeared in the 7th programme, 15-9-52, as compère: with Joy Nichols, The
Five Smith Brothers, Dick James, Winifred Atwell, Fred Yule, Graham Stark, The
George Mitchell Glee Club and the BBC Augmented Dance Orchestra conducted by
Stanley Black. Script by Spike Milligan and Larry Stephens; produced by Dennis Main
Wilson. Recorded 14-9-52 on SLO 15268.

'ALL-STAR BILL'

*Took over the same slot after eight editions of 'Forces All-Star Bill'; again, with varying
compères.*

Hancock appeared in the 3rd edition, 13-10-52, as compère; with Edmund Hockridge,
The Beverley Sisters, Stephane Grappelly, The Hedley Ward Trio, Graham Stark, The
George Mitchell Glee Club and the BBC Dance Orchestra conducted by Stanley Black.
Script by Ray Galton and Alan Simpson; produced by Dennis Main Wilson.
Recorded 12-10-52 on SLO 16839.

'FORCES ALL-STAR BILL'—SECOND SERIES

*Took over from 'All-Star Bill' after 13 editions, but in a new slot—Tuesdays 2000-2100,
LP—and fortnightly, alternating with 'The Forces Show' (with Richard Murdoch,
Kenneth Horne and Sam Costa).*

Scripts by Ray Galton and Alan Simpson; nos 1-6 produced by Dennis Main Wilson;
nos 7-11 produced by Alistair Scott-Johnston.
Recorded the previous Sunday; repeated Saturdays at 1155 HS.

1   6-1-53   SLO 20678   Ted Ray (compère); with Tony Hancock, Graham Stark
                          and Joan Heal; and Josef Locke, Betty Driver, Kenny
                          Baker, The George Mitchell Glee Club, and Stanley
                          Black and his Concert Orchestra.
2   20-1-53   SLO 20950   No compère (the show was in effect compèred by the
                          announcer, Robin Boyle); with Tony Hancock, Graham
                          Stark and Joan Heal; and Bonar Colleano, Zoe Gail,
                          Edmund Hockridge, Stephane Grappelly, and mus-
                          icians as in no. 1.

| 3 | 3-2-53 | | without Hancock. |
| 4 | 17-2-53 | | |

5   3-3-53   SLO 23538   Michael Howard (compère); with Tony Hancock, Graham Stark and Joan Heal; and Anne Shelton, Dick James, and musicians as in no. 1.

6   17-3-53   SLO 24429   Bonar Colleano (compère); with Tony Hancock, Graham Stark and Joan Heal; and Josef Locke, Mary Small, The Three Monarchs, and musicians as in no. 1.

No compère for the remainder of the series; the regular team was Tony Hancock, Graham Stark and Geraldine McEwan; The George Mitchell Glee Club; and Stanley Black and his Concert Orchestra.

7   31-3-53   SLO 25528   with Terence de Marney, The Beverley Sisters, Jimmy Young, and Monia Liter.

8   14-4-53   SLO 25990   with John Slater, Wilbur Evans, Tessie O'Shea, and Harold Smart.

9   28-4-53   SOX 90300   with Dennis Price, Rawicz and Landauer, Muriel Smith, and The Five Smith Brothers.

10   12-5-53   SLO 28243   with Max Bygraves, Bruce Trent, Jean Carson, and The Ray Ellington Quartet.

11   26-5-53   SLO 29035   with Arthur Askey, Vanessa Lee, The Radio Revellers, and Eddie Calvert.

'STAR BILL—THE BEST IN BRITAIN'S SHOW BUSINESS'

Returned to the Sunday placing, 2100-2200 LP, weekly; odd numbers repeated Saturdays at 1155, HS (details in brackets, below); even numbers not repeated.

Regular team: Tony Hancock, Graham Stark and Geraldine McEwan; The George Mitchell Glee Club; and (except where stated) Stanley Black and his Concert Orchestra. Scripts by Alan Simpson and Ray Galton, except nos 5-8, details given below. Produced by Alistair Scott-Johnston.

1   7-6-53   Live   with Ted Ray, Lizbeth Webb, David Hughes, and
(rpt. 13-6-53 on SLO 29704)   Semprini. Orchestra conducted by Philip Martell.

2   14-6-53   Live   with Charlie Chester, Anne Shelton, Harry Davidson, and The Hedley Ward Trio.

3   21-6-53   SLO 30396   with Richard Murdoch, Elizabeth Welch, Dick James,
(recorded earlier same day)   and Tommy Reilly.
(rpt. 27-6-53)

4   28-6-53   Live   with Alfred Marks, The Tanner Sisters, Edmund Hockridge, and Eugene Pini; The George Melachrino Orchestra.

5   5-7-53   Live   with Dennis Price, Adelaide Hall, Lee Lawrence, and
(rpt. 11-7-53 on SLO 31500)   Rawicz and Landauer. (Script by Eric Sykes and Larry Stephens.)

6	12-7-53	Live	with Derek Roy, Vivian Blaine, Josef Locke, and The Malcolm Mitchell Trio. (Script by Eric Sykes and Larry Stephens.)
7	19-7-53 (rpt. 25-7-53 on SLO 32244)	Live	with Jack Watling, Carole Carr, The Five Smith Brothers, and Robin Richmond. (Script by Eric Sykes and Spike Milligan.)
8	26-7-53	Live	with Gene Autrey, Dorothy Squires, Bruce Trent, and Eddie Calvert; The George Melachrino Orchestra. (Script by Eric Sykes and Spike Milligan.)
9	2-8-53 (rpt. 8-8-53 on SLO 31999)	Live	with Dick Bentley, Pat Kirkwood, 'Hutch' (Leslie A. Hutchinson), and Jack Brymer; The Geraldo Concert Orchestra.

From the 10th programme (9-8-53) Hancock was replaced by Alfred Marks in the regular team until the end of the series.

| 21 | 25-10-53 (rpt. 31-10-53 on SLO 37146) Last of series. | Live | Guest appearance by Tony Hancock; with Alfred Marks, Geraldine McEwan, Graham Stark, Anne Shelton, Terry-Thomas, The Deep River Boys, and usual musicians. |

Replaced by 'Top of the Town', with Terry-Thomas, which ran until 21-2-54.

'STAR BILL'—SECOND SERIES.

Regular team: Tony Hancock, Moira Lister and Graham Stark; Joan Turner, Eddie Calvert, The Mitchell Millionaires led by Tony Mercer, and Stanley Black and his Concert Orchestra (except nos 8 and 9, Geraldo and his Orchestra) (From programme 5 onwards, *Radio Times* also billed 'Higgins': this was an off-stage character, referred to by Hancock, but who never actually spoke.) Scripts by Ray Galton and Alan Simpson, with additional lyrics by Jimmy Grafton. Produced by Dennis Main Wilson.
Sundays at 2100-2200 LP; no repeats.

1	28-2-54	Live	with James Robertson Justice.
2	7-3-54	Live	with Ted Ray.
3	14-3-54	Live	with Jack Buchanan.
4	21-3-54	Live	with Josef Locke.
5	28-3-54	Live	with Jimmy James, and Raymond Glendenning (who was pre-recorded).
6	4-4-54		Hancock absent, replaced by Terry-Thomas.
7	11-4-54	Live	with Bonar Colleano.
8	18-4-54	Live	with Richard Greene.
9	25-4-54	Live	with Vic Oliver.
10	2-5-54	Live	with Jimmy Edwards.

Last of series.

Replaced by 'The Forces Show', in which Hancock did not appear; this ran from 9-5-54 until replaced in October by 'Grand Hotel'.
2 sketches from number 4 of this series are in BBC Sound Archives on 78 rpm pressed disc number 20284.

'HANCOCK'S HALF-HOUR': RADIO

The six series of 'Hancock's Half-Hour' are listed here with dates of first transmission, original tape numbers, recording dates (in brackets below the tape numbers), titles, cast details, and a brief synopsis of each show.

All programmes were first transmitted on the Light Programme, at times and on days listed in the heading to each series. Scripts written by Ray Galton and Alan Simpson. Theme and incidental music composed by Wally Stott, pre-recorded by the BBC Revue Orchestra conducted by Harry Rabinowitz (first three series) and Wally Stott and his Orchestra (4th, 5th and 6th series).

None of the programmes originally had titles. Ray Galton and Alan Simpson have a list of titles, but in many cases these are meant to remind them of what the script is about, rather than being a satisfactory title. Later repeats have been given titles in *Radio Times*, but many of these are unsatisfactory—for example, they persistently refer to Hancock as 'Tony', whereas the characters in the shows almost always address him as 'Hancock', 'Mr Hancock', or 'Tub'. I have therefore taken the liberty of inventing titles where necessary, adopting some of the *Radio Times* titles, but trying to choose a title which will identify the show easily.

In-series repeats are listed in the headings to each series; out-of-series repeats are listed following the series lists; followed by details of programmes retained in BBC Sound Archives, and a list of issues for use by BBC Transcription Services.

'HANCOCK'S HALF-HOUR': RADIO, 1st SERIES

Tony Hancock, Bill Kerr, Moira Lister, Sidney James and Alan Simpson (except 6). Produced by Dennis Main Wilson.
Tuesdays at 2130, except no. 15, at 2000. No repeats.

1   2-11-54   TLO 65677   THE FIRST NIGHT PARTY
        (30-10-54)   (with Gerald Campion and Kenneth Williams) Hancock rents a posh flat from Sid James in order to hold an impressive party launching his new radio series. Unfortunately Sid has omitted to get permission from the owner.

2   9-11-54   TLO 65942   THE DIAMOND RING
        (6-11-54)   (with Kenneth Williams) Hancock, begging 'a penny for the guy', finds a diamond ring in his takings. He wants to take it to the police and claim a reward, but Moira assumes it is for her—so Hancock asks Sid to make a copy.

3   16-11-54   TLO 66835   THE IDOL
        (13-11-54)   In an attempt to cure Hancock of an attack of big-headedness brought on by one fan letter, Moira and Bill hire the girls from a local factory to mob him. The trouble is *stopping* them . . .

4   23-11-54   TLO 66369   THE BOXING CHAMPION
        (20-11-54)   (with Kenneth Williams and Paul Carpenter) Under doctor's orders to lose weight, Hancock goes to Syd's Gym and gets involved in a boxing bout. He defeats Sid's champion by accident, and finds himself in a full-scale championship match.

| 5 | 30-11-54 | TLO 66648 (27-11-54) | **THE HANCOCK FESTIVAL** Three short plays, adapted for radio from the pen of 'A. Somerset Hancock'. |

5   30-11-54   TLO 66648   **THE HANCOCK FESTIVAL**
               (27-11-54)   Three short plays, adapted for radio from the pen of 'A. Somerset Hancock'.

6   7-12-54   TLO 67590   **THE NEW CAR**
               (4-12-54)   (without Alan Simpson; with Kenneth Williams) Hancock buys a car from Sid, little realizing that not only is it stolen, but that it is a police car.

7   14-12-54   TLO 68533   **THE DEPARTMENT STORE SANTA**
               (11-12-54)   (with Kenneth Williams) Forced by the Ministry of Labour to stop drawing unemployment benefit and take a job, Hancock reluctantly becomes a Santa in Sid's department store.

8   21-12-54   TLO 68580   **CHRISTMAS AT ALDERSHOT**
               (18-12-54)   (with Kenneth Williams) Hancock's plans for a luxurious Christmas are upset by the arrival of his and Bill's Z-reservist call-up papers. They face the prospect of an Army Christmas under Sergeant James.

9   28-12-54   TLO 68581   **THE CHRISTMAS EVE PARTY**
               (18-12-54)   (with Kenneth Williams) Hancock's party was so noisy that he has been brought to court by the entire district. In flashback we hear both their and his versions of what happened.

10   4- 1-55   TLO 67900   **CINDERELLA HANCOCK**
               (3-1-55)   (with Dora Bryan, Kenneth Williams and Paul Carpenter) Hancock, forced to do the house-work by Bill, and forbidden to go to the National Film Ball, manages to go in disguise—as Sheikh Aly Aga Khancock—in a costume rented only until midnight.

11   11- 1-55   TLO 70167   **A TRIP TO FRANCE**
               (10-1-55)   (with Kenneth Williams) Hancock gets a touch of sea fever, and sets sail for France with Sid—who has a little smuggling planned.

12   18- 1-55   TLO 70443   **THE MONTE CARLO RALLY**
               (17-1-55)   (with Bryan Johnston and Raymond Baxter (both prerecorded) and Kenneth Williams) Hancock takes part in the Monte Carlo Rally, in an 1896 car supplied by Sid.

13   25- 1-55   TLO 70741   **A HOUSE ON THE CLIFF**
               (24-1-55)   Hancock wants to build a house—but Sid takes a hand, and he finishes up building three.

14   1- 2-55   TLO 71084   **THE SHEIKH**
               (31-1-55)   (with Kenneth Williams) Hancock is signed up by Sid's film studio to appear as a dramatic actor—in films shot with a box camera.

15   8- 2-55   TLO 72688   **THE MARRIAGE BUREAU**
               (7-2-55)   (with Peter Sellers, replacing Williams) Hancock has the chance of a job—but he has to be

married before they will employ him. So he goes to Sid James's Marriage Bureau—and finishes up being left in charge.

16   15-2-55   TLO 78466   THE END OF THE SERIES
           (14-2-55)   (with Kenneth Williams)
                      After the end of the final programme of the series, Hancock, Bill, Sid and Moira reminisce on how they first met.

'HANCOCK'S HALF-HOUR': RADIO, 2nd SERIES

Tony Hancock (except nos 1-3), Bill Kerr, Sidney James, Andrée Melly, Kenneth Williams and Alan Simpson (except no. 10).
Produced by Dennis Main Wilson.
Tuesdays at 2130, except no. 2 at 2000; repeated Sundays at 1500, LP (except no. 10, replaced by a further repeat of no. 7 because of an unfortunate topical connotation).

1   19-4-55   TLO 77717   A HOLIDAY IN FRANCE
           (17-4-55)   (without Hancock; with Harry Secombe)
                      Hancock/Secombe and Bill mean to go to Southend—but their aim is bad and they finish up in Paris—where they first meet Andrée.

2   26-4-55   TLO 78205   THE CROWN JEWELS
           (24-5-55)   (without Hancock; with Harry Secombe)
                      In Hancock's absence, Bill is staying with Harry Secombe. They show Andrée round London—and get involved in Sid James's plot to steal the Crown Jewels.

3   3-5-55   TLO 76754   THE RACEHORSE
           (1-5-55)   (without Hancock; with Harry Secombe)
                      Bill has bought a racehorse with Harry's last ten bob. The fact that it has three legs doesn't deter Sid from entering it in the Britannia Steeplechase.

4   10-5-55   TLO 78564   A VISIT TO SWANSEA
           (8-5-55)   (Hancock returns; guest appearance by Secombe)
                      Hancock returns to find Bill and Andrée in his flat. They persuade him that he ought to thank Harry Secombe for standing in for him, so they set out for Swansea, eventually finding Secombe down a coalmine.

5   17-5-55   TLO 79213   THE HOLIDAY CAMP
           (15-5-55)   (with Dennis Wilson—piano)
                      Hancock is hired by Sid to run a holiday camp—a converted Army Camp on an artillery practise range.

6   24-5-55   TLO 79309   THE CHEF THAT DIED OF SHAME
           (23-5-55)   The cast depart from their usual characters to tell the story of 'Iggins, the pie-stall cook who rises to the heights of haute cuisine and falls again through drink.

7   31-5-55   TLO 79278   PRIME MINISTER HANCOCK
           (30-5-55)   Hancock stands for Parliament—and dreams that he has been elected, and has become Prime Minister.

8	7-6-55	TLO 79568	THE RAIL STRIKE
	(6-6-55)		With no trains running due to a national rail strike, Sid and Hancock run their own train—pulled by the original 'Rocket', stolen from the Science Museum.

9	14-6-55	TLO 80086	THE TELEVISION SET
	(13-6-55)		Unable to afford a television set, Hancock buys a home construction kit from Sid—and, surprisingly, manages to make it work. All goes well until a neighbour calls . . .

10	21-6-55	TLO 80909	THE THREE SONS
	not repeated	(20-6-55)	(without Alan Simpson) The story of old Ebadiah Hancock and the respective careers of his three sons—Rodney, in the Navy; Gideon, a gangster; and Anthony, a doctor (all played by Hancock).

11	28-6-55	TLO 81125	THE MARROW CONTEST
	(27-6-55)		Hancock's marrow, lovingly grown for the vegetable competition, is threatened by Mayor James's road-widening scheme.

12	5-7-55	TOX 27302	THE MATADOR
	(2-7-55)		In search of a cheap holiday, Hancock approaches Sid, who suggests a holiday in Spain. Little does Hancock know that Sid is looking for a bullfighter . . .

'HANCOCK'S HALF-HOUR': RADIO, 3rd SERIES

Tony Hancock, Bill Kerr, Sidney James, Kenneth Williams, Andrée Melly and Alan Simpson.
Produced by Dennis Main Wilson.
Wednesdays at 2000. Repeated Sundays at 1700 LP.

1	19-10-55	TOX 32078	THE PET DOG
	(16-10-55)		Hancock buys Andrée a puppy for her birthday. To his alarm the puppy grows rapidly until it is two inches taller than he is.

2	26-10-55	TLO 90311	THE JEWEL ROBBERY
	(23-10-55)		Sid uses Hancock's new Rolls-Royce as the getaway car in a smash-and-grab robbery—with Hancock and the others still inside it.

3	2-11-55	TLO 91436	THE BEQUEST
	(30-10-55)		Hancock's rich Uncle Ebadiah dies, leaving him £40,000 on condition he gets married. The trouble is, no-one will have him; then, a later will turns up . . .

4	9-11-55	TLO 91435	THE NEW NEIGHBOUR
	(30-10-55)		The new next-door neighbour has Hancock worried—he keeps bringing in bodies and dumping them in the incinerator. In fact, he melts down old wax-works to make new ones; but Hancock is determined to investigate . . .

5	16-11-55	TOX 32689	THE WINTER HOLIDAY
	(23-10-55)		Hancock is given a fortnight off from his job as a lift

attendant. Accompanied by Bill and Andrée, he spends it on Brighton beach—in November!

6 23-11-55 TOX 35145 THE BLACKBOARD JUNGLE
          (20-11-55) The cast present the story of a young schoolmaster in a school full of juvenile delinquents. (A skit on the 1955 film of the same name.)

7 30-11-55 TOX 34038 THE RED PLANET
          (27-11-55) Hancock's interest in astronomy turns to panic when he thinks he sees a red planet approaching the Earth. Anticipating a cataclysm, he makes arrangements with Sid for a rapid departure—to Mars.

8 7-12-55 TOX 34371 THE DIET
          (4-12-55) Hancock is too fat for the part he is playing in a film, so he goes on a diet—and to the Turkish Baths.

9 14-12-55 TOX 34083 A VISIT TO RUSSIA
          (11-12-55) As a gesture of East-West goodwill, Hancock decides to do his next broadcast of 'Hancock's Half-Hour' from the Bolshoi Theatre, Moscow.

10 21-12-55 TLO 93836 THE TRIAL OF FATHER CHRISTMAS
          (18-12-55) (with Graham Stark and Ray Galton)
                      Hancock dreams that he is Father Christmas, on trial in the Celestial Court—and being prosecuted by Mephistopheles (Sid).

11 28-12-55 TLO 93837 CINDERELLA HANCOCK
          (18-12-55) (with Dora Bryan)
                      (A new production of the 10th of the 1st series).

12 4- 1-56 TOX 35671 THE NEW YEAR RESOLUTIONS
          (1-1-56) Hancock's New Year's resolutions are undermined one by one as he has to borrow money, tell lies, and when he visits Sid James's night club.

13 11- 1-56 TOX 35594 HANCOCK'S HAIR
          (8-1-56) Imagining that he is going bald, Hancock goes to Sid for treatment, with the result that his hair turns green.

14 18- 1-56 TLO 95615 THE STUDENT PRINCE
          (15-1-56) Hancock is lured to Moravia under the impression that he is playing in 'The Student Prince'; in fact he is impersonating the Crown Prince, who is in danger of assassination.

15 25- 1-56 TBS 17792 THE BREAKFAST CEREAL
          (22-1-56) Hancock takes the claims made in a 'Crunchyflakes' cornflakes advertisement seriously, and sues the firm when the results don't come up to his expectation.

16 1- 2-56 TLO 96268 HOW HANCOCK WON THE WAR
          (29-1-56) Andrée sees a scar on Hancock's chest, and he invents a story of how he got it in the war, as a Commando in Africa and Japan.

17 8- 2-56 TLO 97230 THE NEWSPAPER

		(5-2-56)	Hancock takes over the running of the family newspaper 'The Sentinel', with Sid as the crime reporter—reporting the crimes before they happen.
18	15-2-56	TLO 97704 (12-2-56)	THE GREYHOUND TRACK Hancock's country mansion, newly decorated, is imperilled when Mayor Sid James decides to build a greyhound track on the site. In an attempt to evict Hancock, Sid discovers that a public footpath runs right through the house.
19	22-2-56	TLO 98434 (19-2-56)	THE CONJURER Hancock takes up conjuring, and is hired by Sid to give a performance at Dartmoor Prison—little suspecting that he is part of an escape plan.
20	29-2-56	TLO 98658 (26-2-56)	THE TEST MATCH (with John Arlott, Godfrey Evans, Colin Cowdrey, and Frank Tyson) Sid James, now Chairman of MCC, makes Hancock Captain of the English team—and bets on Australia to win.

'HANCOCK'S HALF-HOUR': RADIO, 4th SERIES

Tony Hancock, Sidney James, Bill Kerr, Kenneth Williams and Hattie Jacques (no. 5 onward).
Produced by Dennis Main Wilson.
Sundays at 1600; repeated Tuesdays at 2000 LP, except no. 11, repeated 24-12-56 at 2130 LP.

1	14-10-56	TLO 14193 (7-10-56)	BACK FROM HOLIDAY (with Alan Simpson and Ray Galton) Hancock and Bill return from a Continental holiday to find that Sid has rented their house to a tenant who won't move. They repair to the doss-house . . .
2	21-10-56	TLO 14194 (14-10-56)	THE BOLSHOI BALLET (with Alan Simpson and Ray Galton) Hancock's desire to see the Bolshoi Ballet is frustrated by a long queue, Sid James's black market tickets, and an incompetent policeman.
3	28-10-56	TLO 15915 (21-10-56)	SID JAMES'S DAD (with Alan Simpson) Sid is expecting a visit from his father, and, being ashamed to admit his true profession, has explained his appearances in court by telling the old man he is a judge.
4	4-11-56	TLO 15926 (28-10-56)	THE INCOME TAX DEMAND (with Alan Simpson and Ray Galton) Rather than pay an income tax demand for £14 12s 3d, Hancock takes the advice of Sid James, chartered accountant—with expensive results.
5	11-11-56	TLO 15927 (4-11-56)	THE NEW SECRETARY (with Alan Simpson; Hattie Jacques joins) Hancock decides to hire a secretary—and gets lumbered

with the outsized, incompetent, aggressive Grizelda Pugh—who starts work by muddling up his mail.

6 18-11-56 TLO 15928 **MICHELANGELO 'ANCOCK**
(11-11-56) (with Alan Simpson and Ray Galton)
Hancock enters a sculpture competition, with Miss Pugh as the model, and Sid supplying the stone.

7 25-11-56 TLO 16299 **ANNA AND THE KING OF SIAM**
(18-11-56) (with Alan Simpson, Ray Galton, and Max Harris—piano)
The release of the film 'The King and I', based on 'Anna and the King of Siam', inspires the cast to present this unmusical and argumentative version of the story.

8 2-12-56 TLO 16988 **CYRANO DE HANCOCK**
(25-11-56) Sid has fallen in love with Miss Pugh. Hancock, showing him how to propose, finds *he* has proposed to Miss Pugh. She *insists* on a wedding . . . .

9 9-12-56 TLO 17087 **THE STOLEN PETROL**
(2-12-56) (with Alan Simpson and Ray Galton)
Sid throws a party to celebrate the return of petrol rationing—and sets Hancock up as a garage proprietor selling siphoned petrol.

10 16-12-56 TLO 18607 **THE EXPRESSO BAR**
(9-12-56) (with Ray Galton)
Hancock rents a cellar from Sid and opens a coffee bar. All goes well until Sid realizes that the cellar is next door to the cells in the local nick—and four of Sid's lads are inside . . .

11 23-12-56 TLO 18730 **HANCOCK'S HAPPY CHRISTMAS**
(15-12-56) (with Michael Anderson, Dorothy Marks, Alan Simpson and Ray Galton)
Hancock, approaching Christmas with all the enthusiasm of Scrooge, finds himself entertaining two children from the local orphanage.

12 30-12-56 TLO 19236 **THE DIARY**
(23-12-56) Browsing in his diary for 1956, Hancock imagines himself as a surgeon, a lion-tamer, and a test pilot whose flight is disastrously upset by the unexpected presence of Kenneth Williams.

13 6- 1-57 TLO 20040 **THE 13TH OF THE SERIES**
(30-12-56) Sub-Druid Hancock superstitiously refuses to do his 13th radio programme. When he is threatened with action for breach of contract, the 'Head Druid' (Sid) arranges a ceremony at Stonehenge.

14 13- 1-57 TLO 20098 **ALMOST A GENTLEMAN**
(6-1-57) Annoyed by his omission from the New Year's Honours list—again—Hancock takes lessons from Sid on how to become a gentleman.

15 20- 1-57 TLO 20694 **THE OLD SCHOOL RE-UNION**
(13-1-57) Returning to his old school with Sid and Bill, Hancock

regales them with stories of his successes as a scholar and athlete.

16	27-1-57	TLO 21507 (20-1-57)	**THE WILD MAN OF THE WOODS** Hancock's desire to 'get away from it all' leads him to camp in a bus shelter on Clapham Common, and then in a bit of forest rented from Sid.
17	3-2-57	TLO 23446 (26-1-57)	**AGRICULTURAL 'ANCOCK** Needing to prove that he is an agricultural labourer in order to maintain his low rent, Hancock buys Lords Cricket Ground from Sid and starts farming it.
18	10-2-57	TLO 23088 (7-2-57)	**HANCOCK IN THE POLICE** As a policeman on the beat in Bond Street, Hancock unwittingly causes a series of robberies by conversationally leaking security information to Sid. A trap is set—with Hancock disguised as a woman.
19	17-2-57	TLO 23037 (14-2-57)	**THE EMIGRANT** Wishing to emigrate, Hancock is met by refusals from Australia, Canada, South Africa, India, and even Baffin Land. With Sid's help, he leaves the country—on Harold Macmillan's passport.
20	24-2-57	TLO 22505 (21-2-57)	**THE LAST OF THE McHANCOCKS** (with James Robertson Justice) Left a castle in Scotland by an uncle, Hancock is forced to defend his claim to it in a Highland Games contest against Seamus McNasty and Bonnie Prince Sidney.

'HANCOCK'S HALF-HOUR': RADIO, 5th SERIES

Tony Hancock, Sidney James, Bill Kerr, Hattie Jacques and Kenneth Williams. Produced by Tom Ronald, except no. 1, produced by Pat Dixon.
Tuesdays at 2000, except nos 10, 12 and 14, at 2031; repeated Thursdays at 2100, LP.

1	21-1-58	TLO 47307 (19-1-58)	**THE NEW RADIO SERIES** Big-headed from the success of his television series, Hancock decides to retire—until he discovers that the BBC intend to replace him with 'Kerr's Half-Hour'.
2	28-1-58	TLO 47555 (26-1-58)	**THE SCANDAL MAGAZINE** (with John Vere) 'Blabbermouth', a scandal magazine run by Sid James, features an exposé of Hancock's supposed carryings on with a cigarette girl. Hancock sues.
3	4-2-58	TLO 47742 (2-2-58)	**THE MALE SUFFRAGETTES** Hancock and Sid take a sudden dislike to women, and start a movement intended to re-establish male dominance.
4	11-2-58	TLO 48544 (10-2-58)	**THE INSURANCE POLICY** Sid persuades Hancock to take out a comprehensive insurance policy—at a premium greater than Hancock's income.

5	18-2-58	TLO 49423 (16-2-58)	THE PUBLICITY PHOTOGRAPH

5 18-2-58 TLO 49423 **THE PUBLICITY PHOTOGRAPH**
(16-2-58) Persuaded to have a new—and heavily re-touched—publicity photograph made, Hancock's pleasure at the good looks of the result turns to horror when he has to undergo plastic surgery and gruelling training to make him match the picture.

6 25-2-58 TLO 49663 **THE UNEXPLODED BOMB**
(23-2-58) (with Alan Simpson)
An unexploded bomb is discovered in Hancock's cellar—to the delight of Sid, who wants the site for a used car lot.

7 4-3-58 TLO 50039 **HANCOCK'S SCHOOL**
(2-3-58) Sid escalates Hancock's attempts to teach Bill to read into an expensive private school—with the pupils packed into the house, and Hancock, Sid, Miss Pugh, and even Bill as teachers.

8 11-3-58 TLO 51223 **AROUND THE WORLD IN EIGHTY DAYS**
(9-3-58) Hancock is bet £2,000 that he cannot emulate Phineas Fogg and get round the world in eighty days. Bedevilled by cancelled planes and refused visas, he eventually books on a world cruise . . .

9 18-3-58 TLO 50768 **THE AMERICANS HIT TOWN**
(16-3-58) (with Jerry Stovin)
When the US Air Force sets up a base in Cheam, Hancock joins the rush to rent them rooms at exorbitant prices; but the sudden appearance of a Council Inspector forces them to masquerade as unexploited Yanks . . .

10 25-3-58 TLO 51442 **THE ELECTION CANDIDATE**
(23-3-58) (with Alan Simpson)
Hancock's preoccupation with collecting a complete set of plastic guardsmen given away with cornflakes is interrupted by his local Liberal Party, who want him to stand as their candidate in the East Cheam by-election.

11 1-4-58 TLO 52226 **HANCOCK'S CAR**
(30-3-58) (with Alan Simpson)
Hancock's car has been parked outside his house for ten years—to the annoyance of the Council, who haven't been able to resurface the road in that time.

12 8-4-58 TLO 53529 **THE EAST CHEAM DRAMA FESTIVAL**
(23-2-58) (with Kathleen O'Hagan—piano)
The cast perform three short plays—'Jack's Return Home', 'Look Back in Hunger', and 'The Life of Ludwig Van Beethoven and the Songs that Made him Famous'.

13 15-4-58 TLO 52835 **THE FOREIGN LEGION**
(6-4-58) Hancock is booked to entertain the troops in Malta, but is diverted by Sid, and unwittingly joins the French Foreign Legion.

212

14	22-4-58	TLO 53939 (20-4-58)	SUNDAY AFTERNOON AT HOME 23 Railway Cuttings is a scene of boredom and inactivity as the occupants try to while away a British Sunday.
15	29-4-58	TLO 54577 (27-4-58)	THE GRAPPLING GAME Sid is now promoting all-in wrestling, and discovers a new champion—Miss Pugh.
16	6-5-58	TLO 54871 (4-5-58)	THE JUNK MAN While having a tidy-up, Miss Pugh sells rag-and-bone-man Sid James some of Hancock's treasured heirlooms. Hancock is determined to get them back . . .
17	13-5-58	TLO 54948 (11-5-58)	HANCOCK'S WAR Hancock impresses the Vicar with tales of his exploits in Military Intelligence—including his escape from a prisoner-of-war camp and his arrival in Berlin just before the Russians.
18	20-5-58	TLO 55393 (18-5-58)	THE PRIZE MONEY (with Alan Simpson, Patricia Hayes and Christina Horniman) Hancock wins £4,000 in a television quiz. Sid immediately makes plans to relieve him of it—with the aid of two 'deserted wives'.
19	27-5-58	TLO 55573 (25-5-58)	THE THREATENING LETTERS (with Alan Simpson) Hancock receives several anonymous letters threatening his life; failing to get any help from the police, he barricades himself in his house . . .
20	3-6-58	TLO 56291 (1-6-58)	THE SLEEPLESS NIGHT Hancock intends to get a good night's sleep, but events—and the other occupants of the house—keep him awake all night.

'HANCOCK'S HALF-HOUR': RADIO SPECIALS
CHRISTMAS SPECIAL
Tony Hancock, Sidney James, Bill Kerr, Hattie Jacques and Warren Mitchell.
Produced by Tom Ronald.
Christmas Day at 1630, repeated Boxing Day at 1430 LP.

| SP | 25-12-58 | TLO 74408 (7-12-58) | BILL AND FATHER CHRISTMAS
Bill's belief in Father Christmas is shattered when he discovers Hancock dressing up on Christmas Eve. He is so upset that, on a doctor's instructions, the others have to recreate his childhood Christmases in Australia. |

SPECIAL RE-MAKE SERIES FOR TRANSCRIPTION SERVICES
Tony Hancock, Sidney James, Bill Kerr, Hattie Jacques and Kenneth Williams.
Produced by Tom Ronald.
Sundays at 1830, no repeats. Both Broadcasting House and Transcription Services tape numbers are given. The series is numbered in the actual order of recording and transmission, rather than the order originally planned and followed in the Transcription Services issues.

TS1	4-1-59	TLO 73628	THE 13TH OF THE MONTH
		TTU 2250	(re-make of 'The 13th of the Series', 13th of 4th series.
		(23-11-58)	The script is re-written so that the plot does not hinge round the show being number 13 of a series as broadcast.)
TS2	11-1-59	TLO 73629	THE NEW SECRETARY
		TTU 2251	(remake of the 5th of the 4th series; Hattie Jacques's arrival
		(23-11-58)	is presented in flashback, again so that the show can be placed anywhere in a series.)
TS3	18-1-59	TLO 71337	THE BALLET VISIT
		TTU 2254	(re-make of 'The Bolshoi Ballet', 2nd of the 4th series;
		(30-11-58)	the ballet company in question is changed to the Covent Garden Ballet, in order to avoid the topical references to the Bolshoi's 1956 visit, and the script goes into less detail as to where in central London the queue extends to.)
TS4	25-1-59	TLO 73630	THE ELECTION CANDIDATE
		TTU 2253	(re-make of the 10th of the 5th series; instead of standing
		(30-11-58)	for the East Cheam Liberal Party Hancock stands for the local Independent Party.)

'HANCOCK'S HALF-HOUR': RADIO, 6th SERIES

Tony Hancock, Sidney James and Bill Kerr (except no. 13).
Produced by Tom Ronald.
Tuesdays at 2000, repeated Sundays at 1830, LP. No. 13 also repeated at 1310 on Friday 29-12-59, HS.

1	29-9-59	TLO 87609	THE SMUGGLERS
		(7-6-59)	(with Kenneth Williams, Patricia Hayes and Noel Dryden)
			Returning on the cross-Channel ferry from a Continental holiday, Sid inveigles Hancock and Bill into attempting to smuggle some watches into the country for him.
2	6-10-59	TLO 87610	THE CHILDHOOD SWEETHEART
		(7-6-59)	(with Kenneth Williams and Patricia Hayes)
			Twenty-five years ago Hancock made a pact with his childhood sweetheart to meet at the café where they parted. Sid and Bill accompany him as he waits for his Olive . . .
3	13-10-59	TLO 88801	THE LAST BUS HOME
		(14-6-59)	(with Warren Mitchell and Hugh Morton)
			Hancock, Sid and Bill have been to the cinema. They are unable to get on the last bus home, and are faced with a walk of several miles—just as it starts to rain.
4	20-10-59	TLO 88800	THE PICNIC
		(10-6-59)	(with Wilfred Babbage, Patricia Hayes, Anne Lancaster and Elizabeth Fraser)
			The three go out for a picnic with three birds they have picked up the previous evening at the local Palais.
5	27-10-59	TLO 88802	THE GOURMET
		(14-6-59)	(with Warren Mitchell, Hugh Morton and Raymond

Glendenning)
Hancock fancies himself as a gourmet—so Sid enters him for an eating competition.

6   3-11-59   TLO 88804   THE ELOPEMENT
                (18-6-59)   (with Lillian Grasson, Wilfred Babbage, Fraser Kerr and Leigh Crutchley)
                             Bill has fallen in love with a rich girl whose father won't allow him to marry her. Hancock and Sid arrange an elopement.

7   10-11-59   TLO 88803   FRED'S PIE STALL
                (17-6-59)   (with Wilfred Babbage, Hugh Morton and Harry Towb)
                             Fred's Pie Stall, which has stood in Cheam square for sixty years, is threatened with closure by the council—until Hancock sets out to save it . . .

8   17-11-59   TLO 88758   THE WAXWORK
                (21-6-59)   (with Warren Mitchell)
                             Madame Tussaud's want to make a waxwork of Hancock, but Sid has a better idea—to make one themselves.

9   24-11-59   TLO 88759   SID'S MYSTERY TOURS
                (21-6-59)   (with Warren Mitchell, Errol McKinnon and Mavis Villers)
                             Sid talks Hancock into becoming the director of his guided tours company—which doesn't even own a coach.

10   1-12-59   TLO 88760   THE FETE
                (24-6-59)   (with Wilfred Babbage, Jack Watson and Hugh Morton)
                             As a member of the Council, Hancock rashly agrees to persuade Sir Laurence Olivier to open the East Cheam Garden Fête.

11   8-12-59   TLO 88761   THE POETRY SOCIETY
                (25-6-59)   (with Fenella Fielding, Fraser Kerr and Warren Mitchell)
                             A poetry evening with a group of Hancock's new avant-garde friends produces gems of abstract poetry, not only from the group but from Sid and Bill.

12   15-12-59   TLO 98294   HANCOCK IN HOSPITAL
                (28-6-59)   (with Patricia Hayes and Joan Frank)
                             In hospital with a broken leg, Hancock is visited by Sid and Bill—and wishes he'd been left alone.

13   22-12-59   TLO 3183   THE CHRISTMAS CLUB
                (6-12-59)   (without Bill Kerr; with Hugh Morton, Wilfred Babbage and Frank Partington)
                             When Sid accidentally gives the slate club money to the Police Benevolent Fund, he and Hancock face a Christmas of starvation.

14   29-12-59   TLO 89293   THE IMPERSONATOR
                (28-6-59)   (with Anne Lancaster, Peter Goodwright, Ronald

215

Wilson, Jerry Stovin, Wilfred Babbage and Jack Watson)
Hancock's pretensions as a serious actor are undermined
by a TV commercial for cornflakes which uses an
imitation of his voice—so he takes the impersonator to
court.

'HANCOCK'S HALF-HOUR'—RADIO REPEATS

Key to networks: HS = Home Service (London Home Service plus all regions for most
transmissions); LP = Light Programme; R2 = Radio 2; R4 = Radio 4.
Programmes are identified by series/number reference and title.
Normal in-series repeats are not listed here (see series pages).
No titles given in *Radio Times* up to 1971.

Wednesdays, HS at 1900, except last two at 1855.

24- 8-55	2/5	The Holiday Camp
31- 8-55	2/6	The Chef that Died of Shame
7- 9-55	2/7	Prime Minister Hancock
14- 9-55	2/11	The Marrow Contest
21- 9-55	2/9	The Television Set
28- 9-55	2/10	The Three Sons
5-10-55	2/12	The Matador
12-10-55	1/6	The New Car

Mondays, HS at 1900, except 18-6-56 at 1830.

5- 3-56	3/1	The Pet Dog
12- 3-56	3/2	The Jewel Robbery
19- 3-56	3/3	The Bequest
26- 3-56	3/4	The New Neighbour
2- 4-56	3/6	The Blackboard Jungle
9- 4-56	3/8	The Diet
16- 4-56	3/14	The Student Prince
23- 4-56	(no repeat: 'Music to Remember')	
30- 4-56	3/15	The Breakfast Cereal
7- 5-56	(no repeat: 'Starstruck')	
14- 5-56	3/18	The Greyhound Track
21- 5-56	3/16	How Hancock Won the War*
28- 5-56	3/13	Hancock's Hair
4- 6-56	3/11	Cinderella Hancock
11- 6-56	3/16	How Hancock Won the War*
18- 6-56	3/19	The Conjurer
25- 6-56	3/20	The Test Match

* number 16 really did go out twice, due to a misunderstanding of instructions from Dennis Main
Wilson altering the running order. It had been intended that 3/9 (A Visit to Russia) should be
broadcast on 21-5-56.

Saturdays, HS at 1310

6-7-57	4/1	Back from Holiday
13-7-57	4/2	The Bolshoi Ballet
20-7-57	4/3	Sid James's Dad
27-7-57	4/4	The Income Tax Demand
3-8-57	4/5	The New Secretary
10-8-57	4/9	The Stolen Petrol
17-8-57	4/8	Cyrano de Hancock

24-8-57	4/17	Agricultural 'Ancock
31-8-57	4/7	Anna and the King of Siam
7-9-57	4/10	The Expresso Bar
14-9-57	4/12	The Diary
21-9-57	4/14	Almost a Gentleman
28-9-57	4/13	The 13th of the Series

Series continues on Wednesdays, HS at 1310

2-10-57	4/15	The Old School Re-union
9-10-57	4/20	The Last of the McHancocks
16-10-57	4/6	Michelangelo 'Ancock
23-10-57	4/18	Hancock in the Police
30 10 57	4/16	The Wild Man of the Woods
6-11-57	4/19	The Emigrant

Saturdays, HS at 1310: re-run of the entire 5th series, in order apart from numbers 1 and 2 (for titles see main series pages).

12-7-58	5/2	30- 8-58	5/8	18-10-58	5/15
19-7-58	5/1	6- 9-58	5/9	25-10-58	5/16
26-7-58	5/3	13- 9-58	5/10	1-11-58	5/17
2-8-58	5/4	20- 9-58	5/11	8-11-58	5/18
9-8-58	5/5	27- 9-58	5/12	15-11-58	5/19
16-8-58	5/6	4-10-58	5/13	22-11-58	5/20
23-8-58	5/7	11-10-58	5/14		

Mondays, LP at 2100

6-7-59	4/17	Agricultural 'Ancock
13-7-59	4/16	The Wild Man of the Woods
20-7-59	4/12	The Diary
27-7-59	5/12	The East Cheam Drama Festival
3-8-59	5/9	The Americans Hit Town

In series 'The Best of the Best', LP at 1931, Monday
| 24-8-59 | 5/14 | Sunday Afternoon at Home |

Saturdays, HS at 1310: re-run of entire 6th series, except no. 13.

23-1-60	6/1	20-2-60	6/5	19-3-60	6/9
30-1-60	6/2	27-2-60	6/6	26-3-60	6/10
6-2-60	6/3	5-3-60	6/7	2-4-60	6/11
6-2-60	6/3	5-3-60	6/7	2-4-60	6/11
13-2-60	6/4	12-3-60	6/8	9-4-60	6/12
				16-4-60	6/14

In series 'The Best of the Best', LP at 1415, Sunday
| 24-7-60 | 6/12 | Hancock in Hospital |

Fridays, HS at 2130

30-12-60	5/6	The Unexploded Bomb
6- 1-61	5/20	The Sleepless Night
13- 1-61	6/3	The Last Bus Home
20- 1-61	6/11	The Poetry Society
27- 1-61	6/10	The Fête
3- 2-61	6/12	Hancock in Hospital

Fridays, LP at 2031

| 4-8-61 | 4/7 | Anna and the King of Siam |
| 11-8-61 | 5/10 | The Election Candidate |

18-8-61	4/8	Cyrano de Hancock
25-8-61	6/11	The Poetry Society
1-9-61	4/13	The 13th of the Series
8-9-61	4/18	Hancock in the Police

HS	1310	Saturday	20-10-62	6/12	Hancock in Hospital
HS	1930	Christmas	25-12-62	SP	Bill and Father Christmas
HS	1340	Easter Mon.	15- 4-63	5/11	Hancock's Car
HS	1225	Boxing Day	26-12-63	6/13	The Christmas Club

Tuesdays, HS at 2100

4-2-64	5/5	The Publicity Photograph
11-2-64	5/8	Around the World in Eighty Days
18-2-64	5/1	The New Radio Series
25-2-64	5/2	The Scandal Magazine
3-3-64	5/6	The Unexploded Bomb
10-3-64	5/3	The Male Suffragettes
17-3-64	5/4	The Insurance Policy
24-3-64	5/7	Hancock's School

Saturdays, HS at 1930

29-8-64	4/18	Hancock in the Police
5-9-64	4/20	The Last of the McHancocks
12-9-64	6/11	The Poetry Society

In series 'Vintage Show Time', LP at 2130, Sunday

8-11-64	4/17	Agricultural 'Ancock

In series 'Let's Laugh Again', HS at 2130, Friday

23-7-65	5/19	The Threatening Letters

HS at 1150, Spring Bank Holiday Monday

29-5-67	6/12	Hancock in Hospital

R2, 1400 Sunday with a repeat at 2045 on Monday

16-2-69 } 17-2-69 }	4/20	The Last of the McHancocks
23-2-69 } 24-2-69 }	4/18	Hancock in the Police
2-3-69 } 3-3-69 }	6/2	The Childhood Sweetheart
9-3-69 } 10-3-69 }	5/17	Hancock's War
16-3-69 } 17-3-69 }	4/14	Almost a Gentleman
23-3-69 } 24-3-69 }	4/8	Cyrano de Hancock
30-3-69 } 31-3-69 }	5/9	The Americans Hit Town

From this point, most repeats are given titles in *Radio Times*, although they frequently do not tally with the titles which have been chosen for this book. Billed titles are given in brackets; if no bracketed title is given then the title billed agrees with the title given here. Those shows not billed by title are indicated.

R4	1345	Easter Mon	12- 4-71	5/14	Sunday Afternoon at Home (Sunday Boredom)
R4	1345	Monday	30- 8-71	5/15	The Grappling Game

218

R4	0905	Boxing Day	26-12-71	4/11	Hancock's Happy Christmas (*shortened to 25 minutes*)
R4	1345	Monday	3- 4-72	4/18	Hancock in the Police (Hancock Joins the Police)
R4	1345	Monday	29- 5-72	4/17	Agricultural 'Ancock

From this point, most repeats, which are all taken from Sound Archives copies, are shortened slightly to allow them to fit into a 28 minute slot.

Sundays, R4 at 1900

3-9-72	4/6	Michelangelo 'Ancock
10-9-72	6/9	Sid's Mystery Tours
17-9-72	6/14	The Impersonator (Anthony the Actor)
24-9-72	4/15	The Old School Re-union

In series 'The Great Shows 1938–1963', R2 Sunday 1430, repeated Friday 2002

| 17-12-72 } | 5/19 | The Threatening Letters (*not billed by title: shortened to allow introduction by Ted Ray*) |
| 22-12-72 } | | |

In compilation programme 1030-1300 on Christmas morning, R4

| 25-12-72 | 6/5 | The Gourmet (Hancock the Gourmet) (*abridged to 23′ 32″*) |

In series 'The Late Show' (during TV early closedowns due to the miners' strike); R4 at 2300, Saturday

| 2-2-74 | 4/12 | The Diary (Walter Mitty Hancock) |

Sundays, R4 at 1902

8-12-74	5/11	Hancock's Car (Hancock the Motorist) (*TS version*)
15-12-74	4/8	Cyrano de Hancock
22-12-74	6/13	The Christmas Club (The Christmas Club Hand-out)
29-12-74	1/19	The Emigrant (Emigration Might Help)
5- 1-75	4/14	Almost a Gentleman (How to be Posh and Influence People)
12- 1-75	5/4	The Insurance Policy (The Sidney James Life Insurance Company)

In compilation programme 'Christmas Morning', R4 1030-1255

| 25-12-75 | 6/14 | The Impersonator (*not billed by title*) |

Mondays, R4 at 1817

26- 7-76	6/2	The Childhood Sweetheart (Tony's Childhood Sweetheart)
2- 8-76	5/17	Hancock's War (Tony's War Memoirs)
9- 8-76	6/6	The Elopement (The Love of Bill's Life)
16- 8-76	6/1	The Smugglers (Anything to Declare?)
23- 8-76	5/6	The Unexploded Bomb
30- 8-76	4/4	The Income Tax Demand (Tony and the Taxman)
6- 9-76	5/2	The Scandal Magazine (Tony Exposed)
13- 9-76	5/7	Hancock's School (Professor Hancock)
20- 9-76	5/9	The Americans Hit Town (The US Air Force Comes to Cheam)
27- 9-76	6/9	Sid's Mystery Tours (Sid's Tours of Cheam)
4-10-76	5/19	The Threatening Letters (Tony's Threatening Letter)

Tuesdays, R4 at 2230. (The first three shows are from the TS 27-minute versions, but with the cut sections copied from the original TS 16″ discs and re-instated.) (*Untitled*)

6-9-77	3/2	The Jewel Robbery
13-9-77	3/19	The Conjurer
20-9-77	3/14	The Student Prince
27-9-77	4/20	The Last of the McHancocks

R4 at 2215, Saturday

| 7-1-78 | 4/17 | Agricultural 'Ancock |

'HANCOCK'S HALF-HOUR'—RADIO—SHOWS IN BBC SOUND ARCHIVES

Listed chronologically with series/number reference.

Prefixes: T = tape. LP = pressed long play record. MT = tape from original 16" disc. No prefix = 78 rpm disc. X or MX = 33⅓ rpm coarse groove 16" disc. Some tapes have two shows on them; the shows are identified as (i) or (ii) after the tape number. Three shows are copied from the Transcription Services (TS) master tapes as edited to 26' 30" approx. for the re-issues.

MT 21325	1/6	The New Car (originally X 21325-6)
T 33727(i)	4/1	Back from Holiday
T 33727(ii)	4/4	The Income Tax Demand
T 33728(i)	4/6	Michelangelo 'Ancock
T 33728(ii)	4/8	Cyrano de Hancock
T 33729(i)	4/11	Hancock's Happy Christmas
LP 24991	4/12	The Diary
T 33729(ii)	4/14	Almost a Gentleman
T 33730(i)	4/15	The Old School Re-union
T 28896	4/17	Agricultural 'Ancock
T 28927	4/18	Hancock in the Police
LP 23457	4/19	The Emigrant
T 28926	4/20	The Last of the McHancocks
T 33730(ii)	5/2	The Scandal Magazine
T 33731(i)	5/4	The Insurance Policy
T 33731(ii)	5/6	The Unexploded Bomb (TS version)
T 33732(i)	5/7	Hancock's School (TS version)
T 33732(ii)	5/9	The Americans Hit Town
T 33733(i)	5/11	Hancock's Car (TS version)
LP 25535	5/14	Sunday Afternoon at Home (also on MT 25535)
T 33733(ii)	5/15	The Grappling Game
T 33734(i)	5/17	Hancock's War
T 28894	5/19	The Threatening Letters
T 33734(ii)	6/1	The Smugglers
T 33735(i)	6/2	The Childhood Sweetheart
T 33735(ii)	6/5	The Gourmet
T 33736(i)	6/6	The Elopement
T 33736(ii)	6/9	Sid's Mystery Tours
T 28893	6/11	The Poetry Society
T 28895	6/12	Hancock in Hospital
T 33737(i)	6/13	The Christmas Club
T 33737(ii)	6/14	The Impersonator

Also in Sound Archives:

MT 17237	'Educating Archie'; edition of 19-10-51 (12th of 2nd series)
20284	'Star Bill'—2 sketches from edition of 21-3-54 (4th of 2nd series)
LP 28455	Tony Hancock interviewed in 'That Reminds Me', 16-10-63
LP 25808	'Face To Face': soundtrack of the television transmission of 7-2-60
T 33753	'What Happened to Hancock': documentary programme by Philip Oakes. Recorded 16-11-70; broadcast 2-2-71, R4.
LP 36096	Extracts from 'Unique Hancock', recorded 6-12-73, broadcast 23-12-73, R4.

220

'HANCOCK'S HALF-HOUR' — RADIO — TRANSCRIPTION SERVICES ISSUES

The BBC Transcription Services selected the most suitable shows for issue to overseas radio stations, who can buy the right to use them for a limited period, usually about two years from the date of issue. The shows were issued on pressed gramophone records, as detailed below; these records cannot be made available to the public, for contractual reasons.

The shows are listed numerically as issued, with series/number reference.

ORIGINAL ISSUES drawn from 1st, 2nd and 3rd series; issued on 16" coarse groove 33⅓ rpm discs.

1	1/1	The First Night Party
2	1/3	The Idol
3	1/4	The Boxing Champion
4	1/6	The New Car
5	1/10	Cinderella Hancock
6	1/11	A Trip to France
7	1/12	The Monte Carlo Rally
8	1/13	A House on the Cliff
9	1/14	The Sheikh
10	1/16	The End of the Series
11	3/1	The Pet Dog
12	2/5	The Holiday Camp
13	2/6	The Chef that Died of Shame
14	2/8	The Rail Strike
15	2/9	The Television Set
16	2/11	The Marrow Contest
17	3/3	The Request
18	3/2	The Jewel Robbery
19	3/13	Hancock's Hair
20	3/14	The Student Prince
21	3/18	The Greyhound Track
22	3/19	The Conjurer
23	3/20	The Test Match

ORIGINAL ISSUES drawn from 4th, 5th and 6th series; originally issued on 10" LPs; later re-issued on 12" LPs. Nos 24-50 slightly cut to run between 29' and 29' 50"; nos 51-64 cut to 29' 05" approx.; nos 65-73 cut to a maximum of 28' 06".

24	5/1	The New Radio Series
25	4/10	The Expresso Bar
26	4/12	The Diary
27	4/14	Almost a Gentleman
28	4/16	The Wild Man of the Woods
29	4/17	Agricultural 'Ancock
30	4/20	The Last of the McHancocks
31	5/3	The Male Suffragettes
32	5/4	The Insurance Policy
33	5/5	The Publicity Photograph
34	5/6	The Unexploded Bomb
35	5/7	Hancock's School
36	5/9	The Americans Hit Town
37	5/11	Hancock's Car
38	5/12	The East Cheam Drama Festival
39	5/15	The Grappling Game

40	5/16	The Junk Man
41	5/17	Hancock's War
42	5/14	Sunday Afternoon at Home
43	5/18	The Prize Money
44	TS/1	The 13th of the Month
45	TS/2	The New Secretary
46	TS/4	The Election Candidate
47	TS/3	The Ballet Visit
48	5/19	The Threatening Letters
49	5/20	The Sleepless Night
50	SP	Bill and Father Christmas
51	6/1	The Smugglers
52	6/2	The Childhood Sweetheart
53	6/3	The Last Bus Home
54	6/4	The Picnic
55	6/5	The Gourmet
56	6/6	The Elopement
57	6/7	Fred's Pie Stall
58	6/8	The Waxwork
59	6/9	Sid's Mystery Tours
60	6/10	The Fête
61	6/11	The Poetry Society
62	6/12	Hancock in Hospital
63	6/14	The Impersonator
64	6/13	The Christmas Club
65	4/1	Back from Holiday
66	4/4	The Income Tax Demand
67	4/6	Michelangelo 'Ancock
68	4/8	Cyrano de Hancock
69	4/15	The Old School Re-union
70	4/18	Hancock in the Police
71	5/2	The Scandal Magazine
72	5/13	The Foreign Legion
73	4/11	Hancock's Happy Christmas

RE-ISSUES—'HANCOCK'S HALF-HOUR' *CN 887*

12″ LPs; all edited to 26′ 20″ with no playout.

1	4/14	Almost a Gentleman
2	4/17	Agricultural 'Ancock
3	4/1	Back from Holiday
4	4/4	The Income Tax Demand
5	4/6	Michelangelo 'Ancock
6	4/8	Cyrano de Hancock
7	4/15	The Old School Re-union
8	4/18	Hancock in the Police
9	4/20	The Last of the McHancocks
10	5/2	The Scandal Magazine
11	5/4	The Insurance Policy
12	5/6	The Unexploded Bomb
13	5/7	Hancock's School
14	5/9	The Americans Hit Town
15	5/11	Hancock's Car
16	5/15	The Grappling Game
17	5/17	Hancock's War

18	TS/2	The New Secretary
19	6/1	The Smugglers
20	6/2	The Childhood Sweetheart
21	6/5	The Gourmet
22	6/6	The Elopement
23	6/9	Sid's Mystery Tours
24	6/11	The Poetry Society
25	6/12	Hancock in Hospital
26	6/14	The Impersonator
27	4/11	Hancock's Happy Christmas
28	6/13	The Christmas Club

RE-ISSUES—'EARLY HANCOCK' *CN 1985*

12" LPs; taken from the 16" discs, with a considerable amount of work going into clearing up the surface noise. All except no. 5 have the opening bars of the signature tune (as far as the beginning of the announcement) dubbed on from a later recording (using the different orchestration) so that the remaining surface noise does not start until the announcement. All edited to 27′ 00″ (nominally), with no playout.

1	1/3	The Idol
2	1/6	The New Car
3	1/11	A Trip to France
4	1/13	A House on the Cliff
5	2/8	The Rail Strike
6	2/9	The Television Set
7	2/11	The Marrow Contest
8	3/3	The Bequest
9	3/2	The Jewel Robbery
10	3/13	Hancock's Hair
11	3/14	The Student Prince
12	3/18	The Greyhound Track
13	3/19	The Conjurer

'HANCOCK'S HALF-HOUR': BBC TELEVISION

The sixth series under the title 'Hancock's Half-Hour', and the seventh, under the title 'Hancock', are listed here with dates of first transmission, original recording numbers (where applicable), recording dates (in bracket below the recording numbers), titles, and a brief synopsis of each show.

Since the casts for most shows are comparatively large, they have been listed together after the series listing.

A few of the earlier programmes were given titles in *Radio Times*; the 5th, 6th, and 7th series, though not titled in *Radio Times*, have acquired semi-official titles, probably by virtue of their being issued by Television Enterprises for overseas use. Where necessary I have invented titles.

All programmes were first broadcast on BBC-TV (this was before there was a second channel) on days and at times listed in the series headings. All programmes were produced by Duncan Wood; scripts written by Alan Simpson and Ray Galton. Theme music composed by Wally Stott.

The series and cast lists are followed by details of repeat showings, and by a list of the programmes still held in BBC Film Library (which includes the BBC Enterprises copies). The original video tapes (which were on the old 405-line standard) have been destroyed.

'HANCOCK'S HALF-HOUR': BBC-TV, 1st SERIES

Fortnightly: Fridays at 2130, except no. 1 at 2045.

1   6-7-56   live   **THE FIRST TV SHOW**
Hancock's first TV Show is jeopardized by his broken leg, but Sid insists that the show must go on—and arranges a transmission from Hancock's hospital bed.
(cast list on page 232)

2   20-7-56   live   **THE ARTIST**
Up-and-coming artist Hancock buys some old canvases to paint over, little realizing that one of them is a stolen Rembrandt. Sid's 'fence' is forced to buy all Hancock's paintings in an attempt to retrieve the Rembrandt.
(cast list on page 232)

3   3-8-56   live   **THE DANCER**
Hancock is offered a part in a film—provided that he can dance. Sid arranges lessons, and Hancock enters for a dancing Championship Contest—with Sid (in drag) as his partner.
(cast list on page 232)

4   17-8-56   live   **THE BEQUEST**
Hancock is left a fortune by his Uncle Obadiah, on condition that he gets married. With the help of the Sid James Marriage Bureau, he starts looking for a wife.
(Based on the radio programme, 3rd of 3rd series).
(cast list on page 232)

5   31-8-56   live   **THE RADIO SHOW**
From the National Radio Show at Earl's Court. Several sketches, including the British answer to the Red Army Choir.
(cast list on page 233)

6   14-9-56   live   **THE CHEF THAT DIED OF SHAME**
The story of the pie-stall cook who rises to the heights of haute cuisine and falls again through drink. (Re-make of the radio programme, 6th of 2nd series).
(cast list on page 233)

'HANCOCK'S HALF-HOUR': BBC-TV, 2nd SERIES

Fortnightly: Mondays at 2000

1   1-4-57   live   **THE ALPINE HOLIDAY**
After an argumentative flight, Hancock has to dispute possession of his hotel room with an attractive French girl; and then finds himself sharing a room with a yodeller and an Alpine Horn player.
(cast list on page 233)

2   15-4-57   live   **LADY CHATTERLEY'S REVENGE**
The East Cheam Repertory Company gives Hancock a small part in 'Moon Over Tahiti'—and then omits to inform him when the play is changed to 'Lady Chatterley's Revenge'.
(cast list on page 233)

3	29-4-57	live	**THE RUSSIAN PRINCE**

Suffering from temporary amnesia after a bump on the head, Hancock is persuaded by Sid that he is Prince Nicolai, the last heir of the Russian Royal Family's fortune. However, he is not the only claimant . . .
(cast list on page 233)

4	13-5-57	live	**THE NEW NEIGHBOUR**

The new next-door neighbour has Hancock worried—he keeps on bringing in bodies and dumping them in the incinerator. In fact, he melts down old wax-works to make new ones; but Hancock is determined to investigate . . . (Re-make of the radio programme, 4th of 3rd series.)
(cast list on page 234)

5	27-5-57	live	**THE PIANIST**

Hancock dreams that his job as a night-club pianist leads him into a romance with a foreign Baroness—and a duel with her fiancée.
(cast list on page 234)

6	10-6-57 (Whit Monday)	live	**THE AUCTION**

Sid and Hancock auction off their property in order to go to Monte Carlo to try out Sid's infallible roulette system. Then they discover that their stuffed eagle had been stuffed with banknotes . . .
(cast list on page 234)

'HANCOCK'S HALF-HOUR': BBC-TV, 3rd SERIES

Mondays at 2002-2030, except no. 12, 2002-2045

1	30-9-57	live	**THE CONTINENTAL HOLIDAY**

Hancock tells Sid the story of his eventful holiday abroad, in which he foiled an international gang of smugglers.
(cast list on page 234)

2	7-10-57	live	**THE GREAT DETECTIVE**

Hancock dreams of being 'Sexton Hancock', unravelling a complicated murder mystery.
(cast list on page 234)

3	14-10-57	live	**THE AMUSEMENT ARCADE**

Hancock leads an Anti-Vice Campaign to close down Sid's amusement arcade. Sid tries to prevent Hancock's election to the Council, and then—when he *is* closed down—moves his arcade—to Hancock's house.
(cast list on page 235)

4	21-10-57	live	**A HOLIDAY IN SCOTLAND**

Under Doctor's orders to get fit, Hancock drags an unwilling Sid on a hunting holiday in Scotland—where they get snowed in.
(cast list on page 235)

5　28-10-57　live　　**AIR STEWARD HANCOCK, THE LAST OF THE MANY**
Hancock's first flight as air steward is nearly his last—his passengers include four policemen looking for a bank robber, and Sid, who has hidden his loot in Hancock's briefcase.
(cast list on page 235)

6　4-11-57　live　　**THE REGIMENTAL REUNION**
Hancock, permanent junior clerk in a City office for 19 years, is promoted when his Army friends, met at a reunion, place large orders with the firm. Unfortunately, they are all frauds—and Sid has the takings . . .
(cast list on page 235)

7　11-11-57　live　　**THE ADOPTED FAMILY**
Hancock has to produce a wife and four children to get to the top of the list for a Council House—so he adopts Sid and four of Sid's mates—and then can't get rid of them.
(cast list on page 235)

　　18-11-57　　　　Programme postponed and replaced with a telerecording of 1st of 2nd series (THE ALPINE HOLIDAY) on 35/INT/3121. Introduced by Sidney James.

8　25-11-57　live　　**THE ELOCUTION TEACHER**
(postponed from 18-11-57)
Under Hancock's tuition, Jack Hawkins sinks from famous actor to the leader of a rock-and-roll group.
(cast list on page 236)

9　2-12-57　live　　**THE LAWYER: THE CROWN v JAMES S.: HANCOCK QC DEFENDING**
Hancock's impassioned plea for the innocence of an obviously guilty Sidney James results in a verdict of James—innocent; Hancock—guilty.
(cast list on page 236)

10　9-12-57　live　　**HOW TO WIN MONEY AND INFLUENCE PEOPLE**
Hancock has entered—and won—a number of newspaper competitions. However, Sid volunteers to look after the money—and Hancock is foolish enough to let him . . .
(cast list on page 236)

11　16-12-57　live　　**THERE'S AN AIRFIELD AT THE BOTTOM OF MY GARDEN**
Sid has sold Hancock a house on the edge of an airfield. Hancock is dissatisfied, and when Sid refuses to refund his money, tries to sell the house—against considerable difficulties (some of them unscripted!).
(cast list on page 236)

12　23-12-57　live　　**HANCOCK'S 43 MINUTES—THE EAST CHEAM REPERTORY COMPANY**
A special show from the Television Theatre, including a

dramatic rendering of 'The Three Musketeers'.
(cast list on page 236)

'HANCOCK'S HALF-HOUR': BBC-TV, 4th SERIES
Fridays at 2105 (1-3) and 1930 (4-13)

1 26-12-58 35/T/5100   ERICSON THE VIKING
   (16-12-58)   Hancock is worried about the first show of his new TV
                         series—and with good reason, as Sid has starred him in a
                         tattily made film about the Vikings.
                         (cast list on page 236)

2 2- 1-59 35/T/5099   UNDERPAID!, OR, GRANDAD'S SOS
   (2-12-58)   Hancock's millionaire grandfather is dangerously ill in
                        Australia. In anticipation of a large bequest, Sid goes to
                        Australia masquerading as Hancock, only to find that the
                        old man has no money left. Meanwhile, Sid's grandfather
                        is dangerously ill in prison . . .
                        (cast list on page 237)

3 9- 1-59 35/T/5098   THE SET THAT FAILED
   (18-11-58)   Hancock's TV set has broken down. Appalled at the idea
                        of a TV-less evening, he and Sid try various ruses,
                        including joining a family who are so intent on their TV
                        that they don't notice the intruders.
                        (cast list on page 237)

4 16- 1-59 35/T/5101 THE NEW NOSE
   (23-12-58)   Hancock's success with the girls is hampered by his
                        nose—or so he thinks. Humiliated, he barricades himself
                        in the house—until Sid suggests plastic surgery.
                        (cast list on page 237)

5 23- 1-59 live   THE FLIGHT OF THE RED SHADOW
                        With 'The Desert Song' closed prematurely, and the cast
                        after them for money, Hancock and Sid escape with only
                        their theatrical costumes. Disguised as an Indian
                        Maharajah, Hancock is mistaken for a genuine visiting
                        Maharajah, and finds himself addressing a meeting.
                        (cast list on page 237)

6 30- 1-59 live   THE HORROR SERIAL
                        In a nervous state after watching the last episode of
                        'Quatermass and the Pit' on TV, Hancock discovers a
                        strange object buried in his garden. Sid calls in the Army
                        Bomb Disposal Squad, but Hancock is convinced that it
                        is a Martian spaceship.
                        (cast list on page 237)

7 6- 2-59 live   THE ITALIAN MAID
                        Hancock hires an Italian maid, who turns out to be such a
                        beauty that an immediate rivalry develops between him
                        and Sid. Hancock finishes up doing all the housework for
                        her—and then her family arrives . . .
                        (cast list on page 238)

227

| 8 | 13-2-59 | live | **MATRIMONY—ALMOST** |

Hancock meets a girl at a pyjama party arranged by Sid for some upper-class twits. He thinks she has money, and Sid tells her that Hancock has money—and so a marriage is rapidly arranged . . .
(cast list on page 238)

| 9 | 20-2-59 | live | **THE BEAUTY CONTEST** |

Deterred from holding a beauty contest by the low standard of entrants, the East Cheam Council decides to hold a 'Mr East Cheam' contest instead. Hancock and Sid both see themselves as natural winners.
(cast list on page 238)

| | 27-2-59 | |

Programme postponed and replaced with a repeat of no. 3 of this series (THE SET THAT FAILED) on 35/T/5098.

| 10 | 6-3-59 | live | **THE WRONG MAN** |

(postponed from 27-2-59)
Hancock agrees to take part in an identity parade—and is picked out by three witnesses as the man who robbed a tobacconist's. Protesting his innocence, he sets about finding the real thief.
(cast list on page 238)

| 11 | 13-3-59 | live | **THE OAK TREE** |

Hancock's pride and joy—the oak tree in his garden—is threatened with removal. He organizes a protest march, and then a local demonstration to save it.
(cast list on page 238)

| 12 | 20-3-59 | live | **THE KNIGHTHOOD** |

Hancock is determined to get a knighthood, and takes up a career as a Shakespearian actor—interpreting all his parts in the style of Long John Silver. His goal—the Old Vic.
(cast list on page 239)

| 13 | 27-3-59 | live |
| | (Good Friday) | |

THE SERVANTS
The TV series is over, and Hancock and Sid need jobs. They dress up as an elderly couple to get a job as servants; but when they start to take it in turns to be the woman, their employers get suspicious . . .
(cast list on page 239)

'HANCOCK'S HALF-HOUR': BBC-TV, 5th SERIES

Fridays at 2030, except no. 3, at 2045

| 1 | 25-9-59 | T/M/6480 | **THE ECONOMY DRIVE** |
| | (4-9-59) | |

Returning from holiday to find that Sid has left every electrical appliance in the house running, forgotten to cancel the papers and the milk and left the car ticking over, Hancock embarks on an economy drive that leads him into difficulties in a self-service cafeteria.
(cast list on page 239)

228

| 2 | 2-10-59 | T/M/6482 (18-9-59) | **THE TWO MURDERERS** |

2   2-10-59   T/M/6482   **THE TWO MURDERERS**
             (18-9-59)   Hancock refuses to lend Sid the money to open a fish and
                         chip shop. When he sees Sid reading a book about perfect
                         murders he assumes that Sid is out to murder him for his
                         money and manages to give Sid the impression that it is
                         Sid whose life is in danger.
                         (cast list on page 239)

3   9-10-59   T/M/6483   **LORD BYRON LIVED HERE**
             (25-9-59)   The Council will renovate Hancock's dilapidated house
                         only if somebody famous once lived there—so Sidney
                         scribbles some doggerel on the walls where he has
                         stripped the wallpaper off and convinces Hancock that
                         they were written by Byron. The National Trust are not
                         so easily convinced, so Hancock opens his house to the
                         public.
                         (cast list on page 239)

4   16-10-59 VT/T/6484 **TWELVE ANGRY MEN**
             (2-10-59)   Hancock stands out against his fellow jurors in believing
                         a petty criminal innocent. Sid, attracted by the daily
                         payment to jurors, joins him, and they set about
                         browbeating the others.
                         (cast list on page 239)

5   23-10-59 T/M/6481   **THE TRAIN JOURNEY**
             (11-9-59)   Hancock's fellow passengers on the train to Giggleswick
                         quickly get irritated by his efforts to enliven the long
                         journey.
                         (cast list on page 240)

6   30-10-59 T/M/6485   **THE CRUISE**
             (23-10-59) Already fed up with his cruise because the only woman
                         showing any interest in him is large and over-amorous,
                         Hancock wrongly believes the ship is sinking, panics, and
                         has to be locked up by the Captain. Escaping, he and Sid
                         attend the fancy dress ball. So does the amorous lady.
                         (cast list on page 240)

7   6-11-59   VT/T/6486 **THE BIG NIGHT**
             (30-10-59) Hancock's Saturday night out with Sid is an unmitigated
                         disaster—the launderette tears his shirt to pieces, the
                         barber cuts his face to ribbons, the girls Sid has provided
                         disappear at the sight of Hancock, and they get thrown
                         out of the local cinema.
                         (cast list on page 240)

8   13-11-59 VT/T/6487 **THE TYCOON**
             (6-11-59)   Hancock's shares have plummeted in value—all except
                         the East Cheam Building Society. Attending their
                         shareholders' meeting, Hancock falls asleep and dreams
                         that he owns half the world; but even in his dreams, Sid
                         twists him.
                         (cast list on page 240)

9 20-11-59 T/M/6488   SPANISH INTERLUDE
            (14-11-59)   The only work Sid can find for Hancock is standing in
                         national dress outside various foreign restaurants.
                         Deciding to try fresh fields, they go to Spain—where,
                         after an unsuccessful attempt as a night-club comic,
                         Hancock becomes a reluctant bullfighter.
                         (cast list on page 241)

10 27-11-59 VT/T/6489   FOOTBALL POOLS
            (23-11-59)   Hancock needs only one more draw for a first dividend—
                         and the match is a local one with a late kick-off. He and
                         Sid go to the match—to encourage each side equally.
                         (cast list on page 241)

'HANCOCK'S HALF-HOUR': BBC-TV, 6th SERIES

Fridays at 2030, except nos 8-10 at 1930

1   4-3-60   VT/T/7483   THE COLD
            (19-2-60)   In desperation with his sixth cold of the winter, Hancock
                         tries a variety of patent medicines, a local 'witch', a
                         doctor—who has a cold himself—and, at Sid's in-
                         stigation, a keep-fit course.
                         (cast list on page 241)

2   11-3-60 VT/T/7493   THE MISSING PAGE
            (26-2-60)   Hancock is reading a murder mystery from the library—
                         but the last page is missing. After keeping Sid up all night
                         trying to work out 'who done it', he determines to track
                         down a complete copy . . .
                         (cast list on page 241)

3   18-3-60 VT/T/7473   THE EMIGRANT
            (12-2-60)   Hancock wants to emigrate, but no-one will have him.
                         Sid gets him a passage on a disreputable tramp steamer,
                         telling the crew to dump him at the first bit of land they
                         see. (This show is not based on the radio script of the
                         same title).
                         (cast list on page 241)

4   25-3-60 VT/T/7519   THE REUNION PARTY
            (4-3-60)   Hancock has planned a 'fifteen years after' reunion with
                         his wartime Army friends, but times change—and so do
                         people.
                         (cast list on page 242)

5   1-4-60   VT/T/7547   SID IN LOVE
            (18-3-60)   Sid has fallen in love with a clippie on the 93 bus route.
                         Hancock's efforts to help cause chaos, and upset both the
                         clippie and the driver—her husband.
                         (cast list on page 242)

6   8-4-60   VT/T/7551   THE BABY SITTERS
            (25-3-60)   Hancock and Sid are employed as baby sitters in a plush
                         modern house. After raiding the larder, arguing over the
                         television, and failing to soothe the baby, they go to
                         sleep—and so don't notice a visit from two burglars.
                         (cast list on page 242)

230

7   15-4-60   VT/T/7689   THE LADIES' MAN
(Good Friday) (1-4-60)   Hancock's total lack of success with women leads him to take a charm school course. We see his daydreams of what life will be like when he has completed the course—but the reality is somewhat less satisfactory . . .
(cast list on page 242)

8   22-4-60   VT/T/7924   THE PHOTOGRAPHER
(15-4-60)   Having broken his ancient camera, Hancock invests in an expensive array of new equipment. His attempts at candid photography get him thrown out of a restaurant; and then Sid talks him into posing for a 'news' photo—on a high ledge . . .
(cast list on page 242)

9   29-4-60   VT/T/7927   THE EAST CHEAM CENTENARY
(22-4-60)   The Council decides to celebrate the centenary by holding a carnival. Hancock sells exclusive coverage to the BBC—but the Mayor has sold exclusive coverage to ITV. Hancock has to provide his own carnival at short notice.
(cast list on page 242)

10   6-5-60   VT/T/7943   THE POISON PEN LETTERS
(29-4-60)   Hancock is most upset by a succession of unpleasant letters. He calls in the police, but eventually Sid discovers that Hancock is writing the letters himself—in his sleep.
(cast list on page 243)

'HANCOCK': BBC-TV, 7th SERIES

Fridays at 2000; 25 minutes (hence the change in the series title)

1   26-5-61   VT/T/11129 THE BEDSITTER (HANCOCK ALONE)
(5-5-61)   Alone in his Earl's Court bed-sittingroom, Hancock tries to read, fails to get the TV working, and almost gets invited to a party.
(cast list on page 243)

2   2-6-61   VT/T/11183 THE BOWMANS
(26-5-61)   Hancock plays 'Old Joshua Merryweather' in a radio series which sounds suspiciously like 'The Archers'—until his behaviour causes him to be written out of the script. He turns to doing TV commercials—until the listeners demand the return of 'Old Joshua'.
(cast list on page 243)

3   9-6-61   VT/T/11133 THE RADIO HAM (MAYDAY)
(19-5-61)   Hancock exchanges comments on the weather and plays chess with remote parts of the world, but when he intercepts a distress call events conspire to prevent him arranging a rescue.
(cast list on page 243)

4   16-6-61   VT/T/11131 THE LIFT (GOING DOWN)
(12-5-61)   Hancock is the ninth passenger in a lift which is designed to carry eight. When the lift sticks between floors, and

stays there all night, his attempts to cheer everybody up are not appreciated by the others.
(cast list on page 243)

5   23-6-61   VT/T/11186 THE BLOOD DONOR
         (2-6-61)   Hancock's sense of public duty leads him to give blood—although he is alarmed when he discovers that he is expected to part with as much as a pint.
                    (cast list on page 243)

6   30-6-61   VT/T/11318 THE SUCCESSION—SON AND HEIR
         (9-6-61)   Deciding that he needs children to carry on his line, Hancock proposes to three girls—and gets three refusals. He is still arguing with the third when the other two return, having changed their minds.
                    (cast list on page 243)

'HANCOCK'S HALF-HOUR' AND 'HANCOCK'—BBC-TV: CAST LISTS

Tony Hancock present in all shows; Sidney James present in all shows except 1st and 2nd of 2nd series, and whole of 7th series: they are therefore not included in the cast lists, which otherwise list all actors present, including 'extras'.

The programmes are listed in chronological order, identified by series/number reference, and title.

1/1: THE FIRST TV SHOW
Husband .... Harold Goodwin
Wife .... Margaret Flint
Nurse .... Irene Handl
Announcer .... Peter Haigh
Hospital Patient .... Iain Macnaughton
Doctor .... Graham Leaman
Hospital Patient .... Chris Dreaper
Male Nurses................... Kim Corcoran
                    James Bulloch
Seamen .... Ivor Raymonde
                    Frank Pemberton
Workmen....................... Patrick Milner
                    Fraser White

1/2: THE ARTIST
Art Connoisseur............ Valentine Dyall
Model .... Irene Handl
Art Dealer................... Warren Mitchell
Gallery Guides........... Desmond Rayner
                    Ivor Raymonde
Policeman .... James Bulloch
Art Students .... Eleanor Fazan
                    Leslie Cooper
            and
Pat Symons, Pat Horder, Esme Easterbrook, Barbara Grant, Anne Marryott, Daphne Johnson, Patrick Milner, Kim

Corcoran, Chris Dreaper, Malcolm Watson, Arthur Hosking and Grant Duprez.

1/3: THE DANCER
Film Producer............. Warren Mitchell
Dance Instructress .. Hermione Baddeley
Secretary...................... Lorrae Desmond
American .... Frank Lonergan
Teddy Girls .... Elizabeth Fraser
                    Eleanor Fazan
                    Jessica Dent
Dancers (Jitterbug) ...... Michael Boudot
                    Philip Casson
                    Roslyn Ellis
                    Kay Rose
Floor Manager .... Alan Simpson
Professional Ballroom Dancers
                    Harry Smith-Hampshire
                    Doreen Casey
                    Nina Hunt
                    Melville E. Noelly
MC, Indian, etc .... Desmond Rayner
            and
Ivor Raymonde, Fraser White, Murray Kash, Patrick Milner and Kim Corcoran.

1/4: THE BEQUEST
Mr Witherspoon ...... Reginald Beckwith

232

Miss Medworthy................ Irene Handl
Mrs Battleaxe.................. Rose Howlett
Uncle .... Claude Bonser
Aunt.................. Tottie Truman Taylor
Grandad........................ Gordon Phillott
Relative .... Fraser White
Fred .... Ivor Raymonde
Linda .... Elizabeth Fraser
and
Margaret Flint, Veronica Moon, Patricia
Martin, Ann Lancaster, George Dudley,
John Vyvyan, Diana Vernon, Alan Simp-
son, Esme Easterbrook, Paula Delaney,
Mary Collins, Juleen Clow, Terry Scott
and John Pike.

1/5: THE RADIO SHOW
Head of TV Variety .... Warren Mitchell
Army Private .... Eric Sykes
Policeman .... Manville Tarrant
Corporal.......................... Alan Simpson
Lance-Corporal................... Ray Galton
Scottish Private .... Iain Macnaughton
Fat Man.................... George Crowther
Thin Man .... Roy Patrick
Corporal.................... Desmond Rayner
Guardsman .... John Vyvyan
Sergeant, Welsh Guards   Graham Stark
Privates .... Fraser White
Kim Corcoran
Mario Fabrizi
Military Policemen....... Frank Lonergan
Peter Emms
NAAFI Girl .... Elizabeth Fraser
Dancers........................... Terry Gilbert
Leonard Martin
Peter Brownlee
David Hyme
15 members of the George Mitchell Choir
and
Spike Milligan.

1/6: THE CHEF THAT DIED OF SHAME
Gentleman from the Opera ....
Warren Mitchell
Martine Dubois .... Constance Wake
Announcer .... Peter Haigh
Head Chef.................. Raymond Rollett
Rich Man.................... Dennis Chinnery
Rich Man.............................. John Vere
and
Claude Bonser, Leonard Sharp, Gordon

Phillot, George Crowther, Iain Mac-
naughton, Manville Tarrant, Desmond
Rayner, Kim Corcoran, Ivor Raymonde,
Patrick Milner, Hugh Warren and James
Bulloch.

2/1: THE ALPINE HOLIDAY
Without Sidney James
Hotel manager .... Richard Wattis
Yodeller of Dulwich.. Kenneth Williams
Miss Dubois .... June Whitfield
Air Hostess .... Peggy Ann Clifford
Passenger on aircraft .... John Vere
Air Pilot .... Dennis Chinnery
Swiss Gendarme .... Patrick Milner
Swiss Gendarme .... Victor Bryant
Porter......................... Manville Tarrant
Hotel Visitor .... Rose Howlett
Autograph hunter .... Elizabeth Fraser
and
Fraser White, Alan Simpson, Jane Rieger,
Charles Julian, Con Courtney, Harry
Drew, Evelyn Lund and Dorothy Robson.

22: LADY CHATTERLEY'S REVENGE
Without Sidney James
Lew Silver .... Warren Mitchell
Humphrey Clanger .... John Vere
Silver's Typist............... Paddy Edwards
Rep Company Producer.........................
Kenneth Williams
Actress (Gertrude and Lady Chatterley) .
Hattie Jacques
Call Boy .... John Vyvyan
Actor (Theodore) .... Dennis Chinnery
Actor (Roger) .... Desmond Rayner
Actor (Stanley and Lord Chatterley).......
Raymond Rollett
Actress (Cynthia) .... Ann Lancaster
Actresses .... Rose Howlett
Evelyn Lund
Ann Reid
1st Man.......................... Alan Simpson
2nd Man .... Charles Julian
3rd Man.................... Manville Tarrant
4th Man .... Claude Bonser
1st Girl.............................. Lynne Cole
2nd Girl.............................. Jane Rieger

2/3: THE RUSSIAN PRINCE
Prince Nicolai .... Tony Hancock
General Sidski.................. Sidney James

Another Prince Nicolai.............................
　　　　　　　　Kenneth Williams
Countess Olga Romanoff.........................
　　　　　　　　Hattie Jacques
Fred....................................... Bill Fraser
Charlie.......................... Michael Balfour
Prince Paul Alexandrovitch.....................
　　　　　　　　Mario Fabrizi
Grand Duke Peter Ilievitch......................
　　　　　　　　Leonard Sharp
Prince Ivan Ivanovitch........ Harry Lane
Russian Aristocrats ..... Dennis Chinnery
　　　　　　　　Raymond Rollett
　　　　　　　　Janet Barrow
　　　　　　　　Ann Lancaster
Footman .... Iain Macnaughton
1st Flunkey .... Roger Oatime
2nd Flunkey...................... Fraser White
Baron Gregoffski........ Frank Pemberton
Count Petroff Stravinski.........................
　　　　　　　　Gordon Phillott
　　　　and
Claude Bonser, Eileen Delamere, Rene
Roberts, Esme Easterbrook, Harry Drew,
Ralph Covey, Rex Rashley and Con
　　　　Courtney.

2/4: THE NEW NEIGHBOUR
Tony's Secretary............. Hattie Jacques
Policeman .... Kenneth Williams
Neighbour.............................. John Vere
Clerk (Estate Office).............. Bill Fraser
Waxwork Museum Guide......................
　　　　　　　　Mario Fabrizi
　　　　and
Harry Drew, Manville Tarrant, Eileen
Delamere, Claude Bonser, Esme Easter-
brook and Evelyn Lund.

2/5: THE PIANIST
Baroness Helen .... Hattie Jacques
Prince Paul................ Kenneth Williams
Aides................................ Mario Fabrizi
　　　　　　　　Roger Oatime
Policeman .... Manville Tarrant
City Gent.................... Graham Leaman
Bird Lover .... John Vere
Pianist............................ Ivor Raymonde
Undertakers .... Claude Bonser
　　　　　　　　James Bulloch
Ambulance Man .... Harry Drew
Waiter............................ Leonard Sharp
Consul .... Raymond Rollett

Assistant Consul .... Dennis Chinnery
Aide .... Harry Lane
Housemaid........................ Angela Crow
Tap Dancers. Norman and Nicky Grant
　　　　　　　　and
Gwertl Hamer, Joanne Dainton and Eve
　　　　Joyner.

2/6: THE AUCTION
Old Man .... Kenneth Williams
Mrs Witherspoon............ Hattie Jacques
Junior Partner............... Gordon Phillott
Auction Attendant ..... Manville Tarrant
Man at Auction......... George Crowther
Military Gent at Auction..... Harry Lane
Casino Croupier............... Mario Fabrizi
At Auction and as Casino Gamblers:
Gaham Leaman, Claude Bonser, Roger
Oatime, Dennis Chinnery, Con Court-
ney, Rose Howlett, Peggy Ann Clifford
　　　　and Evelyn Lund.

3/1: THE CONTINENTAL HOLIDAY
Mr X .... Anton Diffring
Spanish Dancer............... Tutte Lemkow
Spanish Waiter................. Peter Allenby
Spanish Guitar Player ..... George Elliott
Beggar .... Mario Fabrizi
The Golden Scorpion ... Edouard Assaly
The Black Beetle................. Peter Elliott
The Crimson Alligator..... Alec Bregonzi
The Blue Hedgehog.... Anthony Shirvell
The Green Lizard....... Bruce Wightman
Police Inspector .... David Grahame
Abdul the Nubian .... Arthur Bennett
Spanish Dancer.............. Eugenie Sivyer
Arabs .... Leslie Smith
　　　　　　　　Richard Statman
　　　　　　　　Manville Tarrant
　　　　　　　　Thomas Symonds
　　　　Spaniards:
Philip Carr, Patrick Milner, Pat
O'Meara, Harry Robins, and Len Felix.

3/2: THE GREAT DETECTIVE
Rupert...................................... John Vere
Patricia................... Peggy Ann Clifford
The Colonel.................... Cameron Hall
Mrs Colonel..................... Evelyn Lund
Robert........................ Graham Leaman
John........................ Terence Alexander

234

Jocelyn .... Paddy Edwards
Cynthia .... Tottie Truman Taylor
Matilda .... Pat Coombs
Lord Beaumont............. Gordon Phillott
Police Inspector .... Manville Tarrant
Maid .... Anne Reid
Policemen .... James Bulloch
                            Patrick Milner
                            Peter Emms
                            Basil Beale
Body .... John Vyvyan

3/3: THE AMUSEMENT ARCADE
Educated Albert..................... Bill Fraser
Councillor Sproggs .... John Vere
Lady Councillors .... Evelyn Lund
                            Rose Howlett
                            Elizabeth Gott
                          Peggy Ann Clifford
Councillors...................... Claude Bonser
                            Manville Tarrant
                            Con Courtney
Teddy Boys........................ Leslie Smith
                            Patrick Milner
                            Bruce Wightman
                            Richard Statman
                            Alan Simpson
Listener............................ Alec Bregonzi
Ballot Teller....................... Dick Emery
Voter................................. John Vyvyan
Ambulance Men .... Thomas Symonds
                            Anthony Shirvell
Dancers.............................. Ray Grover
                            Anthony Wiles
                            Pat Wallen
                            Iris Eve

3/4: A HOLIDAY IN SCOTLAND
Doctor .... Raymond Huntley
Weathermen.............. Iain Macnaughton
                            Richard Statman
Nurse............................ Anne Marryott
Mrs Brown .... Eileen Delamare
Patients .... Manville Tarrant
                            John Vyvyan
                            George Crowther
                            Charles Julian

3/5: AIR STEWARD HANCOCK
1st Pilot............................. Leslie Smith
2nd Pilot .... Richard Statman

3rd Pilot.............................. Philip Carr
4th Pilot .... Stuart Hillier
Tannoy Girl.................... Anne Marryott
Catering Officer..................... John Vere
Customs Officer .... Peter Allenby
Passenger .... John Vyvyan
Constable .... Basil Beale
Police Inspector .... Bill Fraser
Security Policeman .... James Bulloch
Police Sergeant........... Manville Tarrant
Police Constable............. Dave Freeman
Pilot .... Alec Bregonzi
                        Passengers:
Rose Howlett, Harry Drew, Cameron Hall, Evelyn Lund, Stella Kemball, Charles Julian, Con Courtney, George Crowther and Susan Cox.

3/6: THE REGIMENTAL REUNION
Mr Spooner .... Campbell Singer
1st Clerk .... Claude Bonser
2nd Clerk .... Alec Bregonzi
3rd Clerk......................... Con Courtney
4th Clerk..................... Bruce Wightman
5th Clerk.................... Manville Tarrant
Office Boy .... John Vyvyan
Ex-Major .... Terence Alexander
Ex-Colonel................. Graham Leaman
Ex-Captain................... Guy Middleton
Ex-Major no. 2 .... Stuart Hillier
Ex-Colonel no. 2 .... Cameron Hall
Mr Filley .... John Vere
Mr Gale .... Raymond Rollett
Inspector......................... Peter Allenby
1st Millionaire........... George Crowther
2nd Millionaire .... Arthur Mullard
3rd Millionaire............... Harry Robbins
Flunkey............................. Harry Lane

3/7: THE ADOPTED FAMILY
Secretary........................ Anne Marryott
Housing Officer................. Ian Fleming
Bertha .... Pamela Manson
Judge .... John Vere
Usher............................. Patrick Milner
Young Wife....................... Anne Reid
Young Husband................. Stuart Hillier
1st Son .... Hugh Lloyd
2nd Son .... Mario Fabrizi
3rd Son .... John Vyvyan
4th Son .... Manville Tarrant

3/8: THE ELOCUTION TEACHER
As himself .... Jack Hawkins
Ponsonby Everest................... John Vere
Mrs Fazakerly .... Nora Nicholson
Miss Perkins .... Mary Reynolds
Announcer .... Stuart Hillier
As himself .... John Vyvyan
Rock'n Roll Musicians:
Don Rendell (tenor sax), Bob Robert (bass), Mickie Greene (drums), Eric Cooke (piano), and Ronnie Hunt (trumpet).

3/9: THE LAWYER: THE CROWN V. JAMES, S.
Judge .... John Le Mesurier
PC Trubshawe.............. Arthur Mullard
Barrister...................... Raymond Rollett
Prosecuting Council.............. John Vere
Clerk of Court.................... Hugh Lloyd
Defendant .... Claude Bonser
Police Sergeant...................... Bill Fraser
Barrister's Clerk............... John Vyvyan
Foreman of the Jury.... Anthony Shirvell
PC............................. Manville Tarrant
Usher.............................. Patrick Milner
Court Official .... Alec Bregonzi
Court Official .... Richard Sullivan
PC.................................. Roger Oatime
WPC............................ Anne Marryott
PC...................................... John Foster
and
Nicholas Sandys, Alistair Audsley, Bert Allisom, John Herrington, Mark Bennett, Collett O'Neill and Joyce Hemson.

3/10: HOW TO WIN MONEY AND INFLUENCE PEOPLE
Newspaper boy .... John Vyvyan
Postman............................ Dick Emery
Policeman .... Campbell Singer
Mr Pools............................... John Vere
1st Assistant .... Bruce Wightman
2nd Assistant...................... Basil Beale
2nd Man .... Alec Bregonzi
3rd Man.............................. Philip Carr
4th Man .... Leslie Smith
5th Man .... Anthony Shirvell
Waiter.............................. Mario Fabrizi
1st Japanese .... Burt Kwouk
2nd Japanese .... Nelson Grostate
3rd Japanese.................. Jimmy Raphael

Policeman .... Manville Tarrant
Last Man .... Hugh Lloyd

3/11: THERE'S AN AIRFIELD AT THE BOTTOM OF MY GARDEN
Vicar .... John Vere
Surveyor .... Dick Emery
Surveyor's Wife ...... Esther MacPherson
Colonel .... Cameron Hall
Emily .... Nancy Roberts
Emily's Husband .... Gordon Phillott
Young Couple.............. Paddy Edwards
Leslie Smith
Henry .... Claude Bonser
Elderly Lady .... Vera Elmore
Sid's Secretary .... Anne Reid
Mrs Farley .... Brenda Duncan
Woman Guest................. Elizabeth Gott
Violin Player .... Alec Bregonzi
Viola Player...................... Evelyn Lund
Bass Player........................ John Vyvyan
and
Dorothy Robson, Philip Carr, Manville Tarrant, Eileen Delamere and Rose Howlett.

3/12: THE EAST CHEAM REPERTORY COMPANY
Guest Star........................ John Gregson
Harmonica Player .... Max Geldray
Juggler .... Alf Silvestri
Chorus Dancers .... The Glamazons
Vocal Group .... The Keynotes
and
Dido the Chimp, John Vere, John Vyvyan, Dennis Chinnery, Mario Fabrizi, Arthur Bennett, Tommy Eytle, John McRay, James Avon, Richard Wharton and Michael Ely.

4/1: ERICSON THE VIKING
1st Electrician .... Laurie Webb
2nd Electrician .... Ivor Raymonde
1st Viking......................... John Vyvyan
2nd Viking .... Mario Fabrizi
3rd Viking.................... Arthur Mullard
Saxon King.......................... John Vere
1st Stagehand............ Manville Tarrant
2nd Stagehand .... Anthony Shirvell
Cameraman...................... Alec Bregonzi
Clapper Boy...................... Louis Adam
Saxon Princess .... Pat Coombs
1st Saxon .... Herbert Nelson

2nd Saxon .... Pat O'Meara
3rd Saxon.................. Rufus Cruikshank
4th Saxon.................... George Crowther
Sound Assistant .... Richard Statman

4/2: UNDERPAID! OR, GRANDAD'S SOS
Street Musicians ....Mario Fabrizi
                                       John Vyvyan
Arthur Biggs .... Harry Drew
Frederick Higgins ...... George Crowther
Sharebuyer..................... Arthur Mullard
City Gent......................... James Bulloch
1st Man in Pub .... Con Courtney
2nd Man in Pub.............. Claude Bonser
3rd Man in Pub .... Anthony Shirvell
Australian Barman .... Rolf Harris
Phyllis.............................. Evelyn Lund
Australian Sharebuyer.......... Len David
Voices on radio:
'D'Arcy Villiers'............. Andrew Faulds
'Grimaldo' .... Warren Mitchell
'Nick' .... Richard Statman
Announcer .... Philip Carr
Tony's Grandfather .... Tony Hancock
Sid's Grandfather .... Sidney James
                     and
Bob Marshall, Arnold Lock, James McCloughlin, Herbert Nelson, Manville Tarrant, Patrick Milner and Stella Kemball.

4/3: THE SET THAT FAILED
1st TV repair man.............. Hugh Lloyd
2nd TV repair man .... John Vyvyan
Mr Biggs............................... John Vere
Mrs Biggs .... Rose Howlett
1st Biggs visitor............... Claude Bonser
2nd Biggs visitor .... Evelyn Lund
Uncle Fred....................... Sidney Vivian
Aunt Edie .... Patricia Hayes
Mr Smith..................... Robert Dorning
Mrs Smith .... Margaret Flint
Albert............................... Mario Fabrizi
Barbara .... Anne Marryott
Herbert .... Ivor Raymonde
Tommy............................ Leslie Smith
Jack............................. Anthony Shirvell

4/4: THE NEW NOSE
Girl at Tony's .... Barbara Archer
Milkman .... Mario Fabrizi

Counterhand .... Roger Avon
Nurse............................. Anne Marryott
Dr Worthington........ John Le Mesurier
2nd Girl at Tony's .... Anabelle Lee
1st Girl in Milk Bar ..... Elizabeth Fraser
2nd Girl in Milk Bar..... Pamela Manson
1st Man at Bus Stop......... Alec Bregonzi
2nd Man at Bus Stop .... Ivor Raymonde
                     and
Arthur Mullard, Herman Miller, Bill Matthews, Tom Payne, Joseph Levine, and John Scott Martin.

4/5: THE FLIGHT OF THE RED SHADOW
Singer .... Louise Howard
Arab................................ Mario Fabrizi
Warder/Barracker .... Alan Simpson
Barracker .... Ray Galton
Manager....................... Robert Dorning
Balloon Seller................... Alec Bregonzi
Toy Seller .... Ivor Raymonde
Sailor .... Rolf Harris
Policeman .... Arthur Mullard
Arab.......................... George Crowther
Civic Dignitary .... Con Courtney
Vicar .... John Vere
Mayor .... Bert Simms
Mayoress........................... Evelyn Lund
Colonel .... Harry Drew
Maharajah............................ Guy Mills
Prison Governer............. James Bulloch
Maharajah's Attendant........ Ben Bowers
Arab.................................... Louis Adam
Foreign Leigonnaires ...... Patrick Milner
                             Herbert Nelson
                             Stanley Segal
Strong Man..................... Stanley Ayres
Civic Dignitaries........ Frank Littlewood
                             Anna Churcher
                             Ann Jay

4/6: THE HORROR SERIAL
Lieutenant .... Dennis Chinnery
Colonel .... John Le Mesurier
1st Soldier....................... Alec Bregonzi
2nd Soldier .... John Vyvyan
3rd Soldier .... Laurie Webb
Sergeant................................ Hugh Lloyd
Mr Biggs....................... Arthur Mullard
Mrs Biggs .... Phyllis Norwood
Nurse............................. Anne Marryott

237

4/7: THE ITALIAN MAID

Domestic Agent .... John Vere
˙Italian Father .... Harry Lane
1st Man .... Michael Stainton
2nd Man .... James Bulloch
Italian Maid .... Marla Landi
Lady Plunkett .... Elizabeth Gott
Secretary .... Jeanette Edwards
Italian Mother .... Betty Lloyd-Davies
Swiss Man .... Frederick Schiller
Telegraph Boy .... John Vyvyan
Italian Daughters and Sons:
Mary Abbott, Anita Loghade, Virginia
Mollett, Sandra Robb, Jenny Jones,
Biddy Lennon, Harry Wright, Louis
Adam, Anthony Wiles, Ronnie Robinson,
Dennis Mallard and Francis Lennon.

4/8: MATRIMONY—ALMOST

Reggie/Guest .... Terence Alexander
Elizabeth .... Vivienne Martin
Percy/Guest .... Cardew Robinson
Mr Wetherby .... Cameron Hall
Vicar .... John Vere
Nigel/Guest .... Philip Carr
Freddie/Guest.................. Alec Bregonzi
Bandleader/Guest .... Mario Fabrizi
1st Broker's Man........... Ivor Raymonde
2nd Broker's Man .... Arthur Mullard
Mrs Wetherby .... Edith Stevenson
Maid .... Elizabeth Fraser
Mr Wetherby's friend ....
Frank Littlewood
1st Guardsman/Guest ....
Michael Greenwood
2nd Guardsman/Guest.. Lionel Wheeler
1st Musician....................... John Vyvyan
2nd Musician .... Louis Adam
3rd Musician/PC............. Patrick Milner
4th Musician/PC........... Philip Howard
Butler/Sergeant............... James Bulloch
Harmonium Player .... Evelyn Lund
and
Gwenda Ewan, Anne Maryott, Paddy
Edwards, Patricia Veasey, Deirdre Bellar,
Judy Nash, Con Courtney, Harry Drew,
Shirley Patterson, Edna Stevens, Alan
Simpson, John Caesar and Bill Matthews.

4/9: THE BEAUTY CONTEST

The Mayor............................ John Vere
Alderman Biggs .... Robert Dorning
Alderman Jones .... James Bulloch
3rd Alderman............. Frank Littlewood
4th Alderman...................... Harry Lane
5th Alderman.................. Charles Julian
6th Alderman....................... Bert Simms
Gym Instructor................... Roger Avon
Entrants in Competition:
Jim Banstead .... John Vyvyan
Percy Whyteleafe.......... Mario Fabrizi
Arnold Nonsuch........ Arthur Mullard
Harry Mortlake ...... George Crowther
Baths Attendants........... Herbert Nelson
Richard Statman
Master of Ceremonies.......... John Blyth
Dance Hall Attendants.... Alan Simpson
Patrick Milner
Glamour Girls .... Ann Smith
Phillipa Steward
Competition Winner .... Joe Robinson
Baths Attendant .... Con Courtney

4/10: THE WRONG MAN

Constable .... Roger Avon
Sergeant........................... James Bulloch
Inspector...................... Campbell Singer
Detective Soames.............. Harry Locke
Mrs Haggett................... Nancy Roberts
Mr Hardacre................. Gordon Phillott
3rd Witness...................... Alec Bregonzi
Cinema Cashier............. Pamela Manson
Men in Identity Parade:
Bruiser .... Arthur Mullard
Little Man.................... John Vyvyan
and
Alan Simpson, Laurie Webb, Herbert
Nelson, Con Courtney, Don Matthews
and Anthony Gould.

4/11: THE OAK TREE

Man from Ministry............... John Vere
Clerk of Works......... Reginald Beckwith
Trees Inspector.................. Hugh Lloyd
Timber Merchant .... Robert Dorning
1st workman .... Arthur Mullard
2nd workman .... Laurie Webb
Marcher........................... Mario Fabrizi
Police Inspector .... Graham Leaman
Marcher........................... John Vyvyan
Secretary........................ Gwenda Ewan
Passers by .... Mary Fletcher
Joyce Hemson
Margerie Mason
Sonia Peters
Edwin Morton

238

Albert Grant
Small boy........................ James Langley
Policemen .... John Caesar
Norman Taylor
Robert Pitt
Bill Matthews
Victor Charrington
Anthony Jennett

4/12: THE KNIGHTHOOD

Old Vic Manager .... Richard Wattis
Cheam Rep. Manager .. Robert Dorning
MC .... Mario Fabrizi
Dancer .... Lynne Cole
Pianist............................ Ivor Raymonde
Richard III .... Andrew Faulds
Pub Customer.................. John Vyvyan
Pub Customer.................. Jack Leonard
Barman .... James Bulloch
and
Con Courtney, Doris Littel, Doris Hall,
John Cabot, Michael Middleton and
Diana Walker.

4/13: THE SERVANTS

Colonel Winthrop ..... John Le Mesurier
Mrs Winthrop................... Mary Hinton
Male Secretary .... Alec Bregonzi
1st Old Man........................ Hugh Lloyd
1st Old Woman.............. Nancy Roberts
2nd Old Man .... Charles Julian
2nd Old Woman .... Evelyn Lund
3rd Old Man................. Gordon Phillott
3rd Old Woman.............. Patricia Hayes
1st City Man.................... James Bulloch
2nd City Man .... Con Courtney
3rd City Man .... John Vyvyan

5/1: THE ECONOMY DRIVE

1st Man......................... Arthur Mullard
2nd Man .... Frank Pemberton
3rd Man........................... Laurie Webb
4th Man .... Herbert Nelson
5th Man .... Alec Bregonzi
Cashier........................... Patricia Hayes
Woman in queue Tottie Truman Taylor
Lady Almoner......... Peggy Ann Clifford
1st Counter Girl........... Pamela Manson
2nd Counter Girl .... Elizabeth Fraser
Tea Girl........................ Anne Marryott
Tray Snatcher.................. Mario Fabrizi
1st Waitress............... Beatrice Ormonde
2nd Waitress .... Joanna Douglas

Nurse/Cafe Customer ....
Jeanette Edwards
Man at Lunch .... Michael Ward
and
Margaret Jordan, Tracy Vernon, Anne
Reddin, Judith Pearson, Barbara Adams,
Barbara Ball, Alan Darling, Bill Mat-
thews, Dick Downes, Michael Oaley,
Robin Kildair, Stephen Fawcett.

5/2: THE TWO MURDERERS

Bank Manager.............. Robert Dorning
Librarian........................... Hugh Lloyd
Mrs Cravatte.................. Patricia Hayes
Tony's Doctor .... Mark Singleton
Sid's Doctor..................... Ralph Nossek
1st Bruiser...................... Arthur Mullard
2nd Bruiser .... Tom Clegg
Members of the Public............................
Albert Grant
Betty Miller
John Vyvyan

5/3: LORD BYRON LIVED HERE

National Trust Officer............................
John Le Mesurier
The Disbeliever .... Hugh Lloyd
The American............. Robert Dorning
Mrs American................ Penelope Parry
The Man from the Council....................
William Mervyn
National Trust Attendants ....
Stan Simmonds
Raymond Grahame
Members of the Public............................
Judy Rogers
John Vyvyan
Marylyn Thomas
Frances St Barbe-West
Dorothy Watson
Susan Hunter
Robert Bryan
Michael Wyatt

5/4: TWELVE ANGRY MEN

Prosecuting Council .... Ralph Nossek
Police Inspector .... Robert Dorning
Defending Council......... Leonard Sachs
The Judge........................ Austin Trevor
Usher .... Hugh Lloyd
The Prisoner................. Herbert Nelson
Military Juror .... William Kendall

Company Director Juror... Leslie Perrins
Farmer Juror.......................... Philip Ray
Old Man Juror............... Kenneth Kove
1st Woman Juror .... Betty Cardno
2nd Woman Juror................ Lala Lloyd
Young Man Juror .... Alec Bregonzi
Bank Clerk Juror.............. James Bulloch
12th Juror .... Mario Fabrizi
Old Lady Juror .... Marie Lightfoot
Junior Counsels .... David Grain
                                        James Cliston
                                        Keith Ashley
                                        John Vyvyan
Police Constables .... Robert Pitt
                                        Gilbert McIntyre
                                        Christopher Dyer
                                        Kenneth Cowan
Solicitors............................ Alex Wright
                                        John Tucker

5/5: THE TRAIN JOURNEY
The Doctor.............. Raymond Huntley
The Colonel.................... Cameron Hall
The Vicar................... Henry Longhurst
1st Woman......... Tottie Truman Taylor
The Girl .... Eve Patrick
The Railway Guard ..... Robert Dorning
Railway Ticket Clerk .... Hugh Lloyd
Radio Announcer................. Philip Carr
                              and
Judy Roger, Pauline Walker, Jean Mock-
ford, Anthony Ray, Michael Harrison,
Charles Gilbert and David Graham.

5/6: THE CRUISE
1st Girl............................ Gwenda Ewan
1st Man................................ Philip Carr
2nd Man .... Ivor Raymonde
1st Steward .... Patrick Milner
Amorous Lady................ Hattie Jacques
Old Man .... Harry Brunning
Old Lady .... Evelyn Lund
1st Officer.................... Dennis Chinnery
The Captain.............. John Le Mesurier
Ship's Doctor.................... Brian Oulton
2nd Girl .... Paddy Edwards
Radio Operator .... Richard Statman
Man in Crowd .... Frank Littlewood
Sailor at Wheel.............. Herbert Nelson
1st Junior Officer................. Brian Tyler
2nd Junior Officer .... Astor Sklair
3rd Junior Officer............. Ricky Felgate
Ship's Bandleader .... Mario Fabrizi

3rd Girl...................... Patricia Shakesby
4th Girl......................... Una Trimming
5th Girl......................... Laura Thurlow
1st Airline Steward .... James Bulloch
2nd Airline Steward...... Lionel Wheeler
Steward............................. Hugh Lloyd
Steward............................. Laurie Webb
                              and
Ivor Kimmell, Lee Richardson, Howard
Charlton, Robert Weeden, Anne Clunes,
Viera Shelley, Nancy Adams, Olga Re-
gan, Elizabeth Bergen, Ruby Archer,
Tracy Vernon, Terry Howard, Barbara
Muir, Rex Roland, William White and
                   Alec Wallace.

5/7: THE BIG NIGHT
Mrs Cravatte................... Patricia Hayes
Launderette Attendant....... Hugh Lloyd
Launderette Manager... Robert Dorning
Receptionist .... Ann Lancaster
Man in Launderette............. Sam Kydd
Man in Launderette......... Mario Fabrizi
Cinema Manager......... Michael Balfour
Commissionaire .... Tom Clegg
1st Girl......................... Paddy Edwards
2nd Girl .... Annabelle Lee
Man in Cinema............. Ivor Raymonde
1st Cinema Girl .... Joanna Douglas
2nd Cinema Girl....... Beatrice Ormonde
Policewoman................. Laura Thurlow
Policewoman............. Patricia Shakesby
Police Constable.............. James Bulloch
Policeman .... Leonard Kingston
                              and
Dorothy Watson, Ann Jay, Rosamund
Tattersall, Susan Kay, Vivien Weldon,
Mary Chirgwin, Felicity Peel, Dick
Downs, Bill Matthews and Peter Badger.

5/8: THE TYCOON
Sir Thomas Edgington. William Kendall
Company Secretary.......... Ralph Nossek
Business Man................ Mark Singleton
Art Gallery Man .... Robert Dorning
Tony's Dentist................ James Bulloch
Secretary........................... Hugh Lloyd
Tony's Tailor.................. Alec Bregonzi
Tony's Barber............... Ivor Raymonde
Bootblack .... John Vyvyan
Tony's Manicurist .... Una Trimming
1st Secretary .... Rosamund Lesley
2nd Secretary................. Anne Marryott

240

3rd Secretary......................... Anne Reid
4th Secretary.............. Bernice Swanson
Aristotle Thermopolae .... Harold Kasket
Aide .... Bob Marshall
Aide .... Leonard Graham
and
Glyn Jones, Patrick Desmond, William E. Rayner, Robert Young, Edna Stevens, Shirley Patterson, Susan Kay, Ann Harper, Beatrix Carter, Brian Vaughan, Ryan Jelfe, Stanley Paige, Martin White, Eric Martin, Bernard Dudley, Robert Croudace, Rex Rashley, Charles Western, Charles Gilbert, Royston Tickner, John Caesar, Philip Howard and Frank Littlewood.

5/9: SPANISH INTERLUDE
1st Girl............................ Annabelle Lee
2nd Girl .... Paddy Edwards
3rd Girl.............................. Lynne Cole
Spanish Waiter................ David Lander
Nightclub Manager........... Brian Worth
A Matador .... John Vyvyan
English Bullfighter........... Ronnie Brody
Bull Ring Attendant........ Patrick Milner
Bull Ring Attendant...... Herbert Nelson
Matadors........................... Astor Sklair
Pat O'Meara
Lionel Wheeler
Pianist.............................. Tom McCall
and
Betty Mowles, Carole Brett, Judi Vague, Carmen Capaldi, Nancy Adams, Heather Russell, Astrid Anderson, Colin Dudley, Wilfred Greves, Joe Tregoningo, Alan Vicars, Norman Miller, Ray Marioni, Donald Walker and Roy Spence.

5/10: FOOTBALL POOLS
Rosette Seller............... Robert Dorning
Cashier.............................. Hugh Lloyd
1st Spectator .... Sidney Vivian
2nd Spectator.................... Laurie Webb
Spectator..................... Richard Statman
Footballer .... John Vyvyan
1st Football Player .... Alec Bregonzi
2nd Football Player....... Lionel Wheeler
3rd Football Player .... Patrick Milner
4th Football Player........ Herbert Nelson
5th Football Player.............. Philip Carr
Announcer .... Philip Carr

Goalkeeper........................... Tom Clegg
Footballers .... James Clifton
Edward Willis
Ryan Jelfe
David Bell
Spectators:
John Caesar, Philip Howard, Peter Jesson, Kenneth Alan Taylor, Ronald Mayer, Keith Goodman, Peter Burden, Edmund Dring, Brian Pollitt, Norman Coburn, Michael Lehrer, Leslie Wright, Laurence Archer, Jerry James, Robert Weedon, Charles Gilbert, Alan Darling, Roger Pitt, Roger Williams and Louis Hasler.

6/1: THE COLD
The Doctor.............. John Le Mesurier
Patient................................ Hugh Lloyd
Mrs Cravatte.................. Patricia Hayes
Nurse............................ Anne Marryott
Patient........................ Richard Statman
Boxer .... Herbert Nelson
Boxer's Manager................. Tom Clegg

6/2: THE MISSING PAGE
Librarian............................. Hugh Lloyd
Mr Proctor................ George Coulouris
British Museum Librarian ....
Gordon Phillott
Woman in Library ....
Tottie Truman Taylor
2nd Woman in Library ....
Peggy Ann Clifford
3rd Woman in Library.. Joanna Douglas
Men in Library.............. Kenneth Kove
Gibb McLaughlin
John Vyvyan
Alec Bregonzi
James Bulloch
Frank Littlewood
Ray Grover

6/3: THE EMIGRANT
Australia House Clerk....... Brian Oulton
Canada House Clerk ...... Gordon Sterne
India House Clerk............... Joe Enrikie
Baffin Land Clerk .... Alec Bregonzi
Tramp Steamer Captain . David Lander
Eskimo............................ John Bramley
and

Richard Statman, Hugh Lloyd, Edna Stevens, Louis Stafford, Anne Marryott, Joanna Douglas, Charles Julian, Philip Howard, John Scott Martin, Herbert Nelson, Samuel Manseray, John Vyvyan, Harry Robins and Johnnie Lee.

6/4: THE REUNION PARTY

Licensee	Sidney Vivian
Smudger Smith	Hugh Lloyd
Mavis Smith	Eileen Way
Chalkey White	Cardew Robinson
Man in Off-Licence	Laurie Webb
Ginger Johnson	Clive Dunn
Scrounger Harris	Robert Dorning

6/5: SID IN LOVE

The Clippie	Joan Heal
Bert	Hugh Lloyd
Bus Driver	Robert Dorning
Policeman	James Bulloch
Man in Fish Shop	John Vyvyan
Fish Shop Proprietress	Vi Stevens
Woman in Bus	Peggy Ann Clifford
Man in Fish Shop	John Bramley
Mr Smallpiece	Douglas Robinson
Cynthia Smallpiece	Denny Dayviss

and

Drummond Marvin, Philip Decker, Guy Grahame, Alfred Hirst, John Clevedon, Norman Hartley, Leslie Wright, Louis Haslar, James Clifton, Martin White, Judy Roger, Rosamund Tattersall, Diana Walker, Beatrix Carter, Mary Power, Viera Shelley, Anne Jay, Lizanne Marshall, Alison McMurdo, Jeanette Edwards and Anne Marryott.

6/6: THE BABY SITTERS

Mr Frobisher	Terence Alexander
Mrs Frobisher	Annabelle Lee
1st Burglar	Herbert Nelson
2nd Burglar	Alec Bregonzi
Police Inspector	Robert Dorning
1st Policeman	Patrick Milner
2nd Policeman	Michael Earl

6/7: THE LADIES' MAN

Gregory Chandler	Brian Oulton
Receptionist	Robert Dorning
Muriel	Elizabeth Fraser

Edie	Annabelle Lee
Miss Pringle	Laura Thurlow
The Woman	Honor Shepherd
Bus Conductor	Laurie Webb
The Dancer	Barbara Evans
The Hon Susan Plunket	Gwenda Ewan
Charm School Pupils	Arthur Mullard
	George Crowther
	Herbert Nelson
	Harry Robbins
	Stan Simmons
	John Vyvyan
Pianist (not in vision)	Bert Waller
Choreographer (not in vision)	
	Eleanor Fazan

6/8: THE PHOTOGRAPHER

Business Man	William Kendall
Man in Restaurant	Herbert Hare
Photographer's Assistant	Hugh Lloyd
Manager of Restaurant	Robert Dorning
Woman in Restaurant	
	Tottie Truman Taylor
Secretary	Laura Thurlow
Waitress	Joanna Douglas
Mr Dimwitty	Edward Malin
1st Tourist	Murray Kash
2nd Tourist	Laurie Webb
3rd Tourist	Anthony Shirvell
Waiters	Michael Earl
	Kenneth Firth
	Philip Howard
Man in Restaurant	John Vyvyan
Waitress	Ann Bassett

and

Louise Stafford, May Hamilton, Jennifer Thorne, Una Trimming, Cynthia Marshall, Joy Leggat, Nicholas Hay, Jack Keonard, Keith Goodman, Albert Gant, Norman Kaye and Gavin Reed.

6/9: THE EAST CHEAM CENTENARY

Mayor of East Cheam	Robert Dorning
1st Councillor	Cameron Hall
2nd Councillor	Hugh Lloyd
3rd Councillor	James Bulloch
4th Councillor	Eddie Malin
1st Woman Councillor	Lala Lloyd
2nd Woman Councillor	Evelyn Lund
BBC OB Director	Brian Oulton
Producer	Leslie Perrins

Secretary .... Anne Marryott
Peanut Man .... Sidney Vivian
As Himself .... John Snagge
Scotsman/Scoutmaster .... Astor Sklair
Marcher/Britannia .... Sylvia Osborn
Councillor .... Frank Littlewood
Marcher/Road Sweeper ....
George Crowther
Marcher/Mediaeval Soldier.....................
Herbert Nelson
Marcher/Father Time .... John Vyvyan
Marcher/Mediaeval Soldier....................
John Bramley
Cameraman...................... Michael Earl
Boy Scouts .... James Langley
Michael Phillips
John Bosch

6/10: THE POISON PEN LETTERS
Mrs Cravatte.................. Patricia Hayes
Police Sergeant.................... John Welsh
A Woman .... Anna Churcher
Eccentric Spinster...................................
Tottie Truman Taylor
Police Constable............ Andrew Lieven

All 7th series shows are without Sidney
James.

7/1: THE BEDSITTER
with Michael Aspel

7/2: THE BOWMANS
'Dan Bowman' .... Brian Oulton
'Gladys Bowman'.. Constance Chapman
'George' .... Meadows White
'The dog' .... Peter Glaze
'Fred' .... Alec Bregonzi
'Diane' .... Gwenda Ewan
'The Doctor' .... Ralph Wilson
The Producer.................. Patrick Cargill
Julian Court............. William Sherwood
Postman .... Victor Platt
Florist .... Hugh Lloyd
BBC Official.................. Bruno Barnabe
Reporter..................... Dennis Chinnery
and
Charles Young, James Fitzgerald, Bruce
Wightman, Richard Carpenter, Bernard
Hunter, Richard Simpson, Joan White,
Charles Gilbert, Robert Manning, James
Ure, Frank Littlewood, Laurence Hep-
worth, Andre Ducane, Carl Lacy, Arthur

Lown, Peter Chault, Kevin Davies, David
Franks, Simon Moore, Aubrey Danvers
Walker, Stuart Anderson, Olwen Coates,
Anne Kennedy, Antonita Dias, Carmen
Dias, Moira Flynn, Caroline Aylett, Sian
Price, Norman Hartley, and Donald
Heath.

7/3: THE RADIO HAM
Neighbours .... Bernard Peake
Annie Leake
Policemen .... Edwin Richfield
Bernard Hunter
'Mayday'...................... Andrew Faulds
Other radio voices .... John Bluthal
Geoffrey Matthews
Honor Shepherd
Geoffrey Lewis

7/4: THE LIFT
Mr Humphries........ Charles Lloyd Pack
The Girl .... Diana King
The Producer.................... Jack Watling
The Air Marshall ...... John Le Mesurier
The Vicar........................ Noel Howlett
The Doctor...................... Colin Gordon
Mrs Humphries .... Jose Reed
Lift Assistant .... Hugh Lloyd
Maintenance Engineer ....
William Sherwood
Firemen .... Ralph Wilson
James Fitzgerald

7/5: THE BLOOD DONOR
The Nurse .... June Whitfield
The Doctor.................... Patrick Cargill
Patient.................... Peggy Ann Clifford
Patient................................ Hugh Lloyd
2nd Nurse .... Anne Marryott
3rd Nurse......................... Jean Marlow
Patient.......................... Frank Thornton
2nd Doctor.................... James Ottoway
and
Kenneth Cowan, Frances St Barbe-West,
Michael Earl and Albert Grant

7/6: THE SUCCESSION—SON AND HEIR
Olive Hobbs...................... Myrtle Reed
Veronica Stillwell (the beatnik) ....
June Whitfield
Pamela Ffortescue-Ffrench (the Deb) .....
Gwenda Ewan

'HANCOCK'S HALF-HOUR'—BBC-TV REPEATS

Wednesdays, 1930
20-8-58	3/9	The Lawyer: The Crown v James S.
27-8-58	3/5	Air Steward Hancock, the last of the many
3-9-58	3/2	The Great Detective
10-9-58	3/10	How to Win Money and Influence People

(from 35mm telerecordings, except 3/2, 16mm telerecording.)

Sundays, 1930, except 3-5-59 at 2012
12-4-59	4/4	The New Nose
19-4-59	4/8	Matrimony—Almost
26-4-59	4/5	The Flight of the Red Shadow
3-5-59	4/7	The Italian Maid
10-5-59	4/6	The Horror Serial
17-5-59	4/12	The Knighthood
24-5-59	4/9	The Beauty Contest
31-5-59	4/11	The Oak Tree
7-6-59	4/10	The Wrong Man

(from 35mm telerecordings)

Mondays, 1930; 'The Best of Hancock'
20-6-60	5/1	The Economy Drive
27-6-60	5/2	The Two Murderers
4-7-60	6/1	The Cold
11-7-60	6/6	The Baby Sitters
18-7-60	5/4	The Train Journey
25-7-60	5/10	Football Pools
1-8-60		(no repeat: Film 'Follow the Fleet' at 1930)
8-8-60	6/2	The Missing Page
15-8-60	6/8	The Photographer
22-8-60	5/4	Twelve Angry Men (under the title 'The Juryman')
29-8-60	6/4	The Reunion Party
5-9-60	5/7	The Big Night
12-9-60	6/10	The Poison Pen Letters

(from video tapes)

Sundays, 1930: 'Hancock'
20-8-61	7/1	The Bedsitter
27-8-61	7/2	The Bowmans
3-9-61	7/3	The Radio Ham
10-9-61	7/4	The Lift
17-9-61	7/5	The Blood Donor
24-9-61	7/6	The Succession—Son and Heir

(from video tapes)

Wednesdays at 1930; 'The Best of Hancock'
6-10-65	5/1	The Economy Drive
13-10-65	6/1	The Cold
20-10-65	6/4	The Reunion Party
27-10-65	5/5	Twelve Angry Men
3-11-65	5/7	The Big Night
10-11-65	6/6	The Baby Sitters
17-11-65	6/2	The Missing Page
24-11-65	5/2	The Two Murderers
1-12-65	5/4	The Train Journey

8-12-65	5/10	Football Pools
15-12-65	6/3	The Emigrant
22-12-65	6/5	Sid in Love
29-12-65	6/10	The Poison Pen Letters
5- 1-66	5/6	The Cruise
12- 1-66	5/3	Lord Byron Lived Here
19- 1-66	6/7	The Ladies' Man
26- 1-66	5/8	The Tycoon
2- 2-66	6/8	The Photographer
9- 2-66	5/9	Spanish Interlude
16- 2-66	6/9	The East Cheam Centenary
23- 2-66	7/4	The Lift
2- 3-66	7/5	The Blood Donor
9- 3-66	7/3	The Radio Ham
16- 3-66	7/2	The Bowmans
23- 3-66	7/1	The Bedsitter
30- 3-66	7/6	The Succession—Son and Heir

(This series of repeats comprises the entire 5th, 6th, and 7th series; all from 16mm telerecordings, except 'The Bedsitter', from video tape.)

Mondays at 2155 (approximately); 'Hancock'
6-1-69	7/5	The Blood Donor
13-1-69	7/3	The Radio Ham
20-1-69	7/4	The Lift
27-1-69	7/1	The Bedsitter
3-2-69	7/2	The Bowmans
10-2-69	7/6	The Succession—Son and Heir

(from 16 mm telerecordings, except 'The Radio Ham', from video tape)

Monday at 1940, BBC-2, in 'Festival 40' (celebrating 40 years of BBC Television— various Archive programmes repeated during August)
| 23-8-76 | 7/5 | The Blood Donor |

(from 16mm telerecording.)

'HANCOCK'S HALF-HOUR'—BBC-TV—SHOWS IN BBC FILM LIBRARY

Listed chronologically with series/number reference.

The numbers given represent the project number, and apply to all copies of the programme in each case (including the video tapes, which, however, no longer exist). Each individual roll of film also has its own number, which is not listed here as it is only of interest to the Film Library staff. All programmes exist in negatives, from which positive prints can be made and kept for viewing or transmission.

Prefixes: the first number indicates the gauge (film width) of the *negative*—16 or 35 millimetres. (Some 35mm negatives have been printed to 16mm viewing copies.)

The letter prefix indicates the purpose for which the film recording was originally made: T=transmission (either pre-recorded for transmission, or recorded off transmission for repeat), INT=for internal use (e.g. for the producer to view as a check on the success of the transmission), OI=outside interest (e.g., at the request of a member of the cast), and TU=made for BBC Television Enterprises to sell abroad.

All these films are telerecordings; i.e. they are filmed from a television screen rather than being made in the same way as a cinema film.

All negatives are complete with an optical soundtrack; in some cases there is also a magnetic recording of the soundtrack available, which can be run in synchronization with the picture to give better quality sound—these are indicated by an asterisk (which is *not* part of the official film library number).

All numbers are preceded by the initials F/R (film recording); these have been omitted in this list.

35/INT/3121	2/1	The Alpine Holiday
35/OI/3711	3/5	Air Steward Hancock
35/T/3827	3/9	The Lawyer: The Crown v James S.
35/T/3834	3/10	How to Win Money and Influence People
35/T/3842	3/11	There's an Airfield at the Bottom of my Garden
35/T/3858	3/12	Hancock's Forty-three Minutes
35/T/5100*	4/1	Ericson the Viking
35/T/5098*	4/3	The Set That Failed
35/T/5101*	4/4	The New Nose
35/T/5109*	4/11	The Oak Tree
35/T/5110*	4/12	The Knighthood
16/TU/6480	5/1	The Economy Drive
16/TU/6482	5/2	The Two Murderers
16/TU/6483*	5/3	Lord Byron Lived Here
16/TU/6484	5/4	Twelve Angry Men
16/TU/6481	5/5	The Train Journey
16/TU/6485*	5/6	The Cruise
16/TU/6486	5/7	The Big Night
16/TU/6487*	5/8	The Tycoon
16/TU/6488*	5/9	Spanish Interlude
16/TU/6489	5/10	Football Pools
16/TU/7483*	6/1	The Cold
16/TU/7493	6/2	The Missing Page
16/TU/7473	6/3	The Emigrant
16/TU/7519	6/4	The Reunion Party
16/TU/7547	6/5	Sid in Love
16/TU/7551	6/6	The Baby Sitters
16/TU/7689*	6/7	The Ladies' Man
16/TU/7924*	6/8	The Photographer
16/TU/7927*	6/9	The East Cheam Centenary
16/TU/7934*	6/10	The Poison Pen Letters
16/TU/11129*	7/1	The Bedsitter
16/TU/11131*	7/2	The Bowmans
16/TU/11133*	7/3	The Radio Ham
16/TU/11183*	7/4	The Lift
16/TU/11186*	7/5	The Blood Donor
16/TU/11318*	7/6	The Succession—Son and Heir

(Note that the film and video tape numbers for 7/2 and 7/4 have become transposed, because the programmes were originally recorded in the reverse order, but transferred from video tape to film in the order in which they were transmitted.)

Also in BBC Film Library:

35/TU/3972	The Government Inspector (broadcast 9-2-58).
35/T/5232*	Christmas Night With The Stars (broadcast 25-12-58). Includes Hancock performing the budgerigar sketch, pre-recorded 2-12-58.
16/TU/7178	Trailer for 6th series (2nd for overseas viewers): Hancock talks briefly about some of the family heirlooms at 23 Railway Cuttings, and

introduces Sid James, his agent, manager, and owner. About $2\frac{1}{2}$ minutes.

16/TU/7610   Face to Face (broadcast 7-2-60).
16/INT/35166* Hancock at the Royal Festival Hall (recorded 22-9-66, broadcast 15-10-66).

JACK HYLTON PRESENTS 'THE TONY HANCOCK SHOW': 1st SERIES FOR AR-TV

Tony Hancock with June Whitfield (except no. 6), Clive Dunn, John Vere, and The Teenagers, plus additional cast as shown below. Scripts by Eric Sykes, with Larry Stephens on nos 1 and 2; musical numbers staged by Deirdre Vivian; original music and lyrics by Christopher Hodder-Williams, with additional music by Kenny Powell (nos 3, 4, and 5) and Basil Tate (no. 5); musical director Cyril Ornadel. Executive producer Roland Gillett. Directed by Kenneth Carter. An Associated-Rediffusion Network Production.

Fridays at 2030-2100. No titles billed; details given below are brief identifications of the sketches.

1	27-4-56	live	with Dick Emery, Pamela Deeming, and guitarist Emil Bibobi.
			Opening party/Coffee bar/A Street Car Named Desire/Spanish Dance
2	4-5-56	live	with Dick Emery, Bernard Livesey, Jimmy White and Roy Bartley.
			Massage/Library/Armand and Michaela Denis/Balinese Dancing
3	11-5-56	live	with the Barney Galbraith Singers.
			Audition/Agent's office/Theatrical costumier/Dressing Room/Musical Comedy
4	18-5-56	live	with Ronan O'Casey, Valerie Frazer, Cyril Renison, Lizbeth Cassay, and Eric Sykes.
			Office/Courtroom/Nightclub (Chez Hancock)
5	25-5-56	live	with Robert Arden, Sam Kydd, Dorothy Blythe and Neale Warrington.
			Albert Hall/Embankment/Gun Law/Conjuror/Calypso Dancing
6	1-6-56	live	with Hattie Jacques, Ray Browne, Neale Warrington and Valentine Dyall.
			Auctioneer/'Death of a Duchess'

The entire series exists on 35mm telerecordings.

JACK HYLTON PRESENTS 'THE TONY HANCOCK SHOW': 2nd SERIES FOR AR-TV

No regular cast details available.
Scripts by Eric Sykes, except nos 5 and 6 by Alan Simpson and Ray Galton (uncredited). Produced by Eric Fawcett. An Associated-Rediffusion Network Production.

Fridays at 2030-2100, fortnightly. First four had billed titles; for nos 5 and 6 brief identifications of the sketches are given. Cast details given where known, but these are incomplete.

1	16-11-56	live	'Hancock—the Man of the Moment' with Bill Shine.

2	30-11-56	live	'Honneur et Fidèlité'
			with Hattie Jacques and Charles Heslop.
3	14-12-56	live	'The Further Adventures of Hancock'
			with Bill Fraser and Helen Boult.
4	28-12-56	live	'Weather or Not'
5	11- 1-57	live	with Sam Kydd, John Vere, Dennis Bowen, Terence Alexander, and Betty Huntley-Wright.
			Napoleon and Josephine/The Tailor/The Fireman.
6	25- 1-57	live	*The Odd Job Man/The Woolwich Ferry/The Court Jester.*

'HANCOCK': 1963 SERIES FOR ATV

Directed by Alan Tarrant; a MacConkey Production (i.e. produced by Hancock); ATV Network presentation, by arrangement with Bernard Delfont.

Thursdays 2030-2100, except no. 12, 2145-2215. Programmes listed below in order of transmission; numbers in brackets in column one refer to the order of the programmes as recorded. Cast lists for the series begin opposite.

1 (7)	3-1-63	TR/5085 (13/14-12-62)	THE ASSISTANT (story by 'Ray Whyberd' (Ray Alan), script by Terry Nation) Hancock is challenged to work in a department store for a week without being rude to any customers.
2 (1)	10-1-63	TR/5002 (4-11-62)	THE EYE-WITNESS (by Godfrey Harrison) Hancock witnesses a bank robbery—and insists on aiding the police in their investigations.
3 (2)	17-1-63	TR/5003 (11-11-62)	SHOOTING STAR (by Godfrey Harrison) A film director, looking for 'realism' by hiring non-professional actors, gives Hancock a part in a film. Instead of realism, he gets incompetence.
4 (3)	24-1-63	TR/5015 (18-11-62)	THE GIRL (by Godfrey Harrison) Hancock makes the acquaintance of a pretty nurse—but doesn't know her name. So he invades the local hospital looking for her.
5 (5)	31-1-63	TR/5038 (30-11-62)	THE MAN ON THE CORNER (by Godfrey Harrison) Hancock is convinced that he has seen a spy. He reports to MI5, who 'enrol' him, just to keep him quiet.
6 (4)	7-2-63	TR/5027 (25-11-62)	THE MEMORY TEST (by Godfrey Harrison) Hancock is asked to take part in an edition of 'This Is Your Life' for his old Wing-Commander—whom he can't remember.
7 (9)	14-2-63	TR/5164 (17/18-1-63)	THE EARLY CALL (by Richard Harris and Dennis Spooner) Hancock has to get up early the next day—but his alarm clock is unreliable; so he books an alarm call—and then worries about it.

248

8 (8)	21-2-63	TR/5153 (10-1-63)	**THE CRAFTSMAN** (by Richard Harris and Dennis Spooner) After watching a master carpenter on TV, Hancock is convinced that he can do as well—and offers his services to an aquaintance.
9 (10)	28-2-63	TR/5187 (24/25-1-63)	**THE NIGHT OUT** (by Terry Nation) After a heavy night's drinking, Hancock wakes up in a hotel suite—with a crowd of strangers as his guests.
10 (6)	7-3-63	TR/5066 (6/7-12-63)	**THE POLITICIAN** (by Godfrey Harrison) Hancock strikes up an aquaintance with a street-corner speaker—and decides to try his own powers as an orator.
11 (13)	14-3-63	TR/5249 (14/15-2-63)	**THE REPORTER** (by Terry Nation) Hancock takes a job as reporter on the local paper and causes havoc at a Society wedding.
12 (11)	21-3-63	TR/5222 (31-1 and 1-2-63)	**THE WRITER** (by Terry Nation) Hancock persuades a TV comic to fire his writer and hire Hancock; and then retires to his room to try and think of a few jokes.
13 (12)	28-3-63	TR/5236 (7-2-63)	**THE ESCORT** (by Richard Harris and Dennis Spooner) Hancock demands to be employed by an escort agency—who send him out with a boisterous Australian millionairess.

16mm telerecordings of the entire series are held by Tony Hancock Enterprises Ltd.

CAST LISTS FOR 1963 ATV SERIES.

Hancock present for all shows; listed in transmission order.

1: THE ASSISTANT
Mrs Hart.......................... Martita Hunt
Owen Bowen.............. Kenneth Griffith
Little Girl .... Adrienne Poster
Mr Stone .... Patrick Cargill
Uncle Bunny................... Mario Fabrizi
Edna .... Annie Leake
Window Dresser .... Jennifer Tippet
Workmen.................... Rory McDermot
Alex Farrell
and
Maisie Grant, Charlton Julian, Douglas Grant, Alice Greenwood, Vicki Gate, Sheila Knight, Cara Stevens, Barbara Howard, Stella Maris, Laurence Hepworth, Geoff Shang, Gordon Lang, Ivor Kimmel, Donald James, John Simpson and Alf Mangan.

2: THE EYE-WITNESS
Det. Sgt. Hubbard.......... Peter Vaughan
Ian Fairblow............. Allan Cuthbertson
Det. Con. Tom Flagg .... John Cater
Dulcie Main..................... Pauline Yates
Lady Passer-by .... Joan Benham
Frank Hope......................... Keith Pyott
Theodore Reed .... Maitland Moss
City Gent.................... Geoffrey Denton
Reporter........................ Lane Meddick
Det. Con. Bane .... Robin Chapman
Small Boy .... Gareth Robinson
and

Bill Burridge, Phil Arthurs, Vi Johnstone, Violet Dix, Bill Davies, Tony Starr, Bill Earle, Henry Prina, and Michael Rathborne.

3: SHOOTING STAR
Peter Dartford.............. Denholm Elliott
Diana Pride..................... Frances Rowe
Old Lady .... Hilda Barry
Lucille Frame .... Sally Anne Shaw
Billy Watts...................... Robin Hunter
Clapper Boy................. Stuart Guidotti
Prop Man........................... Alf Mangan
Lady Passer-by .... Tracy Vernon
Continuity Girl .... Irena Rodzianko
Electrician...................... Donald Groves
Film Cameraman.................. Bud Strait

4: THE GIRL
Nurse April Rawlings .... Judith Stott
Doctor Grayne.................. Dennis Price
Sister Fitch .... Edna Petrie
Outpatient................. Norman Chappell
Husband .... Robin Wentworth
Wife..................................... Patsy Smart
Waitress .... Dany Clare
Porter..................... Fred MacNaughton
Poppy .... Nancy Nevinson
and
Michael Sammes, Alf Mangan, Patricia Matthews, John Newbury, Betty Duncan, Grace Dolan, Vi Delmer, and Diana Irvine.

5: THE MAN ON THE CORNER
Colonel Beresford .... Geoffrey Keen
Captain Mainwaring .... James Villiers
Paper Man .... Wilfrid Lawson
Eric Matthews................. Tenniel Evans
PC Glover.......................... Peter Welch
Boris .... John Bluthal
Maggie............................ Moyra Fraser
Vi.................................. Sheila Bernette
Mary................................ Pamela Greer
Joan .... Geraldine Sherman
1st Stranger......................... John Evitts
2nd Stranger .... Basil Beale
3rd Stranger..................... Jack Howlett
and
Alf Mangan, June Hansant, Betty Richardson, and John Devant.

6: THE MEMORY TEST
Wing Commander Bartlett......................
Edward Chapman
The Paper Man............. Wilfrid Lawson
Peter Penrose .... Gerald Harper
Brian Lawrence................. Shaw Taylor
Reg Arnold .... Anthony Sagar
Porter.............................. John Rutland
Mrs Gregory................. Maureen Pryor
Farmer Brown .... Reginald Green
and
Toby Perkins, Alf Mangan, Cyril Cross, Alan Shire, Ernest Blyth, Sidney Woolf, Patrick Hagan, Donald McCallum, John Adams, John Priestman, Mark Bennett, John H. Moore, Stella Maris and Mary Denton.

7: THE EARLY CALL
Voice on Radio................... John Bluthal
and
Rex Rashley and Alf Mangan.

8: THE CRAFTSMAN
Shop Assistant .... Thomas Heathcote
Tradesman........................... Glyn Dale
2nd Lamplighter .... Harry Brunning
Stan Lovegrove................... Brian Wilde
and
Eddie Malin, Godfrey James, Barbara Mitchell, Bernard Davies, Peter Stockbridge, Bill Cornelius, Andre Ducane, Gertrude Kaye, Beverley Cohen, Marylyn Thomas, Margaret McKechnie and Alf Mangan.

9: THE NIGHT OUT
Gavin.............................. Derek Nimmo
Hotel Receptionist .... Donald Hewlett
Waiter................................. Billy Milton
Norma .... Patsy Smart
Sarah............................. Marina Martin
Mason............................ Donald Tandy
Assistant Receptionist ...... Ian Anderson
Spanish Dancer............. Pedro Navarro
Tumbler .... John Pugh
Page Boy .... Leslie Taussig
Plate Spinner .... Eva May Wong
Spanish Dancer................ Karen Carina
and
Pat Dane, Sheila McGrath, Doris Littlewood, Joy Norton, Andrea Lawrence, Sean Barry, Edmund Dring, Frank Lit-

tlewood, Alex Donald, Cyril Cross, Astley Harvey, Darrell Richards and Patrick Milner.

10: THE POLITICIAN
Ambrose Butterfield.. John Le Mesurier
Maud Crispin .... Nora Nicholson
Vic .... John Ronane
Fiona.................................. Diane Clare
Jessica Pinchard .... Hazel Hughes
Malcolm....................... Richard Waring
Schoolboy .... Gareth Robinson
Postman .... Ronnie Brody
Ursula............................. Sheila Raynor
Nick .... Thomas Kyffin
Jonah .... John Herrington
Police Constable............. George Curtis
Passers-by:
John Scott Martin, Rex Roland, June Speight, George Curtis, and Alf Mangan.

11: THE REPORTER
Ron Roberts....................... Olaf Pooley
MC .... David Lander
Editor........................ Michael Aldridge
Mavis, the bride .... Clare Owen
MP........................ Wilfrid Carter
Wilson, the critic.................. John Kidd
Irishman .... Kendrick Owen
and
Fred Powell, Dennis Powell, Julian Holdaway, Paul Holdaway, Pauline Winter, Frances Cohen, Edwin Richfield, Joyce Marlowe, Monty Bond, Bill Matthews, Robert Pitt, Ernest Jennings, Don Fraser, H. V. Diamond, Harry Davis, Tony Starr, Shaun Howard, Gustav Craig, Barry Wallman, Mary Power, Peggy Ler, Elaine Williams, Helen Hurst, Betty Duncan, Mary MacMillan, Andrea Lascelles, Jacqui Noone, Liz Ferguson and Alf Mangan.

12: THE WRITER
Elmo Dent .... Francis Matthews
Jerry Spring .... John Junkin
Barmaid .... Jean Burgess
Compère .... Pete Murray
Landlord.................... Stuart Saunders
Wrestler .... Frikki Alberti
and
Alf Mangan, Edward Argent, Bert Leane, Wilfred Willis and Barbara Bernol.

13: THE ESCORT
Jeweller.................... Reginald Beckwith
Fiona....................... Maggie Fitzgibbon
Irishman .... Harry Towb
Cafe Owner.............. Arthur Lovegrove
Mr Latache .... Anthony Dawes
Receptionist .... Joy Stewart
Lavinia .... April Wilding
Keith.................................. Robert Mill
Ronnie .... Michael Oxley
Secretary........................ Valerie Cooney
and
Patricia Kerry, Richard Holden, Clive Kemp, Rex Dyer, Makki Marsailles, Peter Thompson, Bill Cornelius, David Hartford, Bernard Egan, Robert Croudace, Ivor Kimmel and Alf Mangan.

251

'THE BLACKPOOL SHOW': 1966 SERIES FOR ABC-TV

From the stage of the ABC Theatre, Blackpool. Tony Hancock as compère, with John Junkin, Peter Gordeno and the dancers, Bob Sharples and the ABC Television Showband, and guests as shown below. Scripts by John Muir and Eric Geen. Directed by Mark Stuart; an ABC-TV Network Production.

Sundays 2205-2305, recorded 2030 the same evening.

Pilot programme, not broadcast	VTR/5789 (12-6-66)		with Keith Harris, Gordon and Bunny Jaye, Toni Eden, and Al Saxon.
1	19-6-66	VTR/ . . .	with Matt Munro, Hope and Keen, Marian Montgomery, Ray Alan with Lord Charles, and Deryck Guyler.
2	26-6-66	VTR/5896	with Kathy Kirby, Arthur Askey, The Dallas Boys, and Lee Allen.
3	3-7-66	VTR/5898	with The Bachelors, Allan Sherman, Tony Cawley, and Barbara Law.
4	10-7-66	VTR/5899	with Frankie Howerd, The Kaye Sisters, and Lenny the Lion with Terry Hall.
5	17-7-66	VTR/5900	with Mike and Bernie Winters, Roy Castle, Arthur Worsley, and Elaine Taylor.
6	24-7-66		Hancock absent, replaced by Dave Allen.
7	31-7-66	VTR/5902	with Jeannie Carson, Bob Monkhouse, Freddie Davis, and The Rockin' Berries.
8	7-8-66		Hancock replaced for last show of the series by Bruce Forsyth.

A 16mm telerecording of show no. 7 is in the National Film Archive.

'HANCOCK'S': 1967 SERIES FOR ABC-TV

Tony Hancock with June Whitfield, Joe Ritchie, and Nat Temple and his Orchestra, plus additional cast as shown below. Scripts by John Muir and Eric Geen. Directed by Mark Stuart; an ABC-TV Network Production.

Nos 1-3 Fridays at 2140-2210; nos 4-6 Tuesdays at 2130-2200.

The programmes were not transmitted in the same order as that in which they were recorded.

1	16-6-67		with Edward Evans, Bernadette Milnes, Bob Todd, Harry Davis, and guest star Vikki Carr.
2	23-6-67		with Kenneth J. Warren, Harry Davis, Michael Lomax, Nicholas Brent, Jerry Homes, Joan Crane, Margot Maxine, and guest star Carmen MacRae.
3	30-6-67	VTR/6686 (7-4-67)	with Damaris Hayman, Frank Crawshaw, Jane Hann, John Terry, and guest star Dick Haymes.
4	4-7-67		with Nora Nicholson, Arthur Hewlett, Damaris Hayman, Jay Denyer, Harry Davis, Yvonne Horner, and guest star Vikki Carr.
5	11-7-67		with Richard Caldicot, Jack Allen, Tottie Truman Taylor, Robert Cawdron, Amy Dalby, Barry Kennington, Janet Webb, and guest star Marian Montgomery.
6	18-7-67	VTR/6742 (28-4-67)	with Arthur Mullard, Tottie Truman Taylor, Robin Hunter, Carmel Cryan, Frank Littlewood, Anthony Dawes, Walter Horsbrugh, Robert Raglan, Claire Davenport, Dickie Martin, Parnell McGarry, and guest star Frankie Randall.

(VT numbers and floor dates for nos 1, 2, 4, and 5 are not available)

252

1968 SERIES FOR AUSTRALIAN TELEVISION (INCOMPLETE)

The three episodes completed up to the time of Hancock's death were assembled into a ninety-minute special, and transmitted on Channel HSV7, Melbourne, 2030-2200 on 25-1-72.

Music composed and conducted by Tommy Tycho; editor John McPhail; lighting Bob Fletcher, audio Weston Baker and Bill Woolford. Script by Hugh Stuckey with additional material by Michael Wale. Produced and directed by Edward Joffe for ATN7. Eastman Colour, 35mm.

Mrs Gilroy	Gloria Dawn
Mervyn	Don Crosby
Miss Bancroft	Georgie Sterling
Milkman	Lex Mitchell
Captain	Kenneth Laird
Bandsman	Brian Barrie
Entertainments Officer	Don Philps
Bikini Bancroft	Mimi Dixon
Boy	Marshall Crosby
Colonel	Edward Howell
Customs Officer	Don Reid
Hotel Clerk	Max Phipps
Landlord	Nat Levison
Man in Pub	James Elliott
Maid	Doreen Warburton
Herbie	Kevin Leslie
Ken	Graham Rouse
Pete	Roger Ward
Chips	Brian Nyland
Barmaid	Maxine Wyatt

and

Bettie Crosby, Christina Daniel, Patsy Flanagan, Ron Golding, John Hilton, John Hopkins, Maudie Jacques, Bob Karl, Joanne Neville, Stan Nicholls, John Quinlan and Roy Waterson.

FILM APPEARANCES

Hancock's film career consisted of only five films; one as a supporting player, two as star, and two (whose casts are listed in less detail below) as guest artist.

ORDERS ARE ORDERS
(Group 3/British Lion, 1954)
Directed by David Paltenghi; Produced by Donald Taylor.
Screenplay by Donald Taylor and Geoffrey Orme,
from the play by Ian Hay and Anthony Armstrong

Wanda Sinclair	Margot Grahame
Joanne Delamere	Maureen Swanson
Veronica Bellamy	June Thorburn
Colonel Bellamy	Raymond Huntley
Private Slee	Bill Fraser
Private Goffin	Peter Sellers
Captain Harper	Brian Reece

```
Ed Waggermeyer ............................ Sidney James
Lieutenant Cartroad ..................... Tony Hancock
                                          (78 minutes)
```

Bilchester Barracks is invaded by Waggermeyer Pictures, who have plans for a science-fiction film. The entire barracks is persuaded by the female film stars to take part in the film—to the annoyance of the Divisional Commander, who makes a surprise inspection. He is mollified only when the Band performs a pseudonymous composition of his. In the end he persuades the film company to finish their work in a nearby haunted house.

This dire comedy, loosely based on a play of 1932, is enlivened only by Sidney James's unlikely American accent, and Hancock's droll performance as the Bandmaster.

THE REBEL
(Associated British/Warner-Pathé, 1960)
Directed by Robert Day; Produced by W. A. Whittaker.
Screenplay by Alan Simpson and Ray Galton, from a story by themselves and Tony Hancock.
Music by Frank Cordell; Paintings by Alistair Grant.
Technicolor.

```
Anthony Hancock ......................... Tony Hancock
Sir Charles Brouard ..................... George Sanders
Paul .................................... Paul Massie
Margot................................... Margit Saad
Carreras ................................ Gregoire Aslan
Jim Smith ............................... Dennis Price
Mrs Crevatte............................. Irene Handl
Manager of London Art Gallery.... Mervyn Johns
Manager of Paris Art Gallery............. Peter Bull
Office Manager ...................... John Le Mesurier
Waitress................................. Liz Fraser
Coffee Bar owner ........................ Mario Fabrizi
Josey ................................... Nanette Newman
Madame Laurent........................... Marie Burke
Yvette .................................. Marie Devereux
Poet .................................... John Wood
Artists:
Sandor Eles, Oliver Reed, Garry Cockerill, Neville
                   Becker.
                                      (105 minutes)
```

Frustrated by office routine and his landlady's lack of sympathy for his painting and sculpting, Hancock moves to Paris, and falls in with an artistic set. His dreadful paintings are acclaimed by a collection of weird bogus intellectuals, and his room-mate, Paul, a genuinely good painter, returns to England in despair. Paul's paintings are mistaken for Hancock's by Sir Charles Brouard, an art critic and dealer, and Hancock finds himself acclaimed as a great painter on the strength of them. Commissioned to produce a statue of a rich patron's apparently nymphomaniac wife, Hancock presents another version of the monstrosity he had been working on in London. It is not appreciated. In London, Hancock finds himself having to produce a set of paintings in a hurry for a show arranged by Sir Charles. He calls in Paul—who is now painting in Hancock's infantile style. In Paul's hands, however, the results are once again acclaimed. Hancock abandons the pretence, introduces Paul to Sir Charles, and defiantly returns to his old rooms to resume his sculpting.

The classic Simpson and Galton Hancock character is allowed less room to breathe in this film than in the more confined TV programmes, but the film is entertaining, with some sharp digs at the beatnik and fashionable art scenes; Hancock's performance is assured, losing only slightly from the different pace and absence of an audience.

THE PUNCH AND JUDY MAN
(MacConkey Productions/Warner-Pathé, 1962)
Directed by Jeremy Summers; Produced by Gordon L. T. Scott.
Screenplay by Philip Oakes and Tony Hancock, based on an original idea by Tony Hancock.
Music by Derek Scott and Don Banks.

Wally Pinner	Tony Hancock
Delia Pinner	Sylvia Syms
Mayor	Ronald Fraser
Lady Jane Caterham	Barbara Murray
Sandman	John Le Mesurier
Edward	Hugh Lloyd
Nevil (the photographer)	Mario Fabrizi
Mayoress	Pauline Jameson
Committee Men	Norman Bird
	Peter Vaughan
	John Dunbar
First Escort	Brian Bedford
Second Escort	Peter Myers
Ice Cream Assistant	Eddie Byrne
Bobby Batchelor	Russell Waters
Landlord	Kevin Brennan
Peter (the small boy)	Nicholas Webb
	(96 minutes)

It is the end of the summer season at Piltdown, a small southern coastal town. Wally Pinner (the Punch and Judy Man), and his friends the Sandman (who sculpts figures in the sand), and Nevil (the street photographer), are snubbed socially by the locally important figures. This is one of the reasons for the strained relationship between Wally and his wife Delia, who has social aspirations. The Council plans an official reception for Lady Jane Caterham, who is to switch on the illuminations, and at the Mayoress's suggestion invite Wally to present his Punch and Judy Show at the gala dinner. He is reluctant to appear, but Delia is anxious to increase her social standing, and she and the Sandman pressurize Wally into giving a performance. However, the dinner degenerates into a bun-fight, and when Lady Jane rounds on Wally, Delia knocks her out with a strong punch to the jaw. Her chance of being accepted socially has gone, but she and Wally come to a better understanding and acceptance of each other.

Despite the flaws in this underrated film, largely caused by difficulties on the set with Hancock, and the director's imperfect grasp of comic tempo, the result is a pleasant, quiet, and sometimes sad comedy with several very effective sequences.

THOSE MAGNIFICENT MEN IN THEIR FLYING MACHINES
(20th-Century-Fox, 1965)
Directed by Ken Annakin; produced by Stan Margulies.
Screenplay by Jack Davies and Ken Annakin.
Technicolor, Todd-AO.

Tony Hancock appears as Harry Popperwell in a large cast including Sarah Miles, James Fox, Stuart Whitman, Alberto Sordi, Robert Morley, Gert Frobe, Jean-Pierre Cassel,

Irina Demich, Eric Sykes, Terry-Thomas, Benny Hill, Yujiro Ishihara, Flora Robson, Karl Michael Vogler, Sam Wanamaker, Norman Rossington, William Rushton, Fred Emney, Red Skelton, Eric Barker, John Le Mesurier and Graham Stark.

(132 minutes)

Hancock's appearances in this mammoth, expensive, spectacular, and usually ham-footed comedy blockbuster are confined to a couple of short scenes in which, as one of the contestants in a 1910 London–Paris air race, he is proposing to fly backwards ('less wind resistance'). He seems hardly to be trying to act his part at all. The real stars of the film are of course the aeroplanes themselves, and the stuntmen.

THE WRONG BOX
(Salamander/BLC/Columbia)
Directed and produced by Bryan Forbes.
Screenplay by Larry Gelbart and Burt Shevelove, based on the novel by Robert Louis Stevenson and Lloyd Osbourne.
Technicolor.

Tony Hancock appears as the detective who attempts to unravel the plot at the end of this adaptation of the novel. The cast includes Ralph Richardson, John Mills, Michael Caine, Peter Cook, Dudley Moore, Nanette Newman, Peter Sellers, Wilfrid Lawson, Thorley Walters, Cicely Courtneidge, Irene Handl, John Le Mesurier, The Temperance Seven, Norman Rossington, James Villiers, Graham Stark, Valentine Dyall, and Totti Truman Taylor. (110 minutes)

Hancock is given little enough to do, merely expressing exasperation when faced with the convolutions at the end of this extremely complicated plot involving a Tontine, mistaken identities, and a corpse in a grand piano. He attacks his part with gusto, but tends to be swamped, as are many of the cast, by the inclination of the writers to 'improve' the original by the addition of a wide variety of intrusive comic devices.

GRAMOPHONE RECORDS
There are about forty different tape and disc issues of Hancock, presenting in various permutations a total of about $6\frac{1}{4}$ hours of material drawn from 24 different performances. In order to clarify the complicated situation as much as possible, the performances have been listed first, acting as an index to the list of actual records, which are coded by reference letters to simplify the matter.

Performances from which the record issues have been drawn.
Shows are listed here under their original titles; in most cases excerpts have been taken from them, usually under different titles which are listed with the records themselves. Shows asterisked are issued substantially complete, under the same titles as are used in the present book. All performances listed are from BBC broadcasts unless otherwise stated.

Series and number	Title	First broadcast	Records, identified by letter-code
Radio 4th series			
No. 6	Michaelangelo 'Ancock	18-11-56	Q
No. 11	Hancock's Happy Christmas	23-12-56	Q
No. 12	The Diary	30-12-56	B, K, R, S
No. 14	Almost a Gentleman	13- 1-57	Q
No. 16	The Wild Man of the Woods*	27- 1-57	A, R, S, extract on L

No. 18	Hancock in the Police	10- 2-57	Q

Radio 5th series

No. 4	The Insurance Policy	11- 2-58	Q
No. 5	The Publicity Photograph	18- 2-58	B, F
No. 11	Hancock's Car	1- 4-58	Q
No. 12	The East Cheam Drama Festival	8- 4-58	B, extracts on E, L
No. 14	Sunday Afternoon at Home*	22- 4-58	A, R, S, extract on P
No. 15	The Grappling Game	29- 4-58	Q
No. 19	The Threatening Letters	27- 5-58	B, extracts on D, K

Radio 6th series

No. 2	The Childhood Sweetheart	6-10-59	Q
No. 12	Hancock in Hospital	15-12-59	Q

BBC-TV, 5th series

No. 4	Twelve Angry Men*	16-10-59	U

BBC-TV 7-2-60 : Face To Face | | | H |

BBC-TV 7th series

No. 4	The Lift*	16- 6-61	U

Specially recorded material for records

Linking material for 'Pieces of Hancock' (recorded circa. June 1960)	B, extracts on R, S
The Blood Donor,* adapted from BBC-TV script, 5th of 7th series; recorded 1-10-61 by Pye	C, extracts on G, L
The Radio Ham,* adapted from BBC-TV script, 3rd of 7th series, recorded 1-10-61 by Pye	C, extracts on L, T, V
'Hancock's Tune': signature tune for 1963 ATV series with comments by Hancock: recorded late 1963 by Pye	J
The Reunion Party,* adapted from BBC-TV script, 4th of 6th series; recorded in 1965 by Decca	M
The Missing Page,* adapted from BBC-TV script, 2nd of 6th series; recorded in 1965 by Decca	M, extract on N

The records and tapes : shows are indicated by series/number reference and transmission date. Special titles given to extracts are listed in italics.

A   'THIS IS HANCOCK'
The Wild Man of the Woods (Radio 4/16, 27-1-57), substantially complete. Sunday Afternoon at Home (Radio 5/14, 22-4-58) substantially complete except for a few small cuts mostly involving music.

First published spring 1960: Pye-Nixa PLP 1039 (12″ mono LP), Pye NPL 18045 and Pye Golden Guinea GGL 0206 (12″ mono LPs)

B   'PIECES OF HANCOCK'
The East Cheam Drama Festival ('Jack's Return Home' and 'Look Back in Hunger' extracted from Radio 5/12, 8-4-58; duration 19′ 40″)
The Secret Life of Anthony Hancock (the 'Test Pilot' sequence from 'The Diary', Radio 4/12, 30-12-56; duration 7′ 05″)
The Publicity Photograph (two extracts from Radio 5/5, 18-2-58; total duration 11′ 15″)
The Threatening Letters (two extracts from Radio 5/19, 27-5-58, total duration 10′ 40″)

First published 1960: Pye-Nixa PLP 1110 (12″ mono LP), Pye NPL 18054 and

Pye Golden Guinea GGL 0245 (12″ mono LPs)

C   'HANCOCK'

The Blood Donor—studio re-make of BBC-TV 7/5, recorded by Pye 1-10-61

The Nurse	June Whitfield
Dr McTaggart	Patrick Cargill
First donor	Frank Thornton
Second donor	Annie Leake
Mr Thomas	Hugh Lloyd
Second Doctor	John Bluthal
Second nurse	Annie Leake

This is a much better performance on Hancock's part than the original, which was marred by the after-effects of the car crash on 26-5-61, and the recording suffers only from the lack of the original incidental music. Duration 28′ 10″

The Radio Ham—studio re-make of BBC-TV 7/3, recorded by Pye 1-10-61

Landlady .... Annie Leake
BBC Announcer/CX3 Birmingham/Police
Car/Landlady's husband .... Deryck Guyler
HBX Belgrade/Voice of America/
Flying Doctor .... John Bluthal
B45 Malaya................................ Frank Thornton
Actor/1st Policeman......................... Hugh Lloyd
Actress.. June Whitfield
Mayday.. Patrick Cargill
HB24D Tokyo/2nd Policeman .... Clive Dunn
Duration 27′ 40″

First published 1961: Pye-Nixa PLP 1092, Pye NPL 18068, Pye Golden Guinea GGL 0270, Marble Arch MAL 872 (all 12″ mono LPs); Hallmark HMA 228 (12″ 'stereo' LP); Marble Arch ZCMA 872 Dolby 'electronic stereo' cassette (under the title 'The Best of Tony Hancock') and Y8MA 872 8-track 'electronic stereo' cartridge (under the title 'Hancock').

D   'LITTLE PIECES OF HANCOCK'—Volume 1
The Secret Life of Anthony Hancock (extract from 'Test Pilot' sequence on record 'B')
The Threatening Letters (extract from sequence on record 'B')
Pye NEP 24146 (7″ mono EP)

E   'LITTLE PIECES OF HANCOCK'—Volume 2
Jack's Return Home ⎱ extracts from 'The East Cheam Drama Festival' (record 'B')
Look Back in Hunger ⎰
Pye NEP 24161 (7″ mono EP)

F   'THE PUBLICITY PHOTOGRAPH'
Two excerpts as on record 'B'
Pye NEP 24170 (7″ mono EP)

G   'HIGHLIGHTS FROM "THE BLOOD DONOR"'
Extracts from record 'C'
Pye NEP 24175 (7″ mono EP)

H   'FACE TO FACE'
Slightly shortened version of the broadcast of 7-2-60, Hancock interviewed by John Freeman; from the video tape soundtrack. (The other side is the interview from the

same series with Stirling Moss OBE)
Pye Piccadilly FTF 38500 (12″ mono LP) published January 1963

J   'HANCOCK'S TUNE'
The signature tune by Derek Scott for the 1963 ATV series, played by the Derek Scott Music in a different orchestration from the original and with overlaid comments by Hancock. The other side is entitled 'Spying Tonight' and does not feature Hancock.
Pye 7N 15500 (7″ mono single) published late 1963.
'Hancock's Tune' was also included on an album of TV themes, Pye Golden Guinea GGL 0196.

K   *Wing Commander Hancock—Test Pilot*—extract from record 'B'
The Threatening Letter—most of first extract from record 'B'
Pye 7N 15575 (7″ mono single) published January 1964

L   'A TRIBUTE TO TONY HANCOCK'
The Blood Donor ⎱ extracts from record 'C'
The Radio Ham ⎰
The East Cheam Drama Festival—'Jack's Return Home' from record 'B'
The Wild Man of the Woods—extract from record 'A'
World Record Club—Pye ST 897 (12″ mono LP)

M   'IT'S HANCOCK'
The Missing Page—studio re-make of BBC-TV 6/2, recorded by Decca, 1965
The Reunion Party—studio re-make of BBC-TV 6/4, recorded by Decca, 1965
Both scripts have been adapted for the studio versions, which, particularly in the case of 'The Missing Page', do not show Hancock at his best. This session was his last professional engagement with Sidney James.
Decca LK 4740 (12″ mono LP) published November 1965; reissued under the title 'The World of Tony Hancock' in 1975 on Decca PA 417 (12″ mono LP) and Decca KCPA 417 (Dolby mono cassette).

N   'THE WORLD OF BRITISH COMEDY'
contains an extract from 'The Missing Page' (record 'M')
Decca SPA 39 (12″ mono LP), KCPA 39 (Dolby cassette)

P   'FIFTY YEARS OF RADIO COMEDY'
includes a three-minute extract from 'Sunday Afternoon at Home' (record 'A').
BBC Records REC 138M (12″ mono LP) published 1972.

Q   'THE UNIQUE HANCOCK'
All extracts on this record are from BBC Transcription Services versions, and therefore may contain occasional small cuts.
Almost a Gentleman (opening scene from Radio 4/14, 13-1-57) 6′ 20″
Christmas—East Cheam Style (brief extract from 'Hancock's Happy Christmas', Radio 4/11, 23-12-56) 3′ 40″
PC Hancock—Have Feet, Will Travel (two extracts from 'Hancock in the Police', Radio 4/18, 10-2-57), 3′ 20″, 2′ 35″.
Michael Hancockelo (opening scene from 'Michaelangelo 'Ancock', Radio 4/6, 18-11-56) 5′ 10″
The Doctor's Dilemma (medical examination scene from 'The Insurance Policy', Radio 5/4, 11-2-58) 5′ 30″
Like a Dog's Dinner (opening scene from 'The Grappling Game', Radio 5/15, 29-4-58) 6′ 20″
Is that your car outside? (extract from 'Hancock's Car', Radio 5/11, 1-4-58) 7′ 15″

With my woggle I thee worship (from opening scene of 'The Childhood Sweetheart', Radio 6/2, 6-10-59) 7'00"

The Hospital, or Hancock Revisited (extract from 'Hancock in Hospital', Radio 6/12, 15-12-59) 6' 00"

BBC Records REB 150M (12" mono LP published 1973), REMC 150 (mono cassette incorrectly identified as a Dolby-coded recording; published 1973) and RCT 8002 (8-track mono cartridge published June 1974)

R 'THE GOLDEN HOUR OF TONY HANCOCK'
The Wild Man of the Woods—slightly re-edited version of record 'A' Sunday Afternoon at Home—re-issue of record 'A'

The Secret Life of Anthony Hancock—most of 'Test Pilot' sequence from record 'B' The items are linked by an edited version of the special narration recorded for record 'B'

Golden Hour GH 577 (12" mono LP) published 1974, ZCGH 577 ('stereo' cassette) and Y8GH 577 (8-track cartridge)

S 'COMEDY'
4-record set, one LP of which is identical to record 'R'
Pye IIPP 201, published late 1974.

T 'COMEDY SPECTACULAR—40 YEARS OF TELEVISION'
includes extract from 'The Radio Ham' (record 'C').
BBC Records REB 249 (12" mono LP published autumn 1976) and RMC 4048 (mono cassette incorrectly identified as a Dolby-coded recording).

U 'HANCOCK'
The Lift—magnetic soundtrack of TV 7/4, 16-6-61, with opening non-dialogue sequence omitted and one extra line of explanatory dialogue ('Watch that door-button—Oh my God') recorded by Hugh Lloyd on 24-8-76 and edited in.
Twelve Angry Men—optical soundtrack of TV 5/4, 16-10-59, with signature tune, incidental music and a few lines of dialogue edited out and some of the pauses shortened.
BBC Records REB 260 (12" mono LP published October 1976), RMC 4055 (mono cassette, incorrectly identified as a Dolby-coded recording) and RCT 8018 (8-track cartridge).

V 'A SILVER JUBILEE OF MEMORIES'
includes extract from 'The Radio Ham' (record 'C')
Pageant SJM 001-2 (2 12" mono LPs published April 1977)

The Wally Stott signature tune for 'Hancock's Half-Hour', in an arrangement by Paul Fenoulhet, is included in a medley of Comedy Show themes on United Artists UAG 29739 (12" stereo LP), recorded in the Pye studios by the London Concert Orchestra conducted by Paul Fenoulhet, and published in 1976.

Bibliography

'THE REBEL'—adaptation by Alan Holmes of the Simpson and Galton screenplay. May Fair Books (paperback), 1961.

'HANCOCK—four scripts for television' by Alan Simpson and Ray Galton.
'The Economy Drive' (1st of 5th BBC-TV series)
'The Train Journey' (5th of 5th series)
'Going Down' ('The Lift'—4th of 7th series)
'Mayday' ('The Radio Ham'—3rd of 7th series)
and including an imaginary dialogue between Hancock, the writers, and a barmaid. Illustrated. André Deutsch Ltd (hardback), 1961; Corgi Books (paperback) 1962.

'FACE TO FACE'—the John Freeman interviews edited by Hugh Burnett, and including the Topolski drawings used as captions. Including an adaptation of the Hancock interview broadcast 7-2-60. Jonathan Cape Ltd (hardback) 1964.

'PLAYBACK—ISSUE 1'
Contains excerpts from the interviews between Hancock and David Frost broadcast 19-1-67 and 20-1-67. Cornmarket Press Ltd (large paperback) Spring 1967.

'HANCOCK' by Freddie Hancock and David Nathan.
William Kimber and Company Ltd (hardback) 1969; Coronet Books (paperback), 1975

'THE WIRELESS STARS' by George Nobbs. Includes a chapter on 'The Lad Himself', largely drawn from the Hancock-Nathan book. Wensum Books (hardback) 1972

'HANCOCK'S HALF-HOUR' by Ray Galton and Alan Simpson with an introduction by Peter Black.
Contains five scripts from the BBC-TV series, illustrated with frame enlargements from the telerecordings. The transmission dates quoted in the book are not all accurate.
'The Missing Page' (2nd of 6th BBC-TV series)
'The Reunion Party' (4th of 6th series)
'Hancock Alone' ('The Bedsitter'—1st of 7th series)
'The Bowmans' (2nd of 7th series)
'The Blood Donor' (5th of 7th series)
Also includes the transcript of an interview with Simpson and Galton by Colin Webb. The Woburn Press (hardback), 1974: Woburn-Futura (paperback) 1975

'THE ENTERTAINERS—TONY HANCOCK' by Philip Oakes. Woburn Press (hardback) and Woburn-Futura (paperback) 1975

'LAUGHTER IN THE AIR—an informal history of British radio comedy' by Barry Took. Includes a chapter on 'Ray and Alan and Tony and Beryl'. Robson Books Ltd with BBC Publications (hardback) 1976.

Addenda to the Paperback Edition

Broadcasts, records and videograms since March 1978

'HANCOCK'S HALF-HOUR' – RADIO REPEATS

Sundays on R4; the first at 0955 on medium-wave only; the next at 1100 on medium-wave and VHF; the remainder at 1100 on long-wave and VHF.

12–11–78	2/11	The Marrow Contest (Tony's Prize Marrow)
19–11–78	3/3	The Bequest (Tony's Inheritance)
26–11–78	6/11	The Poetry Society (Tony the Poet)
3–12–78	4/8	Cyrano de Hancock (Tony's Wedding)
10–12–78	4/18	Hancock in the Police (PC Hancock)
17–12–78	5/14	Sunday Afternoon at Home (Tony's Sunday Afternoon)
24–12–78	4/11	Hancock's Happy Christmas (Tony's Christmas)
31–12–78	4/12	The Diary (Tony's Diary)
7– 1–79	4/15	The Old School Re-union (Tony's Old School)
14– 1–79	6/12	Hancock in Hospital (Tony in Hospital)

Sunday, 1200 R4, in series 'Smash of the Day'

2– 9–79	5/14	Sunday Afternoon at Home

Sundays, R4 at 1200. (All from TS 27-minute versions.) No titles billed.

3– 1–82	4/11	Hancock's Happy Christmas
10– 1–82	4/14	Almost a Gentleman
17– 1–82	4/18	Hancock in the Police
24– 1–82	4/15	The Old School Re-union
31– 1–82	5/2	The Scandal Magazine
7– 2–82	6/6	The Elopement
14– 2–82	6/5	The Gourmet
21– 2–82	6/11	The Poetry Society

'HANCOCK'S HALF-HOUR' – the following have been added to BBC Sound Archives, all from the TS versions.

T37099(i)	1/3	The Idol
T37099(ii)	1/11	A Trip to France
T37100(i)	1/13	A House on the Cliff
T37100(ii)	2/8	The Rail Strike
T37101(i)	2/9	The Television Set
T37101(ii)	2/11	The Marrow Contest
T37102(i)	3/2	The Jewel Robbery
T37102(ii)	3/3	The Bequest
T37103(i)	3/13	Hancock's Hair
T37103(ii)	3/14	The Student Prince
T37104(i)	3/18	The Greyhound Track
T37104(ii)	3/19	The Conjurer

GRAMOPHONE RECORDS

W   'HANCOCK'S HALF HOUR'
     The Poetry Society (Radio 6/11, 8–12–59), substantially complete.
     Sid's Mystery Tours (Radio 6/9, 24–11–59), substantially complete.
     BBC Records REB 394 (12″ mono LP) and ZCF 394 (musicassette) published
     November 1980.

X   'HANCOCK'S HALF HOUR'
     The Americans Hit Town (Radio 5/9, 18–3–58), substantially complete.
     The Unexploded Bomb (Radio 5/6, 25–2–58), substantially complete.
     BBC Records REB 423 (12″ mono LP) and ZCF 423 (musicassette) published
     October 1981.

Y   'WE ARE NOT AMUSED'
     includes excerpt from 'The Blood Donor' (record 'C').
     Ronco/Charisma two 12″ LP set RTD 2067; musicassette 4C–RTD 2067

Z   'THE LAUGHING STOCK OF THE BBC'
     includes extracts from 'Almost a Gentleman' (Radio 4/14, 13–1–57) duration
     2′ 00″: and 'The Americans Hit Town' (Radio 5/9, 18–3–58) duration 4′ 18″.
     BBC Records LAF 1 (12″ LP) and ZCLAF 1 (musicassette), published April
     1982.

AA   'HANCOCK'S HALF HOUR'
     The Scandal Magazine (Radio 5/2, 28–1–58), substantially complete.
     The Last of the McHancocks (Radio 4/20, 24–2–57), substantially complete.
     BBC Records REB 451 (12″ mono LP) and ZCF 451 (musicassettes) published
     October 1982.

VIDEOGRAMS

'THOSE MAGNIFICENT MEN IN THEIR FLYING MACHINES' (20th-
Century Fox, 1965) available for purchase in VHS, Betamax and VCC from
Magnetic Video.

'ORDERS ARE ORDERS' (British Lion 1954)
available for puchase in VHS, Betamax and VCC from Derann Audio Visual.

Index

Page numbers in italics refer to photographs

264